QUALITY
EDUCATION

Other books available from ASQC Quality Press

A Quality System for Education
Stanley J. Spanbauer

A Leader's Journey to Quality
Dana Cound

The Deming Management Method
Mary Walton

Measuring Customer Satisfaction
Bob E. Hayes

To receive a complimentary catalog of publications,
call 800-248-1946.

QUALITY
EDUCATION

Applying the Philosophy of Dr. W. Edwards Deming
to Transform the Educational System

Gray Rinehart

ASQC Quality Press
Milwaukee, Wisconsin

Quality Education
Gray Rinehart

Rinehart, Gray.
    Quality education: applying the philosophy of Dr. W. Edwards
Deming/Gray Rinehart.
        p.   cm.
    Includes index.
    ISBN 0-87389-184-8
    1. Deming, W. Edwards (William Edwards), 1900–   . 2. Education–
United States–Philosophy. 3. School management and organization–
United States. 4. Educational change–United States. I. Title.
LB885.D4352R56 1992
370' . 1 – dc20   92-28992
                                                                CIP

10987654321

ISBN 0-87389-184-8

Acquisitions Assistant: Deborah Dunlap
Production Editor: Mary Beth Nilles
Marketing Administrator: Susan Westergard
Set in Avant Garde and Galliard by Montgomery Media, Inc.
Cover design by Barbara Adams.
Printed and bound by BookCrafters.

For a free copy of the ASQC Quality Press Publications Catalog, including
ASQC membership information, call 800-248-1946.

Printed in the United States of America.

  Printed on acid-free recycled paper

ASQC
Quality Press
611 East Wisconsin Avenue
Milwaukee, Wisconsin 53202
®

To my wife and children,
my classmates and students, and
Ann Altman, because I told her I would.

In Memoriam

Julia Shell, whom we called "Gram,"
who always knew more than she let us think;
and Winyah High School, home of the Gators,
where we learned.

*Train up a child in the way he should go, and when he is
old he will not depart from it.*
—Proverbs 22:6

Alma Mater

Oh, Alma Mater glorious,

Forever more victorious,

We pledge to you undying love and loyalty—

Oh, may your wisdom guide us

And ever stand beside us,

Dear Winyah High we pledge devoted faith in thee!

—Winyah High School
Georgetown, South Carolina

C O N T E N T S

P R E F A C E

My people are destroyed for lack of knowledge.

—Hosea 4:6

There seems to be a predilection in this country to search for scapegoats whenever a system fails to achieve its goals. This is evident in the decline of the U.S. educational system: the fact of its decline has generated a great deal of speculation over the factors that have contributed to that decline. As with any fault-finding exercise, however, the answer is never completely found, the magnitude of the problem being much more complex than the simplicity of the question. Instead, once a "cause" or "culprit" has been found or is suspected a plethora of short-term, quick-fix solutions are presented and all too often thoughtlessly applied.

This mindless search for a nonexistent villain and the reactionary measures that follow are largely wasted effort, sometimes leaving the situation worse in the long run. The energy spent on finding a person or institution on which to place blame could be better spent on improving the system in question. But it somehow serves our sense of superiority if we can find someone or something on which to lay our sins instead of carrying them ourselves.

The book you are now reading does not search for hidden causes or guilty parties; it accepts the challenge of the situation and seeks a solution that will lead to improvement in the educational system. The proposed solution is found in the guiding principles of a management philosophy based on the pursuit of continuous improvement of quality. In different forms and forums, the philosophy has become known variously as total quality control, total quality management, and other names. It was rediscovered in this country in 1980, when the NBC White Paper entitled "If Japan Can, Why Can't We?" examined the quality philosophy, reintroduced the country to W. Edwards Deming, and effectively began the decade of the birth of widespread quality consciousness in the United States. Industry and government rediscovered the teachings of such quality experts as Deming, Walter A. Shewhart, and Joseph M. Juran, and greeted with appreciation the works of Kaoru Ishikawa and Genichi Taguchi. (The development of this quality movement is discussed more fully in Chapter 1.) Management rediscovered that a commitment to quality provides a greater return on investment of time, money, and effort than any other endeavor.

Effective application of this quality philosophy to the problems and processes of education is not a reflexive reaction that creates as many problems as it solves, or a palliative that covers up the problems rather than solving them; instead, it is an underlying cultural change that commits the nation to continuing improvement in education, educators, and students. It is not a program to improve education, but a way of thinking about education. The adoption of this new philosophy will not be accomplished by decree but by degrees, by gradual acceptance of new perceptions of and approaches to education. The change must, however, be precipitated by a major shift in outlook toward and understanding of quality as it relates to education, and as such the transformation of education is more like a revolution than an evolution.

In researching the application of quality principles to the practices of education, I chose to focus my attention on the philosophy of Deming. His approach, while based firmly on theoretical statistics, presents a quite complete and holistic view of quality and organizational success. I believe Deming's emphasis on individual satisfaction and esteem fits well with the aim of education, that is, preparing individuals for the future. Readers who disagree are encouraged to research further the quality philosophy in hopes of finding an approach that better fits their inclinations.

Regardless of the approach selected, change on a large scale will certainly not happen overnight; I recall one estimate that major changes in education take approximately 100 years.[1]

Because of the troubling state of education, we may hope the proposed transformation takes less time, but the results will be well worth whatever time and effort are put into the change.

❧

At this point it may be helpful for me to point out features of this book that may help you tailor your reading of it to your own background and interest. This book was originally intended to introduce educators and educational leaders to the quality philosophy; with that aim in mind, it may also be useful to parents, students, and policymakers as well. Quality professionals may also find its discussions interesting.

If you are an educator or educational administrator, you have endured attacks on education for many years and are probably painfully aware of everything in the Introduction. You may, however, have been unaware of the quality revolution; if so, you will find Chapters 1 and 2 useful for background information. Your primary interest will be in Chapters 3 through 7, where the quality philosophy is translated into educational terms.

As a parent concerned about your children's education, or a student in the midst of your own education, you may be particularly interested in the Introduction, where the benefits of quality education are outlined. Chapters 1 and 2 will give you background on the quality movement, while Chapters 3 and 4 focus on quality in education. Specific parts of Chapters 6 and 7 may also shed light on your important and decisive roles.

If you are a member of a school board or other advisory group, or are in a position to influence educational policy, you may find it useful to read closely Chapters 5 through 7 and the Conclusion. You are in the best position to foster the changes required and build the new quality culture, and these sections focus on leadership for the transformation.

I would advise quality professionals to skip (or perhaps skim) Chapters 1 and 2, as you are probably intimately familiar with this information; you will find no new information on the quality philosophy here. If, however, you are interested in its applicability to education, you may enjoy reading Chapters 3 and 4.

I have included four appendices for those with particular interests. Appendix A explains the traditional tools and techniques of quality management; it is no substitute for more technical materials, and certainly not for learning the tools under a master, but should be useful to educators and others who know little of the quality sciences. Appendix B examines changes in education in the United States through its historical development; such consideration may be useful in avoiding the errors of "throwing out the baby with the bathwater" or maintaining outdated and ineffective structures and practices. Appendix C briefly considers the relationship between values and education, and Appendix D discusses the treatment of "gifted and talented" students.

ea.

I believe this book had to be written by someone. Some may argue, perhaps rightfully so, that the someone should not have been me; this book may be rejected out-of-hand because I am an engineer and manager, not a professional educator.[2] So be it. I believe the state of education today is such that someone on the outside, looking in, had to question in ignorance what the experts have overlooked in familiarity. Following C. I. Lewis, "I draw some comfort from the thought that if the experts find my suggestions unacceptable, at least that is a compliment they also pay to one another."[3] This book therefore presents a unique mixture of naivete and bravado, which may be necessary to solving the problems at hand.[4]

Since it first became known that I had prepared this book, many people have tried to hang on me the title of "expert." Educators have referred to me as an expert on quality, and noneducators have called me an expert on education. I am neither. While it may appeal to the baser instinct of my vanity to be thought of in this way, I make no claim to any authority as an expert.

My purpose in writing this book was not to prove or demonstrate any special proficiency; my learning, like everyone's, is incomplete and still growing. Instead, my aim was to fuse what I saw as two distinct areas, hopefully to the benefit of both. Perhaps, however, "fuse" is the wrong word; I should rather hope to act as a catalyst, driving the reaction between education and the quality philosophy, or a midwife, helping a new educational paradigm emerge. For to bring forth, or be present at the birth of (for example, an idea), is the root of education (from the Latin *educare*).

The changes I propose will undoubtedly be difficult for many to accept. I believe they are necessary to preserving and improving U.S. strength and vitality. While some tentative and piecemeal steps toward educational reform have been made in the past, I believe its transformation must begin in earnest now, with the full support of every segment of society. If started too late or not at all, we must bear the responsibility for our failure. This is our challenge.

Gray Rinehart
Seneca, South Carolina
December 1991

ACKNOWLEDGMENTS

It would be impossible to mention all of the people with whom I have had the pleasure of learning and working. Secure in the knowledge that someone will be left out, I will still recognize a few who bear special mention.

This is a book about education, and I will start with those educators who have affected me significantly, whether for good or for ill. Thank you to Sandra Blake, who knew we really were serious; David Colwell, who called us obnoxious and egotistical; Butler Dargan, who taught us the value of hard work; Steve Eubanks, who gave us room to grow; Sharon Gordon, who opened our eyes; Bob Insley, who took a chance on us; Joe Isaac, who believed in us; Mike Johnson, who taught us dedication; Samuel H. Jones III, who thought we were crazy; Mary McKinney, who loved teaching; Pat Nooft, who put up with us; Jim Parker, who criticized us; Fred Reinartz, who taught us teamwork; Tommie Shubrick, who was our friend; Ruth Wasserman, who taught us to think; Bob Wehmeyer, who taught us courage. Thank you also to Dr. Ahmadian, who liked us; Dr. Dane, who encouraged us; Dr. Huey, who inspired us; Dr. Liburdy, who intimidated us.

I would like to especially thank a few of the many people who encouraged and/or made valuable contributions to this project: Dr. David Bayless, Dr. Dan Brown, Tyler Clements, Carroll Cobble, Jim Croteau, Nancy Duden, Dr. Anne Forester, Dr. Joe Gentry, Gary Goldman, Richard Hail, Theresa May Hicks, Dr. Craig Johnson, Eva Jones, David Langford, Brad Lego, Dr. Paul Messier, Emily Millett, David and Sharon O'Nan,

Linda Quass, Dr. John Surak, Janice Thompson, Robert Turner, and Doug Webb.

For his vision and helpful comments, I thank Dr. W. Edwards Deming.

For giving the impetus to this project and for helping me through the early going, I thank my teacher and friend Rob Gray.

For his support, encouragement, advice, and challenging ideas, I especially thank my friend and brother James H. Galt-Brown.

For putting up with me through over three years of research, writing, and editing, I thank my family.

All of the comments, suggestions, and criticism I have received throughout this project have been invaluable, and this finished work is much better than I could have accomplished alone. I hope I have given credit where credit is due, but I must take responsibility for any errors that remain.

Finally, for giving me the drive to complete this project, I thank God, who gave the world Jesus to show us that we don't know all we think we know.

AN EDUCATED NATION

Knowledge in any country is a national resource. Unlike rare metals, which can not be replaced, the supply of knowledge in any field can be increased by education. Education may be formal, as in school. It may be informal, by study at home or on the job. It may be supplemented and rounded out by work and review under a master.
　　　　　　　—*W. Edwards Deming,* Out of the Crisis

The United States of America has experienced a slow but definite decline in its global economic and political influence, a decline that has occurred in concert with another disturbing trend: the decreasing abilities of U.S. high school and college graduates. Especially at the elementary and high school level, U.S. education suffers in comparison with many other industrialized nations. Evidence shows that students in this country have less factual knowledge, cannot reason as well, and are less aware of the current world around them than their counterparts around the globe. As only one example, many eighth graders in Japan are reportedly more fluent in mathematics than graduates of some

1

U.S. business schools.[1] This state of affairs has evolved while expenditures per student in public schools more than tripled from the 1949–1950 school year to 1985–1986.[2]

The link between this nation's decaying educational system and our declining global influence may be only tenuous, but the total downward trend is not entirely coincidental. Industry and government have been forced to institute costly remedial education and training programs to bring graduates up to minimum levels of performance. In addition to the significant up-front cost of administering such programs is the hidden cost of lost opportunity from the time these individuals are in training and not doing productive work. This situation has saddled both the private and public sectors with a competitive disadvantage that our industrialized neighbors do not share.

It is certain that mediocre education, by producing workers who are inept, has contributed to the crippling of U.S. industry; industry, though, has contributed its share to the decline of education in this country. By investing as little as possible of its own money in research, innovation, and improvement—thereby maintaining a status quo—industry has implicitly shown that increased and improved knowledge is only marginally desirable. And by relying more and more heavily on corporate mergers, leveraged buyouts, and hostile takeovers to boost profits—rather than actually producing valuable goods and services—industry has sent the message that clever manipulation rather than true innovation is the key to success.

The debilitating effects of poor education have also shown up far from the factory floor and corporate boardroom. There is a tendency to point to such phenomena as the crack houses and gang warfare that have entered even small-town life in the United States, the rising numbers of teenage pregnancies and abortions, and the alarming numbers of suicide attempts among young people as further evidence of the decay of our educational system; but to lay all of these problems on the head of education is certainly to find a scapegoat to bear the blame for our societal transgressions. Poor education may have exacerbated some of these problems, but it did not cause them.

For much of the 1980s, educators, parents, and students were bombarded with educational "reforms" designed to foster excellence in education. This move toward quality, or excellence, in education gathered momentum late in the decade but actually started long before the much-heralded publication of *A Nation at Risk* or the activities of the National Commission on Excellence in Education.[3] Many states and municipalities started local reform movements designed to improve school conditions and instruction, but the results of these efforts were mixed, and they were not coordinated enough to effect change on the national level. The collective results of these isolated programs prove that national change will be required to complete the educational transformation; while this became clear in 1989, the resulting Education Summit only served to perpetuate negative elements of the existing system.[4]

We are essentially ignorant about our own educational system and are unfortunately doomed to remain so. We can never know how many students have been shamed into submission by competition, grades, and class ranking, or how many will blossom when these external motivators are replaced by joy in learning. We can never know what revolutionary answers to today's problems are lost forever in the murky depths of poor self-esteem, or what innovative solutions will come from students and teachers whose confidence and self-image are reinforced by parents and administrators. We can never know how much tax money has been spent in futile attempts to correct the failures of the educational system—that is, those "failures" who walked out of the schools having been robbed of the chance at a good education[5]—or how much will be saved by investing in education and its continuous improvement.

Those who hope to lead the education transformation (and by this I am referring to you, the reader) must recognize the elusive nature of these figures. They are among the "unknown and unknowable" figures that are most important to the task of leadership and change.[6] (Of course estimates of the figures may be generated, but such estimates are only useful when we all agree on how they are derived. Still they only serve to call attention to the problems, not to produce useful solutions.) As leaders of the transformation process, we must focus on improving quality in education, knowing it will stimulate successive improvements in every area of life. In the end it will not be necessary to quantify how much the education transformation has accomplished, because we will realize our purpose is not to look backward at where we have been but to look forward to the next improvements we can make.

The desirability of quality in education is rarely debated; no school operates on the assumption that it will provide a poor education.[7] Payoffs of improving educational quality will be many. Students will experience joy in learning, and more will graduate. Teachers will enjoy improved self-esteem and status. Graduates will possess skills valued by their employers; they will be able to learn their jobs quickly, participate in quality improvements in the workplace, and keep up with rapid changes in technology. The literacy rate of the country will rise, resulting in improved communication and understanding between elements of our diverse population. It is entirely possible that the United States will experience a renaissance (or perhaps a reformation) that will carry it into the twenty-first century.

COMPETENCE

In the process of applying the quality philosophy to education, we will pay a great deal of attention to the external customers of education. While their specific needs are not exactly the same, we may divide those needs into groups of skills employees must have to thrive on the job (see Chapter 3). In short, employers want to hire workers who are competent, that is, employees who can analyze and solve problems, work effectively in teams, and decipher and retain complex concepts. Their competence may be specific to a job or task, but more likely will be general and exhibit the ability to be trained in specific areas.[8] Quality education, by providing a sound curriculum of communication, analytical, and human-relations skills, assures that graduates will become competent employees.

As mentioned previously, U.S. businesses and government are spending tremendous amounts of money and time training and retraining young employees—people who have recently graduated from school as well as young people who have entered the workforce without graduating. While the quality emphasis will not remove the need for specialized training, it will give new workers a wide range of skills that will make their training easier. Fewer remedial programs will be needed; thus employees' time will be spent more effectively as they learn job-specific knowledge and skills. In addition, quality education can instill in students the ability to press on toward higher levels of knowledge by providing a modicum of challenge rather than intellectual pabulum. The ability to learn effectively will continue to be important throughout graduates' work careers.

Besides basic skills graduates will carry into the workplace, they will bring other important traits that have been reinforced by the quality ethic. Improved ability to work effectively in groups toward successful completion of projects will have been carefully nurtured by relevant team problem-solving exercises and will help employees whether they work on a production line or in a staff office. The new cultural recognition that all elements of the organization work together toward the ultimate aim of the group will enable employees to participate freely in the optimization of the entire organizational system. Strong self-esteem will give employees the ability to suggest changes and improvements with less fear. These factors will spur continuous improvement and subsequently enhance productivity in our service and manufacturing industries.

In order to effectively prepare graduates for life-long careers, education must have comprehensive guidance from the business community. Clear and continuously updated statements of need from industrial (including service and manufacturing) organizations will help the educational establishment prioritize the needs of industry. Symposia that bring together educators, corporations, and the government (for example, the annual symposia on The Role of Academia in Total Quality Management) could provide this feedback regularly, but their focus must be carefully considered. Academia must not allow itself to be led by the nose by business, but neither may it remain cloistered in its hallways. The sometimes adversarial relationship between education and industry must turn to collaboration and cooperation.

TECHNOLOGICAL AND TECHNICAL EXPERTISE

Many students who choose to pursue jobs and careers in technical fields will find their disciplines changing rapidly as soon as they enter them. As discussed in Chapter 7, changes over which they have no control can create strong emotional reactions in people. Effective preparation for these inevitable technological changes is necessary for psychological survival in the modern world.

Quality and excellence in education will help students comprehend the complex technological world and prepare them to keep up with it. Students must be exposed to technology firsthand, in such a way that they are not awed by it but appreciate and have control over it. Part of the curriculum proposed by many reformers is a course in computer science, in which students learn to understand and use this valuable tool. The use of new technological learning tools is one way to introduce students to technology, but the tools themselves cannot guarantee quality education. A number of industries have turned to expensive and complex machinery to save them, only to find that the devices were not the saviors they thought; education must not make this same mistake.[9] Another good way to expose students to technology is to involve local businesses and utilities in the educational experience through field trips and other exchanges.

Through careful exposure to the technical and social aspects of science and technology (beyond the color television and the compact disc player), students will improve their ability to cope with future advances. Social aspects cannot be ignored; special effort should be made to give students opportunities to consider how improvements in technology have affected previous eras. This is a prime topic through which history, science, and sociology classes may be correlated. By studying how these changes affected previous generations, students will be more able to control their reactions to them. Quality education will introduce students to the excitement and wonder of technology through relevant and personal contact, laying a foundation by which they can find new approaches to and uses for it. Technical expertise and the general competence already discussed form a synergistic whole; because education will give students the intellectual tools they need to keep learning after they leave school, the quality transformation will tend to reduce the crisis of technological obsolescence.

THE INFORMED POPULACE

In a nation where a large variety of culturally distinct populations live and work together, the ability of the different groups to understand and communicate effectively with each other is absolutely essential. Misunderstanding and miscommunication only breed intolerance and hatred, while their opposites make peaceful coexistence at least possible. As E. D. Hirsch and his associates at the University of Virginia have argued, consistent treatment of basic knowledge topics can improve everyone's ability to communicate effectively.[10] Adoption of a standard curriculum like that presented in Chapter 5 would give all students a common set of references and improve their abilities to communicate with other members of society.

In this nation, the majority of the power is supposed to be vested in the hands of the people; therefore, it is vitally important that the people know what issues are at stake when they vote. Participation in a democracy certainly requires active citizen involvement; it also requires citizens who understand each other not only in present situations but in light of their history and future possibilities.[11] We cannot hope to develop a concerned, active, and effective citizenry without developing an informed populace. Respect for all segments of the population must be cultivated if decisions are to be made that do not arbitrarily harm or shortchange any group. Citizens who are intimately familiar with the problems facing society and respectful of the impact of possible solutions on their neighbors will be better able to make appropriate decisions about how to vote on critical propositions and whom to elect as their leaders. The depth of understanding required for this decision making is usually beyond the scope of television; it must be addressed in the schools.

Based on these factors, one positive outcome of improvements in education will be a steadily rising literacy rate throughout the nation. Popular opinion is that the proliferation of television works against such a development, since the visual image has largely replaced the need for reliance on the printed word. Recent scholarship, however, suggests this may not be as much of a factor as once thought.[12] It is nevertheless chilling that increased literacy—the ability to comprehend the written word—might be wasted on a population with easy access to such powerful visual stimulation. (Focusing on the intellectual effect of television, of course, does not even begin to address its moral, social, or emotional impacts.) We must nevertheless work for improved literacy, hoping that increasingly literate adults and children will seek and find enjoyment in newspapers, magazines, and books that stimulate deeper thought and imagination than the shallow television image.

It would indeed be significant if U.S. citizens delved deeper into political issues than we presently do, instead of relying on the mud-slinging or self-aggrandizement of campaign commercials. Careful perusal of the candidates' political platforms, ideologies, and experience would provide voters with particularly acute insight, as candidates who present themselves as leaders might be exposed as puppets controlled by the political machine. In addition, honest consideration of both sides of controversial issues would open the door to improved communication and eventual solutions.

Other areas of life would certainly benefit from increased literacy. Citizens who better understand the vagaries of the nation's economy, as well as the implications of economic situations such as the rising national debt and trade imbalance, would be able to understand the need for restraint in consumerism, the importance of savings, and the benefits of a long-range outlook. Citizens who understand the inherent difficulties in developing alternative sources of energy might be convinced to save oil and reduce pollution by driving more fuel-efficient automobiles, instead of mindlessly screaming at petroleum and other corporations over environmental accidents. Citizens who take the time to read in detail of the atrocities of U.S. slavery, Communist purges, Nazi death camps, and South African prisons might be more inclined to work for the basic rights of all people rather than their own special segments of the population.

Besides basic literacy, a quality education that provides people with the means to assess and construct their own values (discussed in Appendix C) will give the populace an important tool of discernment: skepticism. If citizens can learn to dig deeper into issues rather than accepting them at face value, their ability to divine the kernel of truth and choose their own position accordingly will be greatly enhanced. The trick will be to instill healthy skepticism without it turning into cynicism.

LIFETIME EDUCATION

Each of the three areas we have discussed (job competence, technical expertise, and an informed citizenry) points to education that does not terminate with a diploma. It is no longer enough for the youth of the nation to receive only a quality initial education.

But why should adults continue to learn? The question, while basic, is not as naive as it sounds. Besides the internal enjoyment and fulfillment of learning new things, external factors provide some impetus for continued education (for example, as discussed previously, the rate at which current technology and knowledge is progressing presupposes the need for education throughout one's lifetime, just to keep up). Many people still perceive life as a series of stages in which the first stage is for learning, the second stage for working, and the third stage for playing (that is, retirement). To achieve fulfillment in one's life, it is necessary to combine learning, working, and recreation throughout life.[13] Quality education provides a foundation for the continued education that is essential to personal and professional fulfillment.

Continuing education (alternately called *adult education, informal education, postsecondary education, recurrent education,* and a host of other names[14]) has its own special problems, separate from education in general. Teaching adults can be both easier and more difficult than teaching children. Adult education is easier because many have made a conscious choice to participate and are motivated to learn for one reason or another; the same may not be true of young people who are required to attend school. Difficulty in teaching adults often arises because they have developed more or less concrete ideas about the world from their previous experience, which teachers have less chance to affect; this is why many teachers prefer working with younger students and why teaching young people offers its own unique challenges.[15] Lacking the skepticism of adults, young people can often be swayed by whatever they are taught, regardless of its merit.[16] In contrast, there are obstacles from the beginning when teaching adults, especially when the material challenges some of the students' ideas or prejudices. I have found this to be especially true with emotional or controversial issues.[17]

As with initial education, continuing education suffers from disagreement over its purpose. As you will discover when we consider the meaning of quality in education (Chapter 3), we will consider only briefly its philosophical purpose, instead concentrating on the practicality of pleasing education's customers. When we do, you are encouraged to consider who the customers of continuing education are and how they are affected by what the student learns.

The quality transformation in formal schooling will greatly improve the prospects for continuing education. Once students go through school experiencing joy in learning, they will want to continue learning throughout their adult lives. The transformation of educational operations should also extend to continuing education, providing a favorable learning experience for students whether they are 16 or 60.

MEETING THE CHALLENGE

Looking far ahead to the benefits we expect to reach is important; it gives us a reason to continue working. But we must also look critically at the situation as we find it to understand it completely and propose meaningful solutions.

The education community is steeped in paradigms (of school structure, curriculum design, professional relationships, and other aspects of the educational process) that have become entrenched in the education establishment over many years (see Appendix B). Paradigms are unwritten rules, generally accepted and rarely questioned throughout a field, that define the boundaries of the field and explain how to be successful within the boundaries.[18] The paradigm is a powerful force for solidifying approaches to problem solving in a field, but changes in the operational environment can render old paradigms obsolete.

In many schools across the United States, educators are meeting the challenges of today's educational needs with a new paradigm: the quality philosophy. They are using quality improvement methods to improve administrative functions and the learning environment, and are teaching the quality philosophy and allowing their students to apply its principles to their activities.[19] The resistance they have encountered is only slowly being overcome as more educators learn about the power of the new quality paradigm to improve their schools.

This book will introduce you to the quality philosophy and explain how its new paradigm can transform education to better meet the needs of our nation. If you are a teacher or administrator caught in the middle of reform efforts, this book will give you a clearer picture of the systems within which you work and the paths to improving the systems. If you are a parent, student, or businessperson concerned about education, this book will give you a better understanding of your role in the system and how you can contribute to continuous improvement.

If you are looking for a cookbook to follow as you transform your school, you should look elsewhere; no easy-to-follow recipes for success are included. This book is a guide to the quality philosophy, a book of theory intended to introduce you to the new educational paradigm and prepare you to take a leadership role in the transformation.

OVER THE HORIZON

What changes will improving educational quality bring to life in these United States? Possibly, the advent of quality in education and the incalculable improvement in attitude toward learning and school may spark a resurgence of community life. In the same way that local lyceums were centers of intellectual life in nineteenth-century communities (see Appendix B), today's local schools and community colleges (in addition to libraries, museums, auditoriums, and theaters) may bring more people together to learn and grow. Whether or not a new forum for public learning develops, it is almost certain that the transformation of education will deeply affect U.S. life. The relations between segments of society will be improved, removing fears of hatred and prejudice; many obstacles to personal fulfillment will be removed, and more citizens will finally have the chance to secure the Jeffersonian dream of freedom and happiness; better understanding of the social and political structures of the country will lead to more meaningful public discourse on important issues affecting the entire populace.

Our hope must not be blind, however; we must not fall into the familiar trap of "proclaim[ing] salvation through education" and so neglecting other problems we face.[20] While we recognize that many problems plague our nation, problems that must be addressed soon but will not be quickly solved, we must also recognize that quality education is the foundation upon which much of the future of this nation will be built.

11

But what impetus do we have to enact the changes that the educational system requires? We may be lacking a critical ingredient of change: a clear and coherent vision of the future of our nation. If it is true that "major changes in educational institutions follow major changes in society's future aspiration,"[21] then we need to examine critically what our vision for the future is. If in our vision the United States is strong, prosperous and at peace with itself, education must lay a solid foundation upon which that future may be built. With this in mind, let us examine the quality philosophy and how it may help us reach our vision of the future.

THE QUALITY SHIFT

A skilled commander seeks victory from the situation and does not demand it of his subordinates.

—Sun Tzu, c. 400 B.C.

At the midpoint of the twentieth century, no two countries could have been further apart than the United States and Japan. The United States was hardly affected by World War II, while Japan was devastated. U.S. industry was building down from wartime production, while Japanese industry was in shambles, nearly completely destroyed.[1] Japanese industry, trying to rebuild and enter the world marketplace, battled against a significant liability: the perception of Japanese goods. Japanese war machinery had been first-rate, but *Made in Japan* meant cheap, low-quality consumer goods, more suited to toys and novelties than serious commodities. In contrast, *Made in U.S.A.* connoted high-quality durable goods, consumer items that promised and delivered the highest standard of living.

By the 1980s a dramatic shift had taken place. *Made in Japan* had grown to delineate the highest quality consumer products that could be bought, goods that were available at extremely reasonable and competitive prices and virtually defined high technology. *Made in U.S.A.* had lost its superior meaning, becoming in many cases little more than a patriotic plea to U.S. consumers rather than a seal of corporate or national pride.

In the 1980s some U.S. companies discovered the reason behind the shift in economic power toward Japan. The basis of the shift lay not in such postulated causes as governmental incentives, currency differences, wage discrepancies, or a special Japanese "work ethic;" it was revealed to the U.S. in the 1980 NBC White Paper "If Japan Can, Why Can't We?" The power behind the shift lay in a management philosophy of continuous quality improvement the Japanese had imported from the United States. But while Japan had quickly grasped the quality philosophy out of necessity for its economic survival, managers in this country clung to practices developed early in the era of large-scale manufacturing.

SCIENTIFIC MANAGEMENT

In the United States in the late 1800s, the concept of *scientific management* was developed by engineer and inventor Frederick W. Taylor. Though it did not earn its name until 1911, it quickly became the standard for management of U.S. businesses and other enterprises. The concept was based on reducing each job or task to its smallest independent units, then making those units more efficient through time-and-motion studies and introduction of new or modified tools and techniques. One of Taylor's disciples, a former bricklayer named Frank Gilbreth, together with his wife, developed a pseudoscience called *motion economy* that reduced the number of motions required to perform a task to the bare minimum.[2] It was in this era that surgeons learned to say "Scalpel!" with outstretched hand and nurses learned to slap the instrument into the doctor's palm.

The United States became a land where productivity and quality were second to none. In time, however, economy of scale dominated quality as the measure by which businesses succeeded, and even a 1930s study that demonstrated a major contradiction in the scientific management principle could not detract from it. In the study, various working conditions of telephone assembly teams at Western Electric Company's Hawthorne Works in Chicago were changed, and the effect each change had on the assembly teams was noted. The startling results led the experimenters to conclude that concern for and interest in the work teams was the driving force behind increases in productivity, more than the controlled environmental factors.[3]

It took little time for catch phrases like "If it ain't broke, don't fix it" and "Good enough for government work" to permeate the popular vocabulary. Evidence today shows that the scientific management mind frame and the prevailing attitude of "good enough" have taken their toll. U.S. manufactured goods through the mid-1980s continued to be produced in record numbers, but they were returned, repaired, and finally discarded in equally high numbers. While this phenomenon may be attributed to the U.S. consumer's desire to own the latest model of everything, at least part of the problem was poor quality and "planned obsolescence."

It is somewhat unfair to heap all of the quality problems of this country's industry on the scientific management principle. Early in the 1800s U.S. industry had already begun to manufacture products that were good enough to be sold, but not the best they could be.[4] By focusing on production efficiency rather than product suitability, scientific management simply allowed the extension of an already developed mind-set.

While scientific management was in its heyday, and long before the decline of U.S. competitive position in the world, a few forward-thinking individuals saw that decreased emphasis on the quality of manufactured goods would soon get this country into trouble. Their work in analyzing the ills of U.S. industry went largely unnoticed. Some of their suggestions, in fact, were misinterpreted and misapplied, actually exacerbating the problem.

STATISTICAL QUALITY CONTROL

In 1922, engineer George S. Radford published *The Control of Quality in Manufacturing*, effectively beginning the modern quality era. Radford pointed out that one of the problems of U.S. manufacture was the emphasis on quantity over quality. He challenged the traditional and popular notion that improvements in

15

quality always led to increased consumer prices. His solution to the quality problem—which was not an optimal solution, as we will see—was to install inspection in production systems to assure uniform quality in products going to consumers.[5]

Later, in the 1920s and 1930s, unique applications of statistical methods were developed at the Bell Laboratories, where the theories of Walter A. Shewhart ushered in the quality revolution. Shewhart's genius was to recognize that variation exists in every process, and his prime contribution to what became known as *statistical quality control* (SQC) was the invention of the control chart, a graphical method for tracking the normal and abnormal variation of industrial processes (see Appendix A). The control chart was intended to help producers minimize the losses incurred from two prevalent mistakes: making changes to the process when change was not warranted, and failing to make changes when change was called for.[6] The chart was an important tool that enabled managers and workers to understand when they should take action and when they should allow the process to operate undisturbed. Shewhart's theories were ultimately published in 1931 in his book *Economic Control of Quality of Manufactured Product,* in which he quoted from Radford's earlier work:

> The term 'quality,' as applied to the products turned out by industry, means the characteristics or group or combination of characteristics which distinguishes one article from another, or the goods of one manufacturer from those of his competitors, or one grade of product from a certain factory from another grade turned out by the same factory.[7]

Shewhart's theories were later expanded in his 1939 book *Statistical Methods from the Viewpoint of Quality Control.*[8]

Shewhart's contemporaries also added to the growing SQC field. Harold Dodge and Harry G. Romig developed inspection plans based on statistical sampling which were used during World War II. Their work eventually became known as Military Standard (MIL-STD) 105. Driven by the needs of wartime production without a highly skilled, well-trained workforce, SQC techniques were applied to the manufacture of military goods and weapons. The SQC methods were so effective some of them were actually classified until after the fall of Nazi Germany.[9] Though he helped develop the detailed inspection

16

plans, Dodge knew that inspection does not guarantee quality: "You cannot inspect quality into a product."[10] Thus Radford's reliance on inspection was misguided.

Application of SQC principles promised to produce high-quality goods at prices consumers could afford, but misunderstanding of the quality emphasis—and in some instances the statistical methods themselves—reduced their impact. Manufacturers saw the new methods as a means of maintaining their "good enough" quality level, rather than continuously improving the quality. Much of this resulted from the belief that increasing quality would lead to higher costs and higher consumer prices; later applications, however, showed that the opposite was true.[11] In time SQC techniques were used only in isolated instances, and those who preached the gospel of quality had to find a new audience.

Their new audience spoke Japanese.

QUALITY AND THE JAPANESE

World War II left Japan a shattered country. Once densely populated urban areas lay desolate, and shanties built from broken pieces of buildings and scraps of metal took the place of homes and factories. Tokyo was crowded with homeless people, and everyone waited in long lines for food that grew scarcer by the day. One quarter of the nation's production capacity had been destroyed, and shortages of electricity, fuel, and raw materials made industrial activity that much more difficult. Japanese industrial output was practically nonexistent.[12] From this desperate situation Japan rose to industrial preeminence in the world, largely because of a newfound focus on quality and customer satisfaction.

One of Shewhart's followers gave early impetus to the quality revolution in Japan. W. Edwards Deming, a statistician who had worked in the U.S. Department of War, the Department of Agriculture, and the Census Bureau, traveled to Japan in the late 1940s to teach applied statistics in the area of surveys. He was invited back by the Union of Japanese Scientists and Engineers (JUSE) and in July of 1950 lectured on SQC and quality management. Believing that it was "vital not to repeat in Japan…the mistakes made in America,"[13] Deming outlined the philosophy of continuous quality improvement. He particularly emphasized management's role in optimizing its systems (see Chapter 2).[14] Deming lectured again in Japan in 1951 and 1952, and his lectures formed much of the theoretical basis for Japan's quality emphasis.

When Deming was in Japan lecturing on quality, the economic situation had improved somewhat. Japan was in the process of rebuilding its industrial infrastructure, using investments from abroad to expand and improve its production capabilities.[15] The country was, however, still stuck with a less-than-favorable perception of its manufactured goods. In a remarkable turnaround, by 1980 Japan had risen to a position of power in the global economy that had been almost unthinkable 30 years before.

๛   ๛

THE QUALITY FIELD GROWS

After Deming another U.S. quality expert, Joseph M. Juran, lectured in Japan at the request of JUSE. Juran's lectures were primarily to top and middle management and were very successful. The strength of his lectures was his ability to communicate effectively the importance of quality and quality improvement to managers at that level. Juran successfully translated quality concepts into a language managers could easily understand: the language of money.[16]

Later in the 1950s, Armand V. Feigenbaum added to the growing body of quality control expertise. He coined the phrase *total quality control* to define an all-encompassing philosophy of quality that combined quality development, maintenance, and improvement disciplines. His use of the word "total" was meant to differentiate the integrated system of quality management and engineering from the limited work that had begun the quality control field.[17]

While the quality emphasis seemed to languish in this country during the 1950s and 1960s, Kaoru Ishikawa and Genichi Taguchi translated and modified the quality improvement philosophy in Japan. Ishikawa started *quality control circles* among

Japanese workers; in the U.S. this phenomenon would become the *quality circle movement*.[18] Taguchi stressed the importance of the quality loss function and made statistical design of experiments more accessible to workers and engineers, removing some of the mystery of the statistical methods.[19]

In the late 1970s and early 1980s, Philip Crosby brought U.S. attention back to quality and quality management. Using ideas first developed by Juran and Feigenbaum, he presented the cost of quality—that is the monetary cost to an organization of a lack of quality—as a means of alerting management to the need for quality improvement. In addition, he was a primary proponent of the drive for *zero defects*.[20]

For more in-depth comparisons of the differences between the viewpoints of some leading quality experts, see *What Is Total Quality Control?* by Kaoru Ishikawa, and *The Quest for Quality in Services* by A. C. Rosander.[21]

⁂ ⁂

The Japanese borrowed heavily from quality improvement ideas developed in the U.S., but their acceptance and application was influenced by the strength of their own culture. Cultural aspects of Japanese industrial society have been discussed at length by many experts—they will not be dealt with here—and attempts have been made to find out why the Japanese were able to adopt the quality philosophy so quickly. From *Theory Z* to the use of the *kanji* script, the explanations seem largely unable to capture the subtleties of the cultural acceptance of quality as a way of life.[22]

The Japanese do not deny the influence of imported ideas on their efforts; in fact, they are grateful. Japanese appreciation of U.S. quality guidance is best evidenced by the Deming Prize. First awarded in 1951—using royalties from the sale of one of the books derived from Deming's 1950 lectures—the Deming Prize and the Deming Application Prizes are awarded annually and have grown to become two of the most coveted prizes in Japan. The Deming Prize is awarded to an individual who has made the most significant contributions to statistical theory or has done the most to promote statistical methods. The Deming Application Prizes are awarded to corporations whose efforts to improve quality (along strict guidelines) are especially commendable. Deming Application Prizes are awarded based on examination of the quality program by a panel of judges, and are so highly honored that some companies will express interest in the prize and follow its guidelines as a sort of quest. Even if they are not in a position to compete for the prize, they reap benefits from the quality improvements they institute along the way.[23]

Despite their quick acceptance of the quality philosophy in 1950, the Japanese did at first experience a slight setback. For a short period of time they copied one major mistake of U.S. manufacture: they emphasized the statistical tools themselves instead of the overall quality philosophy.[24] After that false start, and largely because of Juran's lectures, Japanese quality and productivity improved remarkably.

From 1950–1960 Japan's economy grew at the rate of almost 10 percent per year, while the productive output of each worker rose at over 6 percent per year. In one recent comparison with the United States, it was noted that the Japanese economy in that period grew more in nine months than the U.S. economy will grow in 10 years.[25] While some of their phenomenal growth was the result of large foreign investments and not having anywhere to go but up, much of it can be traced to the Japanese quality emphasis.

One way the Japanese adapted the quality philosophy to their society, and made quality the responsibility of every level in industry, was through the *quality control circle*. Begun by Ishikawa in 1962, quality control circles involved volunteers from within a company who met to study statistical methods together.[26] Their success spawned a number of attempts in the United States to copy them; however, rather than studying and learning together, U.S. workers were expected to work together to solve particular problems. The poor results from these attempts led to the conclusion that the cultural aspects of Japanese society were a key to success that this country did not have. In reality, U.S. management copied what it did not fully understand. One major mistake of those trying to start quality control circles (which managers in the U.S. called *quality circles*) in this country was to mandate their use, rather than emphasizing the voluntary nature of the group. In addition, even when circles were started and made valuable suggestions, upper management often refused to use what they offered.[27] Thus what could have been a major boost to quality and productivity in the United States was thwarted by American management misunderstanding and indifference.

Japanese quality management, and the quality improvement ethic it has adopted, has brought the Japanese to the forefront of world trade. It has brought us into what Deming calls "a new economic age"[28] and its impact on the United States has been considerable.

THE U.S. FALL

Estimates put the U.S. share of global manufacturing before World War II at about one third. At the end of the war, the U.S.—whose factories and cities had escaped destruction—produced 40 percent of the world's manufactured goods.[29] Yet as the European and Asian economies rebuilt after the war, the U.S. share of industrial production shrank slowly. It was quite natural for this to happen as other nations' production rose, and the decline was so slow that many in this country took no notice. U.S. citizens were used to their ever-increasing standard of living and had become drunk on consumption of manufactured goods. Economic warning signals were typically either missed, colored by expert opinion, or ascribed to special, short-lived causes such as the energy crisis.

U.S. pride in its technology and achievements soon became U.S. complacency about its infrastructure and capacity. Factories and schools fell into disrepair, roads and bridges showed signs of wear, and industries began to feel competitive pressure from abroad. The United States, having become the ultimate consumer market for the world, bought much and saved little. Deficit spending and growing debts became the norm for the federal government. Industries, in much the same way as the general population, saved little money for investment in new equipment and facilities; their machines, some of which must be held together with tape and baling wire, are simultaneously a tribute to the industries that built them and an indictment of the industries that have run them into the ground. As its infrastructure crumbled, the nation fell behind in its ability to transform new technologies into consumer goods.[30]

Across the Pacific Ocean, Japan was investing money in industry, research, and education, and was beginning to surpass the United States in productivity. Japanese industry successfully took U.S. inventions and turned them into quality manufactured products, deftly judging the needs and desires of consumers around the world. Recently, Japan has relied less and less on imported technology, being able instead to rely on its own technology to develop new, innovative products.

When we realized our position at the top of the economic heap was threatened, responses were many and varied. Believing the massive federal bureaucracy was one source of waste, citizens voted in 1980 to trim back the government, only to see deficits grow as expenditures tied to obligatory entitlements rose automatically.[31] Advertising campaigns enticing consumers to buy goods "Made in the U.S.A." filled the media. Many citizens and commentators blamed the Japanese and other nations for exporting so much of their output without importing U.S. goods; placing blame was easier than accepting that the problem lay within our borders.[32] Congressional bickering about "fair" trading practices, in what had been a largely free (rather than necessarily fair) economy, led to debates over the relative evils of protectionism. Increased tariffs and other penalties were soon used in efforts to restrict imports and artificially open foreign markets to our manufactured goods.[33]

As with the various responses to the situation, many ideas about the causes were expressed. U.S. industry and society, some said, had become increasingly litigious[34]; critics charged this obsession with law stifled innovation and productivity. Another explanation: consumerism in this country had overshadowed investment while Japanese savings and investment had grown. It was reported that Japan added more each year in terms of replacement, repair, or new construction to its inventory of houses, factories, laboratories, and other facilities than the United States; an especially remarkable feat, considering they have only half the population.[35] None of the explanations seemed entirely adequate and served often to aggravate more than motivate.

Fault-finding rather than fault-correcting is wasted effort unless uncovering the causes leads to their correction. The causes examined by politicians, economists, and other analysts during the U.S. fall from economic preeminence gave only cursory clues and did not uncover the basic cause of the problem. Analysts generally missed the salient point that if this country was going to compete in the global marketplace, we could not continue trying to sell inferior goods at exorbitant prices. Some U.S. companies came to this realization during the 1980s and began to apply quality improvement principles to their operations. Their successes have proven that an emphasis on quality makes it possible to rebound from staggering losses and reclaim the market.

The increased interest in the importance of quality during the 1980s also led the U.S. Department of Commerce to propose a national award for quality, to recognize those corporations whose commitment to continuous improvement in quality and service is particularly noteworthy. Today the Malcolm Baldrige National Quality Award is a much sought-after award in the corporate world, though it is much different in nature from Japan's Deming Prize. Where the Deming Prize requires companies to adopt a strict approach to quality improvement under the watchful eye of JUSE, the Baldrige Award allows companies to choose the quality improvement approach that works for them; rather than a "stamp of approval" from an approving agency, the Baldrige Award recognizes companies whose quality efforts have been judged successful in relation to the award criteria.[36]

The aggregate of this quality work—using Deming's philosophy as a foundation and including the contributions of other quality experts—was adopted by the U.S. Department of Defense in 1988, and two years later by the entire U.S. Government. Christened *total quality management* (a term Deming does not recognize and prefers not to be associated with), this quality philosophy applies human resources and analytical methods to continuously improve the quality of goods and services continuously.[37] Its aim, at its most succinct, is to satisfy the needs of customers.

ào

While the quality philosophy leads to remarkable changes in organizational climate and productivity, experience in private industry and the government has shown that improvement in quality does not come easily; it involves conscientious application of the principles of quality management and sincere effort at all levels of the

23

organization to achieve the quality transformation. It will require the same effort to achieve fundamental changes in education.

THE QUALITY
TRANSFORMATION

The foreman should take into account the abilities and limitations of his men, circulating among them and asking nothing unreasonable. He should know their morale and spirit, and encourage them when necessary. This is the same as the principle of strategy.

—Miyamoto Musashi, 1645

Before we apply the quality philosophy to education, we will explore the basic elements of the management transformation from traditional practice to the quality paradigm. Transformation is an appropriate word, implying a drastic change at the most fundamental level, even to the point of changing the corporate culture. Effecting such a change in an established process or organization is a difficult task, and the required change of focus toward quality in service and manufacturing industries is no different. The quality transformation is made all the more difficult because it involves changing the perceptions of human beings. It will undoubtedly be met with resentment and resistance.

Part of the problem in the search for quality is the fact that definitions of quality differ according to perceptions of what quality is or should be. Often the approach to a definition depends on the desired emphasis. If the emphasis is on conformance to specifications, or cost-benefit, or product utility, or user satisfaction, or some esoteric and unreachable ideal, a definition of quality will be chosen to fit that emphasis.[1] The differences in perception between the customer and the supplier of a service or product result in gaps in communication, purpose, and delivery; bridging these gaps is the aim of the quality transformation.[2]

For the purposes of this book, quality does not refer solely to manufactured products, but refers also to quality of service; in addition, it involves customers who are internal to the organization (for example, the technician who installs the electronics in your television set after the chassis has been assembled) as well as external customers (for example, you, when you purchase the television).[3] I will define quality as it relates to the user or customer: the aggregate characteristics of a product or service that satisfy the needs of the customer, where the customer may be either the immediate recipient or the ultimate user of the product or service, or both.

The philosophical foundation for the cultural change that is the quality transformation is expressed first in *A Description of Reality*, then in *Deming's 14 Points*. Following the 14 Points we will discuss the plan-do-study-act cycle and the quality planning road map.

Analytical and statistical tools, while important to conducting the transformation, are secondary to the philosophical foundation. Reliance on the tools and techniques without understanding the basis for the transformation will jeopardize its success; therefore, tools used in the quality improvement effort are treated separately in Appendix A, with special applications to education.

A DESCRIPTION OF REALITY

Understanding quality and the management transformation requires an understanding of reality, that is, why things work the way they do. Deming presents this material as *A System of Profound Knowledge*,[4] a collection of interrelated concepts that togeth-

26

er form what I characterize as a metaphysical paradigm. As such, I prefer to call it a *description of reality*.[5]

Understanding reality, that is, understanding how the world works, involves comprehension of four concepts: appreciation for systems, theory of variation, theory of knowledge, and psychology. The four parts of the description interact with one another; they cannot be separated, and knowledge of one without knowledge of the others results in an incomplete understanding of reality. Leaders and managers must understand the four parts, but need not be expert in any one of them to understand the whole and apply it as a system.[6]

A **system** is defined as any collection of interdependent components that work together toward a specific goal. An organizational system consists of the sets and series of functions or activities that work together toward the organization's goals. Deming explains that an orchestra may be thought of a system with the aim of faithfully reproducing the music; he further points out that schools, "including private schools, parochial schools, and universities, provide an example of components that ought to work together as a system for education."[7] It is for the transformation and optimization of the education system that I have written this book.

Managing a system requires two things: understanding of the relationships between the various system components and a clearly defined aim or goal. Management of a system should be directed toward optimizing the entire system for the benefit of everyone, both inside and outside the boundaries of the system. This involves improving communication and encouraging cooperation between components so that all benefit, and judging the performance of each component by its contribution to the system. No component of the system operates by itself; all the parts are connected in some way and affect one another in a variety of ways. Thus no single component may be managed as if it operated in a vacuum, but must be operated in terms of its role in the organization and how well it supports the overall goals. It is deadly for middle managers to build their own little empires with no concern for the impact on the entire system or even to insist that their areas operate at top efficiency. On the contrary, "some components may operate at a loss to themselves, for optimization of the whole system."[8]

Variation is a natural part of the real world, guaranteed by probability theory.[9] Variation in everyday situations is readily observed. For example, it rarely takes exactly the same amount of time every day to get to work; when the waiter or waitress fills your cup of coffee or glass of tea, the cup is rarely filled to exactly the same level, and the temperature is not exactly the same as the last time. In his landmark work, *Economic Control of Quality of Manufactured Product*, Shewhart includes an example that illustrates natural variation, which I like to use in classes and seminars. On a clean piece of white paper, write the letter "*a*." (This assumes that we both agree on what an *a* is.) Next to the first *a*, write a series of *a*'s—10 or 20 will do nicely. Examining what you have written, you see that all of your *a*'s are not alike. To quote Shewhart:

> Why can we not do a simple thing like making all the *a*'s just alike? Your answer leads to a generalization which all of us are perhaps willing to accept. It is that there are many causes of variability among the *a*'s: the paper was not smooth, the lead in the pencil was not uniform, and the unavoidable variability in your external surroundings reacted upon you to introduce variations in the *a*'s. But are these the only causes of variability in the *a*'s? Probably not.[10]

Recognition of natural variation in outcomes, and following the variation over time, leads to understanding of the capability of processes by separating natural causes of variation from special causes. For example, natural causes of variation in the output of a machine tool might include the hardness of the material being worked and the vibration of the machine itself. Special causes of variation might include a new worker unfamiliar with the machine. Understanding the differences between these types of causes, that is, understanding the capability of a process, provides insight into improving the process. Managers who understand the processes they manage can avoid the two mistakes of (1) treating faults, mistakes, or breakdowns as special causes when they actually come from common causes, and (2) treating them as common causes when they actually come from special causes. Distinction between the two is vital and possible only through understanding of variation.[11]

Theory of knowledge forms the third part of the description of reality. The theory is expounded in great detail in the difficult little book *Mind and the World Order* by C. I. Lewis.[12] Briefly, knowledge is the acceptance or modification of concepts through experience, and forms the framework within which all communication and cooperation are possible. The formulation of a concept, however simple, is necessary before information can be acquired to test it. We form these conceptualizations when we are "confronted with the chaos of the given" and try "to discover within or impose upon this chaos some kind of stable order."[13]

Where Lewis uses the word *concept*, Deming substitutes the word *theory*. Those readers uncomfortable with either word but familiar with the scientific method as it is usually taught may prefer to substitute the word *hypothesis*.

True knowledge, therefore, is impossible without a concept or theory. Concepts are necessary to explain experience and predict future possibilities; therefore, examples from experience cannot by themselves generate knowledge, unless the concept or theory exists to explain them. This is not to say that theory is static; unexplained failures of a theory mean it must be modified, perhaps abandoned. Knowledge, following from theory, is the means by which possible futures are explored: "It is impossible to escape the fact that knowledge has, in some fashion and to some degree, the significance of *prediction.*"[14] Deming draws a concurrent conclusion that prediction is the primary function of management, that is, successful prediction of future outcomes is required for continued operation and is the responsibility of those in charge.[15]

Psychology is required to understand the behaviors and interactions of people. Psychology explains what we already know intuitively: people are different; they act uniquely in different circumstances, learn in different ways, and are motivated by internal and external factors. Management has classically understood enough psychology to stress external motivation, smothering internal motivation in the process; this is the legacy of B. F. Skinner and the behaviorists. This reliance on external factors (for example, pay, awards, time off) to motivate people essentially prostitutes them to the job, robbing them of self-esteem, dignity, and joy in their accomplishments.[16]

Proper application of psychology must stress internal motivation if we are to build people's self-esteem and treat them as human beings. This of course runs counter to traditional management

29

practices. It recognizes that "one is born with a natural inclination to learn and to be innovative. One inherits a right to enjoy his work. Psychology helps us to nurture and preserve these positive innate attributes of people" by relying on their internal motivation.[17]

Without an understanding of psychology, management is certain to alienate workers and rob them of their humanity, thus dooming the transformation process. A. C. Rosander points out how vitally important psychology is to the transformation: "Starting as well as maintaining a quality improvement program is primarily a human relations problem, a people problem."[18]

ॐ

Understanding reality (or, in Deming's parlance, possessing profound knowledge) enables managers to make rational, confident predictions about the short- and long-term consequences of their actions. Managers who understand reality will optimize the systems they manage to provide the greatest benefit to everyone working within those systems. But profound knowledge may not be as easy for managers to acquire as it may seem from this brief discussion, because it flies in the face of some of our conventional wisdom. Therefore, in addition to profound knowledge, Deming has developed his 14 Points.

DEMING'S 14 POINTS

Deming's 14 Points, or 14 management principles, form the basis for the transformation of any endeavor (manufacturing or service, private or public) into a quality-directed and quality-driven effort, and are extensions of the description of reality. The 14 Points are explained briefly here and in much more detail in Deming's book *Out of the Crisis* and in several other references.[19] Some of Deming's points may be considered obvious extensions of common sense, though Deming warns, "There are many hazards to the use of common sense."[20]

Some of the 14 Points may appear redundant, but they are not so much repetitive as they are overlapping. They may be arranged in different categories according to emphasis (that is,

30

human relations, optimization[21]), but here they are presented in the original order. Taken as a whole they provide a secure foundation on which to build quality consciousness and quality improvement. They are incompatible with efforts to undermine quality.

As we examine these keys to the quality transformation, you are invited to ponder how they may apply to education. We will discuss their applications in Chapter 4.

1. *Create constancy of purpose toward improvement of product and service, with the aim to become competitive, stay in business, and provide jobs.* Every task we undertake should have as its ultimate goal the improvement of quality, no matter which of us undertakes it. Wasted effort, wasted materials, and wasted time can be found in any level of any organization, and when that waste is equated to dollars the cost can be staggering. In industry, of course, one of the largest sources of waste is rework: products that do not quite meet specification such that they must go through the process again. A related source of waste is simple scrap—usually good for nothing, it can only infrequently be sold and then for a fraction of its value. The effort wasted producing scrap and reworking products to specification is turned into productive effort when the system is changed to facilitate production of good product.

The first step in moving toward improvements in products and services is to understand the concept of the process. Manufacturing processes are relatively well understood, but the delivery of services is also a process. Figure 2.1 illustrates and defines a process as the transformation of various inputs into an output or group of outputs through the application of work. The inputs may be raw materials, tools or equipment, people, operating procedures or manufacturing methods, and environmental factors. The process puts these inputs together and transforms them into outputs that are delivered to customers (who may be internal or external to the organization).

Improving the process is the key to improving products and services, but the variation within the process can make improvements difficult. If the variation is too great (that is, the system is in chaos), improvement is practically impossible, because the capabilities of the process are unknown. The process must first be brought into statistical control (see Appendix A). Once the system is under control, reduction of the variation in the process

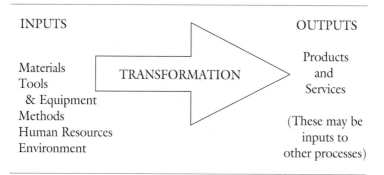

Figure 2.1   A Process: Inputs, Transformation, Outputs

means less effort and resources need to be spent on inspection of the outcomes and rework of rejected items.

The goal to improve processes, however, may lead to emphasis on individual work units rather than the entire organizational aim; Deming calls this *suboptimization*. Optimization (which may be thought of as fine-tuning) of the entire system is necessary to avoid the damaging effects of suboptimization (see point 9). To achieve full optimization, the system must be understood to be made up of interlinked and overlapping processes. Each person within the organization must understand his place within the system, and management must work continuously to optimize the efforts of the entire system (rather than a few single components).

Constancy of purpose is more than everyone knowing how they fit into the system. From the head of an organization to the working level the focus of attention must be on quality and must include the future as well as the present. Despite pressures to focus on the short term—for example, quarterly dividends or weekly production reports—organizations must plan for the long term, putting resources into planning and research. Unless they do not want the organization to exist in the future, all members must be involved in the quest for quality.

2.   *Adopt the new philosophy.* Western managers must awaken to the challenge, learn their responsibilities, and take on leadership for change. Thinking about quality, talking about quality, emphasizing

quality, and focusing on quality are ambiguous terms and do not fully express quality's relationship to the producer. Quality is the key to the producer's rise or fall; without a quality service or product (as perceived by customers and potential customers), producers cannot hope to survive except through cleverness and guile. Quality cannot be a secondary measure of success; ultimately, it is the only measure of success.

I do not wish to mislead you. Perceiving quality as an object to be produced or a state to be reached will produce short-lived efforts and only reap short-term goals. Why? Because quality—like anything else—can only be measured in terms of how it is *defined*, and definitions change over time. Continual emphasis on quality must include long-term adoption of all of the 14 Points and must be a part of a cultural change within the organization.

3. *Cease dependence on inspection to achieve quality.* Eliminate the need for inspection on a mass basis by building quality into the product in the first place. Inspection of work does not provide, improve, or guarantee quality, and inspectors do not produce anything but data. Systems and processes within an organization must be designed so quality is built in at the start, to minimize the need for inspection.

Reliance on inspection in attempts to "assure" quality can have adverse effects. Because inspections heap responsibility for quality on inspectors instead of on workers, employees are stripped of any pride they might have in their work (see point 12). And where multiple inspections are performed, quality almost inevitably suffers, as each inspector may overlook bad items because they have already been passed or "will be checked by the next inspector anyway."

Certainly some inspection will be necessary to determine process capabilities and identify areas for improvement. Even 100 percent inspection may be required if failure of the item costs significantly more than inspecting it. The total amount of inspection performed must be optimized to reduce the total cost to the organization.[22]

4. *End the practice of awarding business on the basis of price tag alone.* Move toward a single supplier for any one item on a long-term relationship of loyalty and trust. Purchasing must be done

33

with consideration of the quality and long-term costs of an item or service. While this seems intuitively obvious, in practice such considerations are rare and purchases go to the lowest bidder. The lowest bidder, however, usually will not provide the highest quality work; it may actually cost more in the long run for the work to be redone. The answer to this problem is long-term partnerships with suppliers, based on the recognition that both customer and supplier need each other and can exist quite well symbiotically. As part of the partnership arrangement, the customer must be willing to facilitate continuous improvement of the supplier's operation. That this involves dramatic changes in the responsibilities of purchasing agents and contract managers is clear, but such changes are required if the aim is constantly improving quality.

5. *Improve constantly and forever the system of production and service, to improve quality and productivity, and thus constantly decrease costs.* Contrary to popular perception, the improvement of quality does not have to result in exponential increases in cost; rather, the emphasis on quality in product or service decreases total costs by reducing waste and scrap. Continuous improvement of quality, therefore, is a perpetually profitable undertaking. Improvements in quality do not have to be drastic—the small, incremental improvements typical of the Japanese *kaizen* philosophy, when carried out faithfully over a period of time, result in significantly reduced waste, improved processes, and increased productivity.

Improving the overall system involves reducing the variation in the system; this provides a reference frame within which management may make predictions about the future. Variation, as discussed earlier, is a natural part of every process or system; the job of management is to separate the common causes of variation (for example, hasty design and production, inadequate testing, unreliable instruments and equipment, ignorance of the capability of the system, environmental conditions[23]) from special causes that result in short-lived perturbations in the system.

To keep improving quality into the future, organizations must strive to understand and build quality into every system at the outset, and must constantly be looking over the horizon at future needs. Ever-improving understanding of the processes in the organization and the needs of the consumers must be coupled with continuous effort to improve quality at every opportunity.

6. *Institute training on the job.* On-the-job instruction at every level must be emphasized. New workers should be taught their jobs not by other workers from whom they learn the job along with mistakes and sloppy work habits, but by personnel competent to teach them correctly. These trainers must recognize that different employees will learn at different rates and will learn better by different means, for example, reading, listening, watching, or doing. Supervisors at every level must be taught not only the importance of good training but the skills necessary to provide good training.

Training in the organization's quality philosophy is a primary component of the quality transformation. Personnel who will be affected by the transformation must first of all understand the need for change. In an industrial setting, many representations of corporate problems may be used to express the need for change: falling profits, impending layoffs, or increasing customer complaints may all be used to generate interest in the quality emphasis. The interest will wane, however, if management does not demonstrate its commitment to quality, that is, if the quality transformation is perceived as "just another management program" along the lines of "management by objective" or "zero defects."[24]

To turn interest into acceptance may require a small-scale application or pilot program that generates measurable results. Interest is a place to start, but acceptance, understanding, consistency, and results are necessary to sustain the change.

7. *Institute leadership.*[25] Leadership is not the same as management; managers must learn not only the difference between the two, but also the craft of leadership. The complete adoption of the quality philosophy requires leaders who are willing to take the steps necessary to bring the organization into the new culture and who are capable of enlisting the support of their workers.

To set the course for the organization, leaders must have a vision of what the organization is and should be. They must be able to communicate that vision to team members, partners, 35 and customers. In relating their actions to the stated vision, leaders must be consistent, especially with regard to quality—the hypocritical plant manager or supervisor who preaches commitment to quality, then pushes through inferior products for the sake of productivity, will not be successful in accomplishing the quality transformation. The conflicting signals will result in ambivalence or disbelief among employees, jeopardizing the entire effort.

As leaders, supervisors must recognize that it is their responsibility to provide workers with the proper tools and materials with which to do their jobs—in other words, they must make sure the systems and processes they manage allow their people to perform at their best. Providing suitable materials when needed, the right tools and the training to use them correctly, a healthy work environment, and an understanding of what is expected are the sole responsibility of management.

One instance in which leadership must be substituted for the inane practices of the day is the periodic performance appraisal. Current performance appraisal systems attempt to divide people into any number of categories of performance, for example, superior, outstanding, excellent, above average, average, below average, and should-have-been-fired-long-ago. Such convoluted systems have two major shortcomings. First, they simply do not recognize that employee performance is dynamic. Rarely is an individual always an outstanding performer; everyone has good days and bad days, good weeks and bad weeks. Second, appraisal systems do not take into account the fact that workers are caught within the systems their management has given them: the ratings workers receive are often based on factors beyond their control.

Performance appraisals, in creating what Deming calls "a shortage of winners"[26] within the organization, do little to motivate employees or enhance their job satisfaction. In fact they are frequently demotivators, resulting in reduced teamwork, stifled initiative, and little innovation.[27] What must be done? Management must replace these antiquated appraisal systems in favor of a new approach.

Like inspection (point 3), evaluation of personnel has a specific and limited usefulness. Small amounts of inspection must be carried on *as measurements of the process with the aim of improving its operation;* likewise, personnel evaluation must be designed with improvement of the system in mind. For example, an evaluation of how an entire group is performing as it moves toward its aim, that recognizes individual differences and the effect of the system on performance, might be considered. Workers would be given specific feedback on the results of their teamwork; individuals would not be rated or ranked. Such a system would be designed to find out what the workers need to perform better. Do they need additional training? Better materials? New equipment? This point has specific and controversial implications for education, which we will cover in detail in Chapter 4.

8. *Drive out fear, so that everyone may work effectively for the organization.* Today's corporate organizations are full of fear. Workers fear losing their jobs, being overcome by new technologies, appearing inept, being blamed for things beyond their control, and being ostracized by their work groups. Middle and upper managers live with their own sets of fears. This may seem to be a natural and unavoidable state of existence, but these fears are crippling our organizations, keeping people from taking pride in their work, and limiting their ability to innovate and add value to their work experience. To achieve the continuous improvement necessary for continued survival, everyone must be able to participate fully in the organization and in the improvement process without fear. Members must be secure in their positions, so they can effectively share their ideas and opinions.

This again points to management. Management must work to reduce the levels of fear and anxiety experienced by employees. One key to this is involving workers in decisions that affect them; this recognizes their natural need to feel some control over their lives, and has been practiced in many circles as *participatory management.* But management must not limit itself to participating with workers; it is essential not only to listen to the ideas and suggestions of workers but to implement as many of them as possible. Unions must be invited and encouraged to participate in the quality transformation to avoid creating additional fears in their ranks—they themselves being products of adversarial relationships and fear run rampant. Unions and management must recognize that they are partners with the common goal of achieving success for the organization.

9. *Break down barriers between departments.* No one area can be responsible for the quality philosophy, and no one area can improve the entire organization's quality alone. The barriers that have been erected within organizations stifle innovation; instead of individual effort behind departmental walls, teamwork at every level and between every area is required to start and maintain the quality transformation.[28]

The existence of barriers can be attributed to many causes. Poor communication creates and is perpetuated by barriers within the organization. Ignorance of the overall aim of the organization can create barriers by leading departments to substitute their own goals for the organization's, resulting in crippling suboptimization. Many organizations actively foster competition between departments, rather than stressing cooperation for the achievement of the common good. The different backgrounds among, for example, factory workers, accountants, and engineers can themselves build barriers between these groups. Excessive levels of management, fear in the organization, jealousies, and many other factors can also result in barriers.[29] Despite the reasons for the barriers, they must be removed if the quality transformation is to be complete.

The need for cooperation rather than barriers within the organization was espoused when Ishikawa coined the phrase "the next process is your customer" to demonstrate the importance of internal customers.[30] Industrial examples are easy to see. The purchasing agent's customers are the workers who must use the materials they purchase; the machine operator's customer is the next person who will use or work on what they produce; the bookkeeper's customers are the workers collecting their paychecks; and everyone's customer is the ultimate user of the product or service.[31]

When we understand systems, we realize every area within the organization overlaps other areas to some extent; these relationships must be nurtured to facilitate the greatest improvements in quality. For example, marketing must communicate with engineering to assure that customer desires are considered in product design, and engineering must communicate with production so the product can be made efficiently, and so on. Communication between the functional areas is not enough, however; management must actively optimize the entire system for the benefit of the whole organization.

Optimizing the complicated systems of a large organization may be difficult, but the payoffs are enormous. The first step is to remove any incentives that recognize the achievements of a single group or individual, or the completion of any single task, over any other. For example, sales representatives must no longer be rated or rewarded on the basis of their individual sales: they may have oversold an item to boost their productivity figures, while floor workers struggled in vain to complete the orders. Purchasing agents must no longer be rated or rewarded on the basis of the money they save: they may have bought materials that are unusable and must be discarded or completely reworked. Such suboptimization pits the elements of the system against one another, to the disadvantage of all members.[32]

10. *Eliminate slogans, exhortations, and targets for the workforce asking for things they cannot deliver.* Is it not evident that signs and slogans requesting superhuman efforts required to achieve ambitious but unattainable goals ask too much? Less obvious but equally true is that even simple posters advertising and inviting participation in the quality improvement process are unnecessary and may in fact be detrimental to the overall effort. Too often such things are aimed at the workforce, implying that poor quality or productivity is the workers' fault. As pointed out previously, workers are trapped within the processes they have been given by management; poor quality is a product of the system, and the system cannot recognize words, only changes.

An example from my own experience may help clarify this. When we evaluated machine shops for safety and health compliance, we noted which machinery produced hazardous noise levels or might throw fragments when operating. In those work areas and on those machines we were required to place signs warning operators of the danger and requiring the use of protective equipment (for example, hearing protection, face shields). How much good would those signs do to protect the workers? By themselves they could do nothing; so as safety management we made sure the proper protective equipment was on hand and in good condition at the machine itself, and that all machine operators understood the need for and use of the equipment. Reminding the workers with obnoxious signs that the equipment was necessary without providing the equipment and training them in its proper use would have been ludicrous.

Posters and signs that are instructional or informational are suitable for use, but those that only exhort are insulting. One type of sign that may be particularly effective as the quality transformation proceeds is one that explains what management itself has been doing to accomplish the transformation or improve working conditions. If the changes are tangible and the workers can relate to them, it would demonstrate constancy of purpose (point 1). In placing such reminders, however, management must be careful to avoid patronizing the workforce.

11a.   *Eliminate work standards (quotas) for the workforce.* Quotas are detrimental to both quality and productivity. Typically workers will be forced to sacrifice quality in order to meet a quota, and the resulting scrap or rework effectively cancels the temporarily increased productivity.

Productivity and quotas are often emphasized through merit pay or incentive pay that rewards workers on the amount they produce. Incentive pay, however, is a cruel hoax played on both the worker and management. The worker, in being rewarded for doing what she knows to be wrong—for example, for doing the work so fast, in order to produce large quantities and receive her merit pay bonus, that she cannot do the work correctly—is being robbed of pride of workmanship (point 12). Management, in turn, pays twice for the same product: once for the employee to turn it out poorly, and again for the product to be scrapped or reworked or for higher costs in warranty repairs. Management may eventually pay for the customers' dissatisfaction through lost sales and lost customers.

Monetary incentives play a much smaller role in motivating employees than current managerial practice would indicate, especially in the realm of innovation. As pointed out by Rosabeth Moss Kanter in her book *The Change Masters:*

> People tackle innovative projects because they have finally received the go-ahead for a pet idea they have always wanted to try, or they feel honored by the organization's trust in them implied in such a big assignment, or they simply want to solve a problem that will remove a roadblock to something else they want to do, or they take

pride in their company and cannot sit still while a problem continues. They do *not* take on this kind of effort because a trinket is dangled in front of them.[33]

The entire emphasis on productivity must be changed to an emphasis on quality; this can only be accomplished by management. Proper guidance, leadership, and especially improved training will increase quality, which will decrease wasted effort; consequently, productivity will fall in line and will increase. In the organization committed to quality, the use of quotas as motivators will become unnecessary. In addition, quotas as measures of performance will be recognized as demeaning to the workforce because they are unresponsive to variations in the processes.

Recall my previous example of training workers in machine shops about safety and protective equipment. Our efforts could easily have been undermined by the shop foremen if they had stressed some level of production over safe operation of the equipment. Workers in pursuit of a quota or time limit might eschew using the protective gear if they felt it added too much time to their task. How many industrial accidents and deaths may be related to quotas and numerical goals? We might be shocked to find out how many workers routinely risk their health, their safety, and even their lives in pursuit of management-mandated performance objectives.

11b. *Eliminate numerical goals for people in management.* Production goals, cost goals, and even safety goals are usually set arbitrarily, with no knowledge of the system's capabilities to reach the goals. Often the goals are simply numbers that are stated without any workable plan or program to meet them. As Deming has pointed out, this begs the following question: if you can meet this goal now, without a plan, why did you not meet the goal before now?[34]

This does not mean goals should not be set; the key is that they should not be set arbitrarily and *never be used as benchmarks for performance.* Only an intimate knowledge of the processes and their capabilities allows a manager to set realistic goals with the confidence that they can be met. The manager will never be able to predict the outcome with certainty, but will with confidence.[35] Because the manager cannot predict success or failure based on an arbitrary goal, to hold anyone responsible

41

to meet or exceed the goal (as with quotas in the previous point) is patently unfair and almost absurd. This point will be much expanded in Chapter 4, with emphasis on the newly adopted National Goals for Education.

12. *Remove barriers that rob people of pride of workmanship.* Giving every member of the operation the proper tools, materials, and environment for the job, as well as all required information for doing the job right, usually allows them to complete the job with their pride of workmanship intact. Investing resources and confidence in employees, providing them with the means to turn out a quality product, and not penalizing them for common variations in the system—over which they have no control—are key to instilling pride of craftsmanship (a term little heard in relation to modern U.S. industry[36]). This pride in a job well done equals increased quality and productivity for the organization.

13. *Institute a vigorous program of education and self-improvement.* Continually improving the quality of an organization's products and services requires continually improving the organization's human resources: its people. People are the most valuable renewable resource an organization has. Is it not clear that an active, involved, and stimulated workforce has more potential to make breakthroughs for the organization than any static resource? Workers and managers at every level of the organization must be given ample opportunities for growth, through advanced training on company time as well as organizational sponsorship of outside education.

   Many organizations have grasped the necessity of continued education and sponsored their employees' efforts. In fact, industry is one of the biggest educators in the country.[37] Some of the organizations, however, have stipulated that the course material must be applicable to the job. Who can say what is applicable to the job? Must it be applicable to the present job, or to the job the person will hold in two years, or five, or ten? In truth, any education is applicable to the job, regardless of subject matter: the mental exercise and the effort of learning improve the employee's alertness, attention to detail, and ability to solve problems creatively. Only employees who are growing personally through continuing education will be capable of handling the increased responsibilities that the quality emphasis gives them.

14. *Put everybody in the company to work to accomplish the transformation.* Management must not rely on words without actions to achieve improved quality. Management must accept its responsibility to chart the course for the organization and take concrete steps to bring every element of the organization into the quality family. Management must take advantage of every opportunity to stress quality improvement and also to *show that managers are practicing it themselves;* in short, managers must learn to *lead.* Insincerity in the adoption of the quality philosophy is deadly to an organization; only with everyone's full support will its systems and processes improve and continue to improve.

ða·

The 14 Points have evolved throughout Deming's career. As better ways of stating the points are developed, the points are updated.[38] In a state of never-ending improvement themselves, the points are the culmination and codification of the quality philosophy.

PLAN-DO-STUDY-ACT

The plan-do-study-act (PDSA) cycle, sometimes called the Deming cycle, the Shewhart cycle, or the plan-do-check-act cycle, is shown in Figure 2.2 and was introduced (in embryonic form) to Japan in 1950 by Deming. Deming credits Shewhart with the cycle, but the four-step quality improvement process is actually Deming's adaptation of Shewhart's earlier three-step production cycle.[39]

The PDSA cycle is an iterative process of study and action that may be applied to experiments or system improvements. *Plan* refers to defining the problem, identifying the processes that affect or are affected by the problem, and devising a process change to solve the problem (or a test to gather more information). This most important step is too often neglected; the more careful and thorough the planning, the better the outcome. *Do*   43

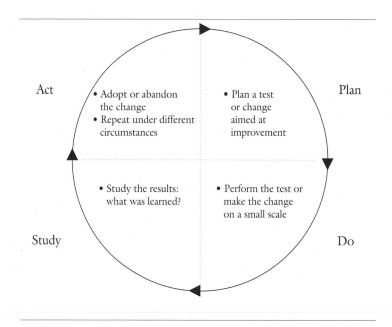

Figure 2.2 PDSA Cycle (From a handout at W. Edwards
Deming's Quality, Productivity, and
Competitive Position seminar.)

involves implementing the change or performing the test, prefer-
ably on a small scale, and collecting data on the results. *Study,* the
third step, consists of data analysis and evaluation; it tells us what
we have learned, both in terms of results and problems encountered. In the fourth step, *action* is taken in one of three ways: (1)
by implementing the change (or accepting the test results), (2)
abandoning the change, or (3) cycling back through the steps
after changing one of the parameters. The cycle eventually leads
back to *planning,* where the refined problem or a new problem is
tackled, each step flowing into the next in a never-ending cycle of
improvement.[40]

ôℓ

A similar approach to an iterative cycle of quality improvement is
the *quality planning road map,* a step-by-step process that guides
managers through the planning process. A key concept developed
by Juran and included in the road map is that of translating quality

44

concepts from the organizational perspective into forms the customer can understand (and vice-versa). The steps in the quality planning road map are as follows[41]:

1. *Identify the customer(s).* Determine who is impacted by or receives the product or service, both inside and outside the organization.

2. *Determine the needs of the customers.* This may be accomplished by customer surveys, lengthy interviews, or simply by intuition. The customers' needs will be stated in their language, that is, language specific to their business. Customers and suppliers are different and may not understand each other's language. To deal with this effectively, read the next step.

3. *Translate customer needs into organizational language.* For example, the customer needs a transmission that runs quietly and lasts reliably over the life of an automobile. These two needs may or may not be mutually exclusive; if the transmission is built to precise tolerances in order to reduce noise, its reliability may suffer (it may very well improve). Such precision may also affect its cost or producibility. The needs must be translated into operational definitions and specifications for the transmission's working parts so the device, when completed, will operate quietly and be reliable.

4. *Develop a product that meets the customers' needs, or at least addresses them.* In the case of the transmission, it must be designed to meet the customers' needs but also must be designed so it can be economically produced and supported once it has reached the field. Recall point 9 of Deming's 14 Points: all of the organizational elements involved in producing the transmission must work together to assure that the product realistically meets the needs of the customer.

5. *Optimize the product so it best meets both the customers' needs and the organization's needs. Quality function deployment* and Taguchi's *quality engineering* are two of the most powerful tools for optimizing products to achieve customer satisfaction economically.

6. *Develop a process to produce and deliver the product.* This is why it is vitally important to involve all phases of manufacturing and/or customer service in the planning stage. 45

Tap the experience of the people who will actually make the product to ensure that the desired product can be produced.

7. *Optimize the process.* Once the process has been developed, it should be optimized so as to produce a minimum of scrap and require a minimum of inspection. Proper training of personnel and the selection and purchase of proper tools and materials are essential; it is the sole responsibility of management to set up the production system correctly.

Note that it may be difficult to optimize both the product and the process in two separate steps—the capabilities of the process must be thoroughly understood in order to optimize the product itself. For example, a product may be designed that simply cannot be manufactured economically. Conversely, it is hard to optimize the process without knowing what the required product specifications are. Thus steps 5 through 7 are very synergistic and not easily separated.[42]

8. *Prove that the process works correctly.* A small-scale experiment should be conducted to prove that the elements of the process work well together and to prove that the output is of uniform high quality. By performing an experiment and measuring the output—either the product's conformance to specifications or the degree of customer satisfaction—the organization may be assured that the product and process are ready. Now you are ready for step 9.

9. *Put the process into operation.* Full-scale operation of the process should now be profitable.

Note that the quality planning road map follows a similar path to the PDSA cycle discussed earlier. Steps 1 through 4 mirror the activities of the planning stage, the next three steps accomplish doing, while studying and action make up the final steps.

Brian Joiner, Deming's long-time colleague, has developed a seven-step model for problem solving that elaborates on the PDSA cycle. It is designed to allow more in-depth analysis of causes, to better assure the root of the problem is discovered and corrected.[43] No matter what version of the problem-solving model is chosen, the steps must be repeated and incremental changes implemented to obtain continuous improvement of quality.

QUALITY CONTROL CIRCLES

As mentioned in Chapter 1, quality control circles were introduced by Ishikawa and are an effective way of tapping the innovative power of the workforce. Like most quality improvement tools and techniques, they must be handled carefully; managers must know the theory behind them before they try to apply them. Circles must be voluntary, formed by a group of employees that wants to solve a particular problem. Management cannot manipulate or coerce its employees into forming them and still hope to reap rewards from them. Successful use of the quality control circle concept involves a commitment by management to support the efforts of the circles, and employees must be given the opportunity to grow through participation.[44] Quality circles (the adopted version of Ishikawa's original concept) did not initially thrive in the United States, where many employers made participation in the circles mandatory. Also, U.S. managers often stifled the participants' esteem and development by rejecting most of the ideas they presented.

As mentioned earlier, quality control circles (or quality circles, if you prefer) were originally formed so shop supervisors could study and learn statistical tools and techniques together. As adapted by many U.S. firms, the circles usually have many purposes. Improvements in quality and productivity through reduction of waste and cost are tangible objectives of circle activities. Less tangible objectives include improved communication among workers and between workers and managers, development of effective teams, and increased worker involvement and job satisfaction. The growth and development of circle members is another primary function, through training in both the need for and the methods of quality improvement.[45]

Like the whole of the quality transformation, implementation and success of quality control circles is never automatic. Management cannot grasp hold of any new idea or method and implement it without understanding it thoroughly.[46] Resistance to the idea—and the entire quality initiative—can come either from managers who feel threatened by the change or from workers who fear exploitation by management. Perhaps the most difficult objection to counter is the catchall, "It won't work here." Those who brush off innovative techniques with such flippant   47 comments are difficult to convince. While they may not be willing or able to offer constructive alternatives, they will usually remain unconvinced until some improvements are made and presented to them.[47] These and other problems with implementing change will be discussed in Chapter 7.

એ

The principles and concepts we have covered form the basis of the management transformation that is sweeping U.S. industry and government. I propose that a similar transformation can vastly improve the quality of our education. But what is educational quality?

DEFINING QUALITY
IN EDUCATION

A human being should be able to change a diaper, plan an invasion, butcher a hog, conn a ship, design a building, write a sonnet, balance accounts, build a wall, set a bone, comfort the dying, take orders, give orders, cooperate, act alone, solve equations, analyze a new problem, pitch manure, program a computer, cook a tasty meal, fight efficiently, die gallantly. Specialization is for insects.

—Robert A. Heinlein

As many approaches may be discovered for defining quality in education as exist for defining the quality of a manufactured good or delivered service (especially since education may be considered a service industry). The disparity of approaches makes it extremely difficult to develop a common approach to educational quality, but such an agreed-upon approach is necessary to fully exploring the topic.[1] The definition of quality presented in Chapter 2 was "the aggregate characteristics of a product or service that satisfy the needs of the customer, where the customer may be either the immediate recipient or the ultimate user of the product or service, or both." We will apply this definition to

49

education; while we will largely confine our discussions to elementary and secondary education, the principles may be applied to education at any level.

Education scholar Alexander W. Astin suggests two criteria for evaluating any conception of quality in education. Astin generally turns his attention to higher education, but I will address his criteria in terms of education in general. The first criterion is that the definition reflect what is generally meant by quality. This is necessary because concepts of educational quality (especially higher education) often hinge on impressions of the reputation of an institution or the resources a school has at its disposal—for example, schools with more money or better facilities are usually considered "better."[2]

This definition of quality, as applied to education, certainly reflects what is generally meant by quality. Though education deals with issues and ideas that are more ephemeral than quality of products or services, this does not mean the concept is not applicable. The outcomes may be harder to measure and the principles harder to visualize, but they are no less valid.

Astin's second criterion is that the definition itself must be useful in enhancing the quality of education.[3] The premise of this entire work is that applying the quality philosophy to education opens many doors toward improvement. But, as discussed previously, quality is a concept that is closely tied to perceptions. The previous definition of quality—and especially this educational application—will certainly be contested by people both in and out of the education system. This very nature of quality and of quality in education makes it a difficult concept on which to reach a consensus.

The consensus that education in the United States requires overhaul has not yet developed into a consensus on approaches to its problems. If agreement on the relationship of quality to education can be engendered and turned into unity and drive toward continuous improvement, the effects on this nation will be overwhelming. The time has come, the Walrus said, to talk of quality in education; let us proceed to examine it in detail.

REALITY IN EDUCATION

Contemporary educational philosophy is generally divided into four schools: *perennialism, progressivism, essentialism, and reconstructionism*. We will not go into detail on the precepts of the philosophies, though progressivism is covered briefly in Appendix B. It should be sufficient to say that each of the philosophies has ardent followers, each has good points and bad, and each is in part correct and in part flawed in relation to the world as described by the reality paradigm.[4]

Because these different approaches tend to fragment educational effort, some synthesis of the four philosophies is required to build a common approach to education. Only educational solidarity will meet the nation's needs in the twenty-first century and beyond. As a first step toward this synthesis, we will apply Deming's profound knowledge (the description of reality presented in Chapter 2) to education.[5] Recall that understanding reality involves appreciation of systems, understanding of variation, theory of knowledge, and understanding of psychology.

Systems. First and foremost we must recognize the simple fact that education is a system, a collection of processes. As seen in the previous chapter, all processes consist of inputs from a supplier or suppliers, work that accomplishes some transformation, and outputs that go to a customer or customers. It is useful to illustrate the educational process as the transformation of inputs (for example, students and information) into outputs (citizens and workers) through the application of teachers' skills, students' interests, and other factors. This is shown in Figure 3.1 in two views: a general view of the overall process and a detailed view of education as a series of such processes.

Seeing the system so simply laid out makes it easy to comprehend that each successive step in the education process depends on the successful completion of the prior step. The education process in Figure 3.1 follows the typical U.S. model (though any other educational model can be displayed in a similar manner), from early education in the home to grammar school to junior high school to high school to perhaps college and beyond. No single element can be treated separately without risk of damaging the entire system. (The system could have been illustrated using individual grade levels; however, broad school divisions

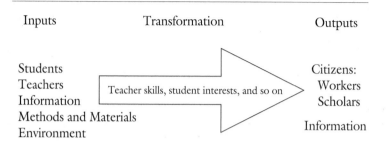

A. Inputs, transformation, and outputs

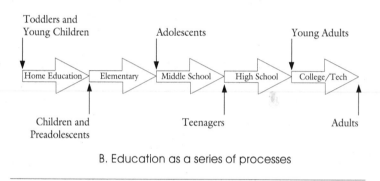

B. Education as a series of processes

Figure 3.1   The Education Process

were chosen because arbitrary grade levels are generally too restrictive to students and teachers.) Using this model, it could be said that the U.S. educational system is no system at all, since the elements are generally treated individually with no concern for systemic effects.

The role of educational managers and administrators is to optimize the overall system, that is, to orchestrate the interrelationships between the elements to maximize the benefits to everyone involved.[6] We might say public school administrators must improve the quality of curriculum and instruction by managing the interdependence of the grade and school levels. We might also say they should concentrate on improving the quality—the skills, talents, and ability to learn—of high school graduates by fine-tuning the entire system the students go through. Suboptimization, the emphasis on individual units rather than the whole, cannot achieve the maximum benefit; optimization of the entire system is

52

necessary. For example, pouring more money into high schools will not improve the elementary schools that supply high school students. School districts trying to divide monies "equitably" between education levels (based on the numbers of students in each or some other arbitrary measure) may not be optimizing the entire system. In some areas, it may be necessary to apply more money for teachers and materials to elementary schools to make up for poor preparation of students in the preschool years. In other areas, it may be necessary to apply more money to middle and high schools to combat the encroachment of drugs and gangs into the school campuses or to repair the crumbling infrastructure. These decisions can only be made by local leaders, but not without guidance and knowledge.

Optimization can only be accomplished in relation to the aim or purpose of the system. What is the purpose of education? Quality consultant Ron Moen, who has worked with Deming for several years, suggests the aim of schools should be "to develop the desire for and the skills necessary for continuous learning—joy in learning."[7] Implicit in this purpose is preparing students for self-sufficiency in the future, that is, preparing them to succeed in life.

Variation exists in every process and every operation, and naturally exists in human performance also. With regard to our total educational system, we must recognize that we cannot expect all students to perform at the same level; always there will be some who grasp material quickly and others who take more time. Simply because they require more time to learn the material does not mean they are incapable of learning it! This variation is perfectly natural and is not necessarily within the students' control, because many factors for which we cannot completely account go into determining their performance. Because the variation is natural, because it exists in any human population according to whatever criteria we choose to adopt, and because it is not completely under their control, we must not arbitrarily reward or punish students by ranking them one against the other. The same rationale applies to treatment of teachers. We must instead study the *process* of teaching and learning to find out what the variation is trying to tell us.

Not only will there be differences between members of the student population. With regard to individual students, we must   53 recognize that each student's performance will vary over time, due to a large number of factors such as extracurricular activities, work, family disputes, and other unquantifiable factors. Because of this simple fact, our emphasis must be on helping students master the subject matter by giving them opportunities to put their knowledge into practice.

Knowledge. The theory of knowledge presented in Chapter 2 holds that theory, or concept, is the basis of knowledge. Theories allow us to extrapolate from the present into the future, as well as explain the past. Whatever action we contemplate, whatever experience we have or learn about, is judged in relation to a concept we have formulated in our minds. The concept or theory may be complex or it may be quite rudimentary, but it is essential to our acquiring new knowledge.

In education, this leads to the proposition that teacher guidance of student inquiry may be the ideal learning situation. Young children, for instance, who are still acquiring and assimilating facts will require mostly knowledge-level learning. Answers to their "What is this?" and "Why?" questions must be clear, concise, and appropriate to their levels of mastery and maturity. Older students, however, may inquire deeper into their subjects; the teacher will be the source of concepts and theories and the students' guide in testing theory against experience. Education to promote joy and accomplishment in learning will empower students to formulate their own theories for explanation of the past or prediction of the future; through research and experiment they will test their own and the teacher's theories. The learning experience will enable them to either accept the theory, reject it, or modify it; they will thus be led to higher levels of learning (for example, comprehension, application).[8] What they learn will become truly theirs.

Psychology is related to two major areas of education. The first involves teaching methods, following the theory of knowledge. Psychology explains that our human differences manifest themselves in many ways, one of which is observed in differences in the way people learn. Educators use this knowledge to adapt learning strategies and teaching plans to best serve the needs of their students, using a variety of teaching methods, organizational patterns, and educational tools. The object is not to discover one "right" way to teach a subject or to develop strategies for teaching the best and brightest, but to build a learning program in which all students work toward their potential.

The second area of psychology we apply in our theory of reality in education is motivation. Psychology shows that motivation comes from many sources, but those sources may be divided into two spheres of influence: internal to the student or external. Traditional educational psychology, like traditional management practice, has relied on external motivators to entice or coerce students into learning; the practice has been called one of the "evils of education."⁹ Better understanding of psychology and motivation allows teachers to use internal rather than external motivation to spur their students' learning, thus building rather than destroying their students' self-esteem and dignity.

In "Miri," an episode of the original "Star Trek" series, we find a look at motivation in education. A group of children is gathered together, playing school. One of them holds a hammer; he is the teacher. "What does a teacher say?" asks another of the children. The boy thinks for a moment before speaking, then emphasizes his words with the hammer as he says, "Study, study, study! Or bonk! bonk! bad kids!" That is external motivation.

Internal motivation is Plato sitting at the feet of Socrates. External motivation is the schoolmaster who raps your knuckles with a ruler. Internal motivation is the children coming to see Jesus. And how did he receive them? He took them in his arms and blessed them.

Many management and education practitioners tenaciously defend their use of external motivators, often for subtle reasons. Some use them because they have done so their entire careers; they were brought up on prizes, grades, and rewards for doing what was expected, and know nothing else. These managers and teachers earnestly believe in the Newtonian and Skinnerian cause-and-effect/action-and-reaction/stimulus-response theory of motivation. Others use them because they have come to rely on the power such rewards give them over their workers and students; while they would rarely admit this, to willingly give up some of that power would entail taking a risk they would rather not face.

The extremes of the argument over the use of external motivators are poles apart. On one end, managers and teachers believe that external motivation (for example, prizes, awards) is good if it helps one person rise above his previous level, no matter how many others are hurt or demotivated. On the opposite end are those who believe that regardless of the number of people who appear to be helped by external motivators, they should be avoided if they hurt even one individual. The reader may have concluded that I fall into the latter category; you are absolutely correct.

An example from my high school career may help explain my position. When I played high school football, I was far from being a star. I played because I enjoyed the game and the camaraderie, not because I had any innate talents I wished to showcase. Every year, an awards ceremony was held to honor a few of the "outstanding" players. It was generally assumed that a good friend of mine would receive a certain award: he deserved it and rather expected it. I still remember the look on his face when they gave the award to me; it was as if a part of him had been destroyed, and the team spirit we had worked so hard to build had been torn apart. Looking back, I would give anything to remove the hurt he must have felt at the time.

We will continue to discuss internal and external motivators throughout the text.

⁊⬤

The metaphysical paradigm, taken as a whole, provides a solid conceptual foundation for leading the transformation of education. According to Lew Rhodes of the American Association of School Administrators, "In a world perceived as increasingly fragmented, Dr. Deming's profound knowledge provides a way of understanding the connectedness of things."[10]

THE CUSTOMERS OF EDUCATION

Often discussions of quality in education revolve around the purposes of education. Education in this country's early history was seen as a method to preserve the freedoms and liberties of the new country, of making good citizens and unifying the nation (see Appendix B). Thomas Jefferson understood the usefulness of education for increasing productivity, promoting good health, and giving every person a better opportunity to respond to her own situations and experiences.[11] This differed markedly from earlier thinking that reserved the benefits of education for a specific class, thinking that evolved in medieval Europe when Latin was the language of academia.[12]

We earlier described the purpose of education as empowering and enhancing joy in learning and preparing students for success, and the definition of quality given at the beginning of the chapter focused on the needs of the customer. If we are to focus on the needs of the customer, the customer must be identified; this is not as straightforward as it may seem.[13] Many tend to immediately identify parents and students as education's customers,[14] but this answer is incomplete. Education affects every part of our society either directly or indirectly, so the ultimate consumers or users of education are the national and international communities. Within these larger communities, certain specific customers of education, both external and internal to the educational system, may be identified. A few of the many external customers of education (and particularly secondary education) are the service industries, manufacturing industries, and government agencies that employ former students, the colleges and universities that build on what former students have learned, and the local community.[15] Internal educational customers at all levels include students, teachers, administrators, and governing bodies; of these internal customers, the student is usually considered most important.

Some readers may object to the use of the term customer with respect to education, preferring instead to use client, user, or shareholder. The principle is the same, regardless of the language.

Two views on customers. Figure 3.2 shows two views of education in the form of a system, corresponding to the two major views on the primary customer of education.[16]

Normally it is thought that the two viewpoints are incompatible. Those who identify students as the primary customers chafe at the thought of students as inputs and outputs of the education process. Those who focus on employers (or some other agent of society) as the primary customer argue that the first group fails to see the economic reality of the situation.

Deeper consideration reveals the two views to be practically synonymous, assuming the *needs* of the students are being given more credence than their *desires*. (I do not mean student desires

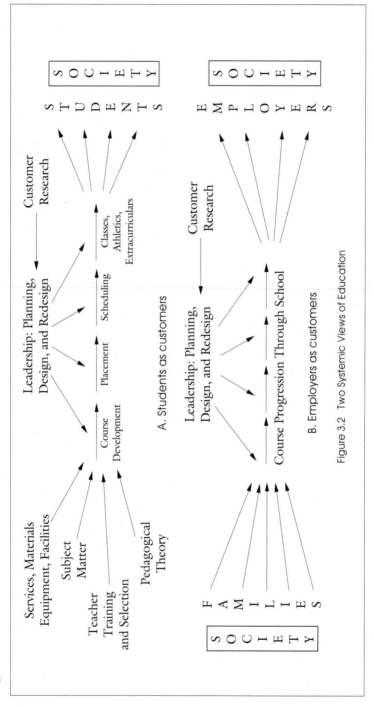

Figure 3.2 Two Systemic Views of Education

should be ignored; rather, I am pointing out that student needs and desires are often diametrically opposed.) Students need to have fun in learning; they need to develop positive self-esteem and take pride in their accomplishments; they need the social interaction of teamwork; they also need to be equipped to support themselves and their families in the future. If these student needs are being met, are not employer's needs also being met? They are indeed if schools are committed to preparing their graduates for life 20 years hence.

Unfortunately this long-term view is rare, the emphasis being more often on the present needs of students and teachers. A more pragmatic argument may then be advanced: successful graduates, gainfully employed, pay taxes that support the public school system (as well as the rest of the community infrastructure). It is therefore in the schools' best interests to prepare their graduates well for employment, that is, to treat employers as their ultimate customers and to meet the needs of the customers.

In addition, students cannot be considered the primary customer of education for the purpose of educational quality, for this simple reason: students have no conception of what they must learn; they are, after all, students. As mentioned previously, their needs and desires may not match. Does a quality education to the student with strong abilities in mathematics include English? Will she not opt to forego serious literature study in favor of her best subject? And the young man who barely got through chemistry but loves history: will a quality education for him include science of any kind? Education is preparation for the long-term future. Students are in school to learn because they do not know what is important for them to know and do in the future. Otherwise they would not need school. This does not mean students' needs are neglected—far from it. Focus on students' needs is incumbent on identifying those needs; the logical source for such knowledge is the world beyond graduation.

Consider again Figure 3.2. In addition to the arguments discussed here, it is conceptually easier to map out the system processes using employers as the primary customer; we will use this convention throughout the book. Understanding then that students are the primary *internal* customers of the system, Figure 3.3 shows an expanded view of the educational system using the education process of Figure 3.1b as a building block. Added to it

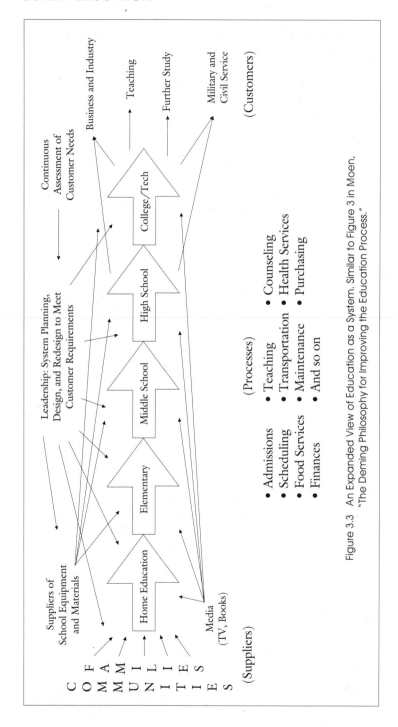

Figure 3.3   An Expanded View of Education as a System. Similar to Figure 3 in Moen, "The Deming Philosophy for Improving the Education Process."

are suppliers of the process, customers of education, and some of the functions necessary for optimizing the system.[17]

The various customers of the educational system certainly have different needs, and different ideas about what constitutes quality education. We now turn our attention to the customers.

External Customers

The variety of external educational customers is as wide as the variety of endeavors undertaken by individuals or society. Every type of service and manufacturing industry, every level of governmental service, every institute of higher learning, and every community is affected by the educational process.

Assuming that both high school and college graduates (and nongraduates) participate in the economy at one time or another, a close examination of the industrial population may shed some light on external educational customers. (This is not an unreasonable assumption, as the number of chronic unemployed in this or any country is quite small). Figure 3.4 shows projected figures for employment in various industries for 1990. This figure is arranged according to the Pareto principle (see Appendix A). As shown, the largest customer of education is the service sector, accounting for almost 70 percent of the total working population. Adding service and manufacturing together, the total jumps to over 87 percent.[18]

The statement that the service and manufacturing industries are the largest direct volume customers of education may be tempting to advocates of business or vocational education. It is not meant to imply that the needs of these industries overshadow any other; in fact, many of the needs of education's customers overlap. It must be realized, however, that industries of various types have the largest stake in education. This places an onus on both education and industry.

Are the needs of service industries radically different from manufacturing? Not anymore. Advances in technology have changed the face of heavy industry and brought the two sectors closer together. Specific skills necessary in the sectors remain different, but those skills are best learned on the job. All industries need employees who have communication and problem-solving skills and are willing and able to learn their specific jobs quickly and effectively. Surveys of business leaders show that such students have a definite advantage in the job market.[19]

&

As we intimated previously, focusing on external customers of education does present some problems. Students in the 1960s rebelled against the model of education we presented in Figure 3.1a,[20] and many educators today are vehemently opposed to the "industrial" model. Perhaps the main problem with the model is the name; it could just as well be called the "systems" model of education, as it treats education as the system of interdependent parts it clearly is (see Figure 3.3). Each level of education is part of the system, a separate process the output of which becomes the input to the next level (for example, the student output of elementary school is one input to the junior high school). This concept of education is not new.[21]

Protest against this analogy may also stem from the perception—often not unjustly held—that manufacturing and service industries view and treat people as disposable commodities. The quality transformation within industry is helping dispel this image, as the industrial sector begins to recognize and treat people as what they are: the most valuable resource in any organization. Understanding that education is the primary early means of nurturing and developing this priceless human resource is the first step in recognizing the overwhelming importance of education in building and strengthening our society. As stated by the National Commission on Excellence in Education:

> The people of the United States need to know that individuals in our society who do not possess the levels of skills, literacy, and training essential to this new era will be effectively disenfranchised, not simply from the material rewards that accompany competent performance, but also from the chance to participate fully in our national life.[22]

Students, therefore, are one input of the learning process, along with teachers, raw information, pedagogical theory and methods, learning materials, and the school environment. This is graphically displayed in the Ishikawa chart in Figure 3.5 (see Appendix A for more information on the uses of Ishikawa charts). Students are a human resource that is being developed for the external customers of education. The propensity toward overlooking this important relationship may be one reason why education has faltered in the United States and prospered in less naturally affluent

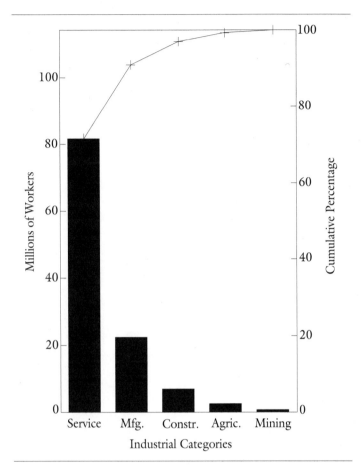

Figure 3.4 External Customers of Education:
Agents of Society

(Source: Statistical Abstract of the United States, 1985.)

countries. Japan, after all, has no natural resources other than its population, and applies great energy and effort in developing its human resources.[23]

❧

Education as an industry is a synergistic mix of product and service orientation. In higher education, the product may be pacesetting research in science or history, or consultative services to farmers and industries, in addition to educated graduates. At the high school and lower levels, however, the product of education

63

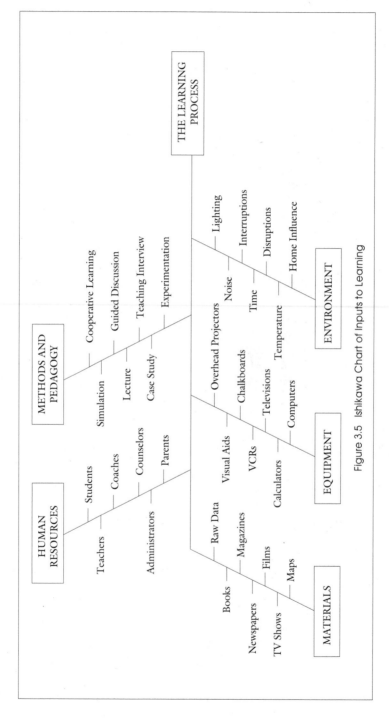

Figure 3.5 Ishikawa Chart of Inputs to Learning

(as perceived by its external customers) is the graduates—or non-graduates—who are to be employed or taught. While the elementary and secondary educational system provides some services to the general public, its service role is largely internal.

As pointed out by Juran, customers state their needs in their own language. Often this must be translated into the language of the producing or servicing industry.[24] The external customers of education are no different. Each has its own needs, its own laundry list of skills it expects (or desires) its employees to have. Those skills are usually stated in specific terms according to each customers' corporate vocabulary, but we will state them in general terms that apply to almost all customers. They are addressed in four broad areas: communication skills, personal skills, group skills, and cognitive skills.[25]

Communication skills include the ability to understand and express ideas clearly and concisely, especially in oral but also in written form. Basic literacy is necessary to every person's individual fulfillment, whatever path they choose to follow, but it is also necessary in almost every work category.

Communication skills also include an important but often overlooked skill: the ability to listen effectively. Listening is the first step toward understanding and is the foundation of effective verbal communication. Sadly, listening seems to be a dying art, as pointed out by Yaconelli and Burns, "There is so much noise today, so much activity, so many advice-givers, but there are very few people who will listen anymore."[26]

Personal skills. The ability to set personal goals and the motivation to work toward them are particularly important skills. They involve analyses of objectives, evaluation of possible methods to achieve them, and planning of strategies and approaches. And while not classified as a skill per se, self-esteem is vitally important to everyone's emotional well-being; it should be reinforced by the educational experience.

Group skills. One of the most important popular myths in this country is that of rugged individualism, and because of its popularity the importance of the group has been diminished. We admire and honor the star quarterback or power forward and bestow upon them the title Most Valuable Player, forgetting the rest of the team, offense and defense, that combines to win the game. This emphasis on individual achievement over group effort permeates our culture, and keeps our corporate—that is, group—activities from reaching their true potential.

The ability to work effectively in a group situation, whether on a production team or a staff committee, is a vitally important skill. Teamwork and cooperation—the ability to work together toward group aims and the ability to negotiate the goals when appropriate and build effective organizations to reach the desired objectives—are necessary to our success and badly neglected by our culture.[27] Another group skill, the ability to lead and motivate groups when necessary, is also important. Leadership instruction and practice are severely lacking in education and industry; we must give students opportunities to develop and gain confidence in their leadership abilities.

Cognitive skills. An important skill that is often taught only in mathematics and science courses, but that applies equally well in history and civics, is problem solving. Controversial issues that require the solution of multifaceted problems have risen in every period of history and are rampant today. Learning how to approach difficult problems methodically and evaluate alternative solutions carefully is a valuable skill that is directly transferable to the workplace.

An accompanying skill that can also be exercised and strengthened is creative thinking. Approaching problems creatively and reaching innovative solutions must be practiced both individually and in groups. Another prime cognitive skill that future employees must have is simply the ability to learn effectively; everyone must be prepared and able to learn the specifics of the career or trade they are entering, and to keep abreast of new developments in the field as time goes on.

ða

To provide the highest quality education, planners and educators must set up a meaningful dialogue with their customers; those customers must in turn be prepared to participate in the continuing improvement of the educational process. This has not happened much in the past and will take time and effort to facilitate now. As pointed out by quality expert William Scherkenbach,

> For years industry has accused academia of not teaching anything relevant. And for years academia has been

replying that they are the bastion of theoretical purity and that industry had better start using it.... It is time for the nonacademic sectors to recognize academia as their most important supplier and either begin to work with them or develop another source.[28]

The final external customer, as previously mentioned, is the general community (society). The community is the largest customer of education, since *every* graduate and nongraduate from education enters some community. Often people influence more than one community, for example, living in one area and working in another, or living in one town and vacationing somewhere else. In addition, every graduate and nongraduate, as a citizen not only of this nation but also of a state, county, or city, is also a member of the larger world community. How well education prepares students for citizenship and community living helps determine whether they will become builders or destroyers, producers or burdens on society.

Internal Customers

While attention to external customers is important, it does not justify neglect of the internal customers. Because every process has both a supplier and a customer, teachers, students, and administrators will always be both suppliers and customers of each other. They must understand each other's needs to improve their relations and the overall quality of education.

Students are the most important internal customers of education; they have been called the "key worker[s] in a school,"[29] but their schools have not always served them well. Students usually enter school with a great desire to learn about the world around them and the things their parents and other adults consider important. Unfortunately, many leave school with that desire crushed, because learning is not the joyful experience it should be; instead, it is a burden.[30] Students learn quickly that the effort they apply in learning is not as important as their innate ability to grasp subjects and concepts—they have tried their best and received only humiliation in return. Many "develop a pattern of academic hopelessness" and give up on education.[31] The quality transformation in education will empower students to learn and greatly enhance their educational experiences.

One of the most frequently heard student complaints is that the subject matter of their classes is not relevant to their lives; they often express it as a question, "What good is this going to do me?"[32] Educators must not make the mistake of ignoring this frustration, even when the answer to the question is not evident. Explaining why familiarity with Shakespeare's sonnets is important to a student's intellectual development may be more difficult than explaining the practical utility of the Pythagorean Theorem,[33] but students need to understand the importance of all of the elements of their education. And the troubling fact is that in this day of continued social rebellion, the explanation that the student needs the material to understand and communicate effectively with other members of society may not be sufficient.[34]

In addition to the need to have fun in learning and the need to understand the relevance of course material, students need experiences that build their self-esteem. They need challenges, opportunities to excel, not against each other but against their own imagined limitations. They need nurturing, time to grow, and teachers who believe in them.[35] Finally, students need to develop the confidence and drive necessary to pursue their dreams and desires. Part of this purpose will be realized by involving students in the transformation process and continuous improvement of their schools; as stated by Anne Forester, "Whether students are seen as users of the system or workers in it, their needs are considered and their opinions and input are taken seriously."[36]

Many of the needs of students and suggestions for meeting those needs are discussed by William Glasser in his books *The Quality School* and *Control Theory in the Classroom,* and by Peter Kline in *The Everyday Genius.*[37] I will not repeat what they have already covered so well; you are encouraged to read their books for their insight and application.

Teachers. This nation must stop treating teachers, who are entrusted with the responsibility of preparing its children for the future, as second-class citizens. Teachers deserve much more recognition and respect for what they do and much less blame for what the system does (or fails to do) than they presently receive. Recognizing teachers' professional status, similar to that of engineers, doctors, and lawyers, would go a long way toward solidifying the position of teachers,[38] but such status cannot simply be granted without being earned. Many excellent teachers are to be found in our nation's schools, teachers who deserve true professional recognition, but their achievements are often overshadowed by teachers who are unfit for the classroom.

It can hardly be denied that the teaching profession has suffered for years from a devastating cycle in which a lack of recognition, compensation, and respect attracts many poorly qualified applicants whose other opportunities are limited; subsequently, their preparation leaves much to be desired, and their achievements as teachers deserve little recognition, compensation, or respect. The cycle has repeated itself almost endlessly, but it must be broken somewhere if we are to enlarge the pool of talent among teachers. We must attract motivated and talented teachers and give them the tools and autonomy—in classroom management, lesson planning, and administrative duties—they need to do quality work. Coupled with continued professional development opportunities, such freedom should greatly enhance teachers' self-esteem and give them improved chances for the recognition they deserve, thereby attracting even more talented applicants. Only educational management is in a position to change the teaching profession to allow this to happen—but it will require leaders with vision to make it a reality.

Besides professional status, one of the most pressing needs of U.S. teachers today is adequate compensation for their work. Many educational reforms have made news boasting about raising the average salary of teachers, but the headlines and stories usually leave out more information than they provide. When they quote an "average" teacher's salary, they usually leave out whether it is the mean (the arithmetic average), the median (the value in the middle of the data set), or the mode (the value that occurs most frequently). Typically, the news also leaves out the salary range (the difference between the lowest and highest salaries), obscuring the fact that starting salaries for teachers are still well below starting salaries for other professions.[39]

Administrators.[40] Like teachers, administrators need improved professional status, proper recognition for their efforts, and increased compensation for their efforts. They need support from parents and the community, but increased autonomy would benefit them as well. Shared feedback from all of the elements of the education system, especially constructive solutions to common problems, would enable them to do their jobs more effectively. 69

The adversarial relationships between administrators and faculty (and between students and teachers) can only be overcome by better understanding the needs and expectations of the groups involved. The relationships must turn away from suboptimization in favor of any one group and toward the optimization of the entire system for the benefit of all. The energy expended in fighting must be turned toward more productive purposes, such as the never-ending improvement of quality.

೫

Being an astute reader, you no doubt have noticed that these discussions of educational customers have not included parents. **Parents**, as customers of education, exist in a nether land. They are not usually the true external customers of education, except as members of the community, and they cannot be considered completely internal customers, as they rarely work intimately within the education system. Though it may be more appropriate to consider parents as the owners of the education system (along with the rest of the taxpaying population), they are, nevertheless, important customers of education. Education is also a customer of the parents.

The primary need of parents is to see their children receive a quality education that will adequately prepare them for the future.[41] Parental interests extend beyond this basic need, however. Parents need to know what their children are learning and how it relates to any special beliefs they espouse; not so they can fight the inclusion or exclusion of particular teachings or lobby for their specific viewpoint to be given precedence over any other, but so they can augment the curriculum with instruction that is specific to their belief and value system (see Appendix C). Parents also need feedback on their children's behavior and progress; not so they can berate and belittle their children, but so they can encourage and help them. Such feedback also gives parents insight into their children's needs and may help parents recognize problems and crises before they end in disaster.[42]

Parental needs may extend to areas that do not directly involve their children. Parents may find that they need help with some aspect of their own lives, for example, changing jobs or living within a budget. Schools wishing to broaden their educational services and improve community relations may help parents and other members of the community by sponsoring seminars or classes to which they are invited.

In much the same way that parents are customers of education, the education system is a customer of the parents. Schools, of course, depend on parents to provide them with students. But a student does not arrive at school as a *tabula rasa*. Students enter the school doors with several years of either deliberate or inadvertent education from their parents. Much of their attitude toward school and themselves will have been formed in these years. Parents who use the preschool years to lay a foundation for future study benefit their children as much as the schools; sadly, relatively few children are given this advantage. Children whose parents regularly converse and interact with them, paying attention to their progress and their school activities, are more likely to succeed in school than those who are denied this home experience. Parental effort is even more influential on their children's achievements than the family's economic status.[43] Schools depend on parents for students, but for students with some propensity toward learning.

CURRICULAR QUALITY

The discussion of quality in education inevitably leads to the question of curriculum, a question that is as old as education itself. What is to be taught? When he proposed his own academy, Benjamin Franklin proposed a long list of subjects, largely falling under the major headings of English, mathematics, and history. To these he also added physical exercises, public speaking, drawing, and the natural sciences.[44]

What is a quality curriculum? It is clear that certain elements of education are necessary to successful living. The ability to communicate is necessary no matter what field of endeavor a person will enter, and some modicum of mathematical skill is necessary to cope in the world, especially a world that relies increasingly on computers. The incredible advancements in science and technology require at least some familiarity with scientific concepts.[45] An often neglected part of education is the values education that explores questions of right and wrong, good and evil; this is addressed in Appendix C. Finally, any education that releases upon

71

a society an individual who would be a citizen must prepare that person with an idea of how the society is organized and what citizenship involves.

Many approaches toward curricula have been taken, many programs offered.[46] In 1983, the National Commission on Excellence in Education offered the following guidelines for high school achievement: English, 4 units; mathematics, science, and social sciences, 3 units each; computer science, 1/2 unit; and optionally (but recommended) foreign language, 2 units. What the Commission did not offer was an outline of what focus the units should have, though some general concepts students should know or master by the time they graduate were included in the discussion.[47] In giving the impetus to the whims of state and local school boards, they missed an opportunity to facilitate real change.

One element of the school curriculum often neglected in studies of academics is physical education. While this country is becoming more and more health conscious and enjoying more physical activities, our schools are not preparing young people for a lifetime of activities. Physical education is usually mandatory for only one or two years in high school and not at all in most colleges. At a time when studies have shown this country's young people to be generally overweight and inactive, the education system must include instruction in the need for and methods of exercise that will carry young people into adulthood and beyond; to do less would be to deny them the advantages of good health and fitness and poorly prepare students for the future.[48] Sports that build teamwork as well as sports that can be enjoyed individually must be emphasized, and sports that even out athletic abilities (in which the aim is pure enjoyment and no one has a clear advantage) should be included most often; youth workers have been developing sports and games along these lines for years.[49]

In Chapter 5, a detailed secondary school curriculum is presented. It builds on the suggestions of the National Commission on Excellence in Education which, while well intentioned, did not go far enough. It includes all of the Commission's recommendations, adding physical education and some specific classes.[50]

LOCAL VERSUS CENTRAL CONTROL

Many local school boards are finding themselves in trouble: school board elections draw few voters, and the community is generally unaware of what the board does and why.[51] To meet the demand for quality in education, the education transformation calls for a radical change in the role of school boards.

Blind adherence to local and state control of education places the needs of the local community and the state above the needs of the nation as a whole, quite simply compromising the future of the country. Local control has in general operated under the premise, developed in Puritan New England, that the education system should serve the needs of the community. This concept was fine while communities differed radically. Education in a mill town in South Carolina like the one I come from could focus on the skills needed to work in the mills or run a small business that served mill workers, while education in a farming community in Iowa focused on teaching students the skills necessary to life on or around the farm. As our nation has grown more homogeneous and the world approaches the status of a global community, this limited outlook satisfies our total needs less and less.

Local and state boards of education should retain the authority and responsibility to operate quality schools, but they must be given guidance that is equally applicable to all localities. With this guidance must come financial resources that will balance out the huge tax base imbalances between rural communities and urban centers. Presently only a small fraction of the total education bill is paid by the Federal government; most of the costs are shared by local and state governments.[52] Only with large amounts of financial aid to communities will the quality of education in rural Louisiana or inner city New York approach that of suburban areas around Denver or Chicago.[53] Without such compensation, "states' rights" in education today are as damaging as they were in civil rights in the 1960s, the Tenth Amendment to the Constitution notwithstanding.

A curriculum basic to every school in the nation, like the one presented in Chapter 5, would not take away local control over the methods and specifics of teaching. It would, as pointed out by E. D. Hirsch, provide a broad base of ideas and concepts common to all graduates throughout the country. Such a base is a

73

necessary element of coherent and effective communication,[54] and would actually go far in improving the performance of all students. As in Japan, the national curriculum could either be accepted verbatim by local authorities, or school districts could apply stronger requirements.[55]

VALUE-ADDED

Education at its best adds to the student's base of knowledge and abilities, helping the student grow and develop. The concept of *value-added* in education has been developed to track this development and focuses on changes in the student as a result of the educational experience.[56] Though it has its roots in economics and is usually applied to higher education, the value-added approach is a useful part of the quality initiative.[57] This quality-based application of the idea is an adaptation of the traditional value-added concept.

Value-added education has the potential to reinforce natural joy in learning to a much greater degree than traditional education. Students' abilities are measured when they enter school or a course of study, to provide them and their teachers with information about their strengths and weaknesses. These evaluations must be carefully used; they cannot become tools for humiliation or result in any type of arbitrary ranking of students against one another (see Chapter 4). As students progress through the term, they focus on weak concepts or abilities and reinforce those that are strong. When measurements of the learning process indicate that the students are ready to move to the next level or the next class, their abilities are again measured—not to rank them or "approve" their promotion, but to measure student growth and achievements and provide information for improvement of the teaching program.[58]

The main problem with the traditional value-added approach is its reliance on single evaluations at the beginning and end of the semester. The entire approach revolves around the assumption that the change can be measured, but this presents definite difficulties. Both the first and last tests will be affected by student motivation and condition, and the results will include random errors and variance due to the test items. Comparing the results will measure what is common to both tests, what is different between the tests, and the random errors associated with the student's responses.[59] A far better approach to evaluating student performance is to gauge the performance over a period of time, that is, to use a series of measures at the beginning and again at the end rather than single discrete measures.[60] The importance of this is addressed specifically in Appendix A.

Perhaps the greatest benefit of value-added education is intangible and largely psychological. The entire concept of value-added, even the name, recognizes that education builds on a cognitive foundation that already exists. To be truly value-added, both teachers and students must recognize *the value that is already present in the student*. This reinforcement of the intrinsic worth of the student will help promote self-esteem and stimulate joy in learning.

ॐ

The pursuit of excellence, of continuous improvement in educational quality, depends for success on a fundamental transformation of the way the system is managed and led. That transformation is the subject of the next chapter.

THE EDUCATION TRANSFORMATION

Then Jesus took his disciples up onto the mountain and gathered them around him; he taught them, saying:
   "Blessed are the poor in spirit, for theirs is the kingdom of heaven;
   Blessed are the meek;
   Blessed are they that mourn;
   Blessed are the merciful;
   Blessed are they that thirst for justice;
   Blessed are you when persecuted;
   Blessed are you when you suffer;
   Be glad and rejoice, for your reward is great in Heaven."

Then Simon Peter said, "Are we supposed to know this?"
And Andrew said, "Do we have to write this down?"
And James said, "Will we be tested on this?"
And Bartholomew said, "Do we have to turn this in?"
And John said, "The other disciples didn't have to learn this."
And Matthew said, "Can I go to the bathroom?"
And Judas said, "What does this have to do with anything?"

Then one of the Pharisees asked to see Jesus' lesson plan, and inquired of Jesus, "Where are your objectives in the cognitive domain?"

And Jesus wept.

—Youthworker *magazine*   77

We have discussed the need for and difficulty of a sweeping transformation of education. Accomplishing the quality transformation in the face of these difficulties is another matter.[1] The combined efforts of educators, students, parents, communities, industry, and the government will be required to effect true reform, but the responsibility for the transformation rests with those who manage the education system. Only those in management can change the system, but first they must understand it thoroughly.[2]

EDUCATION'S 14 POINTS

Just as the quality philosophy in industry focuses effort on the processes and systems within which workers produce goods and services, in education it focuses on the processes and systems within which teachers teach and students learn. The emphasis in each area is to improve the process, and in education the goal is improvement of the process so that teachers and students operate more effectively. With apologies to Dr. Deming, here his 14 Points are applied specifically to education; this is neither the first such application nor the last.[3]

1. *Create constancy of purpose toward improvement of education, with the aim to prepare people for the future by providing joyful learning experiences that develop their potentials fully.* There seems to be some agreement among various sectors of the United States that *something* needs to be done about the conditions of our education system. Agreement on that point has not, however, led to coherence of action. Many individual school districts have made great strides in improving instruction and classroom conditions; their successes, while important, have unfortunately remained localized and have not been transferred to other areas.

The approach to educational improvements for the nation must be more universal. If the talents and abilities developed and nurtured through education are truly vital human resources to the nation as a whole, some comprehensive policy must be in place to guide their development, to assure the pool of national talent is sufficiently skilled to meet the growing challenges of industry and service. Paradoxically, the establishment of national policies, goals, or

78

guidelines does not drastically weaken local control of education. Previously, boards of education determined their local educational objectives in a vacuum; constancy of purpose on a national level requires their participation in the planning process before they take charge of fulfilling national objectives. Local agencies must decide how those objectives are fulfilled, based on their intimate familiarity with the characteristics of their student and teacher populations.

Improvements in education must address future needs. The United States must learn to plan for the long term in such areas as facility renovation and teacher requirements. Statistics on births in any given year are readily available and, along with population movement information, can be used to predict future educational staff and facility needs. If it is known that the school population will grow, efforts to build adequate facilities and hire or educate sufficient teachers can be made; if it is to shrink, more effort can be put into maintenance of current and replacement of obsolete facilities, while the surplus of teachers may allow for smaller classes.

Providing for long-term future needs involves more than a commitment to improvements in school infrastructures and organizations. Educators must also look deeper into issues that demand a forum in the schools, for example, the global economy and the need for foreign language instruction, or environmental problems and the need for new and innovative ecological research. We must put resources into educational research, including development and use of new educational tools and methods. Forecasts of future trends in popular culture—if such things can be forecast—must be made available to educators if they are to prepare themselves and the school system for the future.

Administrators, educators, and the populace at all levels must be aware of the need for constant improvement in the educational system, and they must be committed to that improvement. Such awareness and commitment is growing almost daily. The American Association of School Administrators, many local communities, and other groups have been sending representatives to Deming's seminars and enlisting the aid of quality consultants in improving the educational environment for some time. Recent grass-roots movements in academia, industry, and government have sought to infuse quality into education and the curricula, including the National Education Quality Initiative, the national symposia at West Virginia University, the University   79 of Southern California, and Lehigh University and the Total Quality Alliance.[4] In addition, the American Society for Quality Control (ASQC) has a technical committee that is working to improve the teaching of quality sciences in higher education.

Meetings and symposia are held almost every month throughout the United States to discuss quality and education. This effort should continue, but it should aim at contributing inputs to a National Educational Vision Statement, a bold statement that stresses quality of education through joy in teaching and learning.[5] (The recent "national goals" do not constitute such a vision; see point 11b.) Such a statement, sweeping and inspiring, would provide a basis for constancy of purpose, and is being investigated by the Total Quality Alliance. Once developed and published, it could be adopted verbatim or amended by state and local agencies for their own school programs.

A note to leaders concerning visions. While it is imperative that those involved in the transformation eventually "buy into" the vision, it is unrealistic to expect everyone to agree on *any* initial version; therefore, use caution in involving participants in developing a vision statement. You as leaders have the responsibility to set the course for change. You must be the ones to develop and propagate the vision.

As Scherkenbach points out, "Only top management can establish the constancy of purpose necessary to know and then meet the customers' needs and expectations. Only they can make policy, establish the set of core values, or set the long-term course."[6]

Allowing faculty, staff, students, parents, and other participants to provide inputs as part of the process of developing a vision statement is good and proper. At Mount Edgecumbe High School in Sitka, Alaska, their statement of purpose was built on the agreement of faculty, students, and administration.[7] But their consensus was not arrived at without guidance. Allowing members of the school organization to build a vision statement for themselves is an abdication of the leader's responsibility. Any purely democratic vision statement is almost sure to be weak and diluted, but a consensus guided by a visionary leader can pull all of the members together toward the common purpose.

A second note concerning visions. You should think long and hard before you completely accept any vision statement that is written in the future tense, for two reasons. First, such a statement will be dangerously close to establishing a goal or benchmark which may become the end rather than an indication of success (for example, efforts are focused on becoming "the best" rather than on delivering consistently high quality instruction, service, or research). This is a subtle shift in perception, possibly dangerous because the temptation will be to skew data or observe only those evaluations that indicate what we want to see.

Second, and more importantly, any vision statement written in the future tense begs the following questions: when? how? In two months, two years, or two decades, and why not some shorter (or longer) period of time? With the resources we have on hand now, or only if we receive more money, or teachers, or computers? (See point 11b.)

ea.

The benefits of constancy of purpose toward enhancement of learning have been ably stated by Anne Forester: "When the entire [school] team shifts its purpose, and learning takes center stage, the day-to-day functions are performed in the service of the overall goal and the climate becomes one of meaningful learning for students and staff alike."[8] Thus the pride of accomplishment extends to everyone in the school.

2. *Adopt the new philosophy.* Improvement in education must be understood to be a constant process, a never-ending PDSA cycle of planning, doing, studying, and acting to enhance the quality of education. The educational transformation should not be implemented as if it were simply a new tool or a fad that will give way to other new ideas in the future. It is not a technique but a concept, not a tool but a philosophy.

This philosophy—that such a thing as quality exists, can be defined, and is worth striving for—controls every aspect of our lives, even when we do not recognize it. Our perceptions of and understanding about quality determine what choices we make every day. Informing our suppliers and our customers about quality and the benefits of quality improvement will foster the creativity and confidence that make improvement possible.

The quality emphasis must, however, be firmly grounded in reality. We cannot be led to believe that quality, in education or   81 anything else, is ultimately achievable except as it is defined and accepted. Quality is relative, largely based on perceptions, and must be improved continuously. Excellence, if looked upon as a state of existence to be achieved, can become self-limiting, as one can always find areas needing improvement: better to consider quality and excellence as goals to pursue without end.

3. *Cease dependence on comparative and competitive testing.* Note that this does not read "cease dependence on evaluation." Students must still be evaluated to assess how much they have learned, if they are ready for the next subject or concept, and what the teacher should do to improve the way the material is presented. This is not an easy task.

The idealized learning process can be thought of as an application of the PDSA cycle (Chapter 2), in which lessons are prepared (plan), material is presented (do) and analyzed (study), and new knowledge is applied to future situations (act). Unfortunately, the effectiveness of learning can only be determined once the future situations have been encountered, that is, when the knowledge has been either correctly or incorrectly applied. Testing, in the ideal, simulates the future situation, enabling the teacher to assess the results of the learning process and come to a decision. (This itself is a process that follows the PDSA model: the test is planned, performed, and studied, and the result used as a basis for action.) The decision and action may be different in certain circumstances, for example, to present the material in a new way to a student who has not yet grasped a concept or to allow the qualified student to progress to the next subject or next level.

One problem of this situation is readily apparent. First, few tests are adequate simulations designed to evaluate application of knowledge to new and unique situations. Most are designed to determine whether a student has amassed a collection of certain facts, and some are designed to test the student's ability to relate those facts to each other in more or less predetermined ways. Use of these tests as predictors of success or failure in future situations may require a leap of faith, but development of tests that more appropriately simulate the future, if not impossible, would probably be prohibitively expensive.

A second problem, and one more down-to-earth, is the difficulty of using test results as indicators of intellectual growth or achievement: there are such things as lucky guesses. Especially where, for ease of grading or test construction, tests make it easy for students to guess or contrive correct answers from context, it is practically impossible to ascertain if the student really knew the correct response. This situation is unlikely to change while teachers are required to handle large numbers of students in every class, yet teachers will always be required to determine (predict) if their students are ready to move on to the next level or concept or topic.

Another problem of the testing process is the tendency to use comparisons across an entire class. Almost all teachers indicate to their students what the class average is, and in college courses it is not uncommon for professors to publish not only the average but the standard deviation or other measure of the dispersion as well. While this information might be useful in determining if a student is in need of special help (see Appendices A and D), when broadcast widely it only serves to let everyone know where they stand in relation to everyone else. This point, therefore, calls for the complete abandonment of norm-referenced measurement, in which student performance is measured and students are ranked against one another.

Norm-referenced evaluation systems must be replaced by criterion-referenced systems, in which students are evaluated against the learning objectives and the evaluation becomes a tool for improving the learning process.[9] While this does not remove the difficulties of the testing process, it does remove the pressure of comparison and should apply to both routine and special testing. With norm-referenced testing, numerical grading schemes should also be abandoned.

The elimination of grading is certainly a controversial subject. It has been argued that students need the external motivation of grades and competition to spur them to higher levels of achievement, and that overall achievement (usually undefined, but inexorably linked to testing of some sort) goes down when grading is eliminated.[10] Such arguments usually cannot be substantiated without recourse to attempts to measure performance, aptitude, and achievement, attempts that are fraught with built-in errors and bias. One of the biggest problems, of course, is that grades and other measures are almost exclusively enumerative in nature and cannot be used as predictors of future success (see Appendix A).[11]

Evaluation should only measure students against their previous performance or against the established learning objectives, such as, what was the student supposed to learn from the lesson or class? Where appropriate, measuring against an accepted level of mastery of a subject may be used, but defining the *accepted level* will sometimes be difficult and controversial. Evaluation must not measure students against one another; competition between students must be minimized. Though competition in school is appealing to the popular ideal of the rugged individual, it serves to reinforce both the positive (the superior performer) and the negative (the poor performer), while leaving the vast majority of students in the middle who get little attention, positive or negative. This competitive nature shows up vividly in school assemblies and graduations when lists of superlatives are read; only a few names are called, leaving the nameless majority feeling perhaps proud of their friends but often dejected because they were not recognized.[12] Theodore R. Sizer writes similarly of teachers' use of humiliation: "Test papers are handed back in order of grade received, the highest first, a form of torture in anticipation as well as result."[13]

According to this point, grades and ranking structures must be abolished and replaced with leadership among teachers and administrators that recognizes the differences between students (likewise with respect to ranking of teachers) (see point 7). This will cause special problems in districts that have chosen to offer advanced opportunities to so-called "gifted and talented" students. (In Appendix C, I argue that groups of students usually form a stable system and that norm-referenced, comparative testing dividing the students into small subgroups insults both the students who work within the system and the teachers who are given the task of performing the division.)

The learning process must still be measured, but not to rank students one against the other. The National Commission on Excellence in Education recommended that grades be used as "indicators of academic achievement,"[14] not recognizing that student performance will form a stable system (see Appendix A) as long as teaching and subject matter have been consistent. Because they are stable systems, classes should be taught in relation to curricular standards that are realistic and consistent. Performance standards (that is, grades) must not become paramount, as they rob students of any internal motivation to learn and replace it with the external motivation of "grading and gold stars."[15] To facilitate the use of criterion-referenced measures of performance, the value-added approach that measures growth and development of student abilities and knowledge must be explored and refined to determine its applicability to all levels of education. (Refer to point 11.)

With the abolition of explicit grading, teachers and administrators must still collect information and evaluate their students' potential; in this effort, they must beware and use the information correctly. In Chapter 2, we discussed the necessary role of inspection in industry as process measurements; measurements and evaluations in the classroom must be used in a similar manner. These measurements are taken to determine if the process is working correctly and to produce information helpful in improving the process. Measurements in the classroom should be used to determine if the learning process is proceeding correctly. If it isn't, what changes to the process will result in better understanding of the course material? These process measurements help the teacher design learning experiences that foster quality work and let teachers know if any students require special help.[16]

William Glasser has proposed a novel idea for evaluating student performance that fits in well with this proposal to eliminate competitive grading. He proposes that students and teachers should set criteria together for what will constitute quality schoolwork; then the students themselves should help evaluate their work and determine if it fits the criteria, with only "quality" work being acceptable.[17] This is precisely the method Mount Edgecumbe High School has been using with great success for the last four years.[18]

Special standardized testing (for example, tests, exit examinations) has come under close scrutiny in recent years. Educational specialists have begun rejecting standardized tests as tools for assigning students to special programs, while at the same time tests have been implemented that are aimed at measuring teacher effectiveness and school performance.[19] The education transformation rejects such testing and actually reduces its necessity. Because students will have already demonstrated stable classroom performance based on curricula that are more or less standard across the country, such special tests are simply more single data points (like final exams; see point 7). They are superfluous because they are incapable of generating any useful information about future performance.

4. *Work with suppliers to continually improve the quality of incoming people, equipment, and supplies.* Wherever possible, end the practice of contracting on the basis of price tag alone. This point is both the same and different for the educational quality transformation as for the industrial quality transformation.

School districts that understand the dynamics of the educational system (see Figure 3.3) will work with the suppliers of the district's human resources. While this means working closely with the colleges and universities that provide teachers, on a practical basis it also means working with the suppliers of students (parents and guardians). These relationships are subtly different. While the school district may be able to give colleges of education an idea of the type of teacher it would like to hire, it must be prepared to *help* families develop the kind of students it would most like to enroll. The schools and school boards, therefore, will establish a long-term partnership for the mutual benefit of students, teachers, and the community.[20]

Educational institutions conduct routine business with many entities: printing and office/school supply centers, booksellers, contractors. Purchases are usually made on an as-needed basis and, especially with district or government purchases, typically go to the lowest bidder; the county maintenance shop I worked in between high school and college was often forced to use substandard materials because of purchasing decisions. Wherever possible the sporadic nature of educational purchases must be replaced with long-term agreements based on quality first. If material usage or maintenance or other functions are in statistical control, confident predictions of future needs can easily be made. Ultimate costs of goods and services, including costs of repair and maintenance, must be considered as opposed to basic costs.[21]

≈

In regard to textbooks, the rate of increase in the knowledge base (especially in technical subjects) is such that many textbooks are obsolete almost as soon as they reach the students. Some teachers supplement the texts with magazines and other sources of recent information, but the basic fact is that texts older than five years are usually not sufficient. Schools and publishers must reach cooperative agreements to either replace or supplement textbooks—especially in quickly changing fields—on a regular basis.[22]

What might an appropriate replacement schedule be? Information about how fast the source material changes, the time required to research, prepare, and publish supplements or new books, and the resources available to purchase new materials would all combine to determine a schedule. Long-term, cooperative agreements between school boards and publishing companies would provide a basis for continual improvements of the teaching materials, enhancing the educational experience for students and teachers and providing economic security for vendors.

Using complete and up-to-date texts may have an intangible benefit, also. Many school districts save money by collecting and reissuing textbooks every year; as a result, their students have gone through many classes with books that were falling apart. What message does this send to those students? Do we care so little about their education that we allow them to use old, inferior materials? It may be possible to recycle the old texts, thereby saving money and resources while simultaneously giving students and teachers the best possible resources.[23]

❧

The idea behind long-term agreements with educational vendors must also apply to teacher contracts. The National Commission on Excellence in Education recommended an 11-month contract for teachers, but why stop there? If we are going to consider teachers as professionals, we must treat them as such. Teachers should be employed all year, with their contracts and their pay continuing through their vacation periods. Because of the school schedule, they should use most of their vacation period during scheduled breaks, but they should also have the freedom to reserve part of those school vacations for planning, advanced study, or research. In addition, educators should be rewarded with multiyear contracts, or the equivalent, based on the quality of their service.[24]

This inevitably brings up two subjects: money and tenure. Managers for years have overestimated the motivational effect of money, establishing merit pay and pay-for-performance plans in misguided efforts to spur productivity. Invariably, quality suffers

87

under such programs. In Chapter 5 we will discuss teacher remuneration in relation to teacher career and professional development; in doing so, we recognize that money is not the primary reason people choose to become teachers. It can, however, be a primary reason that people leave teaching. As discussed in the previous chapter, improving the lot of our teachers requires two things: recognition of their professionalism and adequate compensation.

Tenure is another important part of the educator's security package, a recognition of their professional status, and guarantees that teachers and principals will not be fired on a whim or let go when budgets get tight. Ideally, every professional teacher should have the equivalent of tenure. Tenure, however, does not give teachers carte blanche or remove their responsibility to provide quality service in and out of the classroom.

5. *Improve constantly and forever the system of instruction and service.* Quality of education, like quality of anything, must be built in early. It cannot be a by-product, it must be the product. Teams of teachers and administrators must constantly be on the lookout for ways to improve the quality of their services to students, parents, the community, and each other, and must strive to improve the quality of their ultimate output, that is, their graduates who become citizens and workers.

Building in quality at the start in the teaching corps will require improvements in teacher recruiting and training. Retention of quality teachers and retraining of teachers with special problems will be an ongoing concern. Master and senior teachers (discussed in Chapter 5) will be able to help principals provide top-quality ongoing training to teachers and apprentice teachers (see point 6).[25]

Continuous improvement in education into the far future will require not only optimization of the systems that exist, but research and innovation into new techniques and new learning technologies. While continuous, incremental improvement of educational products and services is essential, only innovation (that is, finding new and better ways to accomplish the ends and please the customers) will provide dramatic leaps in educational quality.

Peter Kline's work in integrated learning, as well as new research into how the brain functions, have promising implications for this effort, and may be influential in pedagogy. Other innovations being investigated are improved computer-based learning systems, interactive video learning, and new formats for reference texts (such as center-indexed texts).[26] As mentioned in the Introduction, however, we cannot look to technological or pedagogical innovations as the saviors of our education system.

To keep the quality improvements in education moving forward continuously, educators must improve their understanding of the needs of their customers (for example, businesses, industries, the community). They cannot maintain a limited local outlook, however; they must strive to understand the needs of both their local communities and the larger national and global communities.

6. *Institute training on the job.* The training of teachers, administrators, and other staff members must extend beyond their initial qualification into their tenure. Many state reforms have focused on teacher preparation, placing emphasis on student teaching and assigning new teachers under master teachers to be mentored through their first few years.[27] They recognize that professional education for teachers does not end with their progression beyond their initial apprenticeship. Classes and seminars that bring teachers up-to-date and reinforce their specialties as well as those that improve teaching, counseling, administrative, and leadership skills should be frequently offered and strongly encouraged. They can be taught by local master or senior teachers, or by consultants who are brought in by a school or district. In addition, the quality philosophy itself should become a standard part of teacher preparation, with emphasis on the understanding and use of statistical methods, and should be shared with all employees throughout the education system.

7. *Institute leadership.* Administrators, superintendents, school boards, and master and senior teachers—all of whom are in positions of some authority—establish and communicate the vision for excellence in education. To do so effectively, they must learn to take action where action is required and be willing to set and stay the course for the improvement of their schools. They must clearly understand the differences between management and leadership, and strive for leadership. As pointed out by Thomas J. Sergiovanni:

> Quality schooling will not be achieved by teachers and principals who view themselves as subordinates. Instead, it is necessary to encourage and develop followers, in the truest sense of the word, for followers have the capacity for continued performance beyond expectations.[28]

Leadership that empowers everyone in the school system and is dedicated to helping everyone achieve their full potential is the key to the education transformation.

As part of this process, annual performance appraisals for teachers and administrators, like grades for students, need to be abolished. In their place, those responsible for evaluation (for example, master teachers, principals, superintendents) must take leadership and provide regular, timely feedback that addresses strengths, points out areas for further improvement, and above all recognizes the variation in human performance over time. Leaders must focus on the overall aim of their organizations and try to place every individual's performance within the context of the larger whole. For example, how has this school improved and how has this person contributed? Teamwork and cooperation between teachers as well as their leadership in and out of the classroom are stressed and rewarded, while merit pay, bonuses, and incentive plans that encourage individual efforts are dropped completely.

For two reasons, the concept of merit pay is especially poor in education. First, many different teachers, counselors, and coaches will touch the life of any given student—no single person will be responsible for what a student does (or fails to do) in the future. Second, the ultimate outcome of education remains unknown until years after the student leaves school. To specially reward some teachers over others, when their performance is part of a larger system and their effectiveness is essentially unknown for years hence, cannot be justified.

≈

The application of this point to students has already been discussed in point 3, but it cannot be overstressed. Just as performance appraisals do nothing to enhance work performance for the vast majority of employees, grades are less than motivators for most students. Traditional grading systems are designed to compare students against the "standard," with 70 percent correct (or some other arbitrary number) being "passing" and 100 percent being perfect. All too often they devolve into comparisons of students against each other. While teachers may not always look at grades this way, students certainly do. This reinforces the perception of some students as "brains" and others as "stupid," even when students of like ability are grouped in classes together.[29] The negative motivation sometimes goes so far as to persuade smarter students to perform poorly, so as not to "blow the curve" and risk losing popularity.

Grading schemes also rely, more often than not, on a single data point by emphasizing one grade, the final exam, over any other. Under the guise of being a "comprehensive" measure of the student's grasp of the subject, final exams usually reveal only whether a student studies effectively or takes tests well, rather than whether the student has mastered the subject matter. A far better method is to measure the student's improvement and the effectiveness of the teaching and learning process through a variety of measures (for example, criterion-referenced tests, essays, or other measures of mastery) using the value-added approach.

Improved leadership is desperately needed in this area. Teachers must learn to evaluate the teaching and learning process, recognizing the effects of the system on performance, and provide realistic and useful feedback to individual students without contributing to the destructive practices of student competition, ranking, and single data point management.

8. *Drive out fear, so that everyone may work effectively in school.* This has not been the same type of problem in education that it has been in industry, as the educational forum has traditionally been open to the free expression of ideas. Recent developments regarding particular value systems has eroded this freedom somewhat, but it is largely intact and a great advantage in the educational arena. The education transformation will provide a forum for educators to express their own ideas about and (more importantly) suggestions for improvements in education; educators must be free to suggest improvements and express opinions without fear of retribution or censure.

While fear of suppression of ideas may not be excessive, teachers and administrators have other fears. For many their financial security and job security is in question; for some, the socioeconomic decline of their schools and the prevalence of delinquency have made the school grounds itself a source of fear and anxiety. The recent moves toward higher academic standards have heightened anxiety among educators who see the standards as measures by which they will be judged.[30] Human beings cannot excel if they must operate under fear. Providing financial and job security, through good-faith negotiations between all levels of government, the public, and teachers' organizations, and visionary leadership and cooperative agreements based on the principles of the quality philosophy will help alleviate some of those fears. Conscientious application of quality principles and improvement of education—and, by extension, the improvement of crime prevention, drug rehabilitation, and youth employment services—will also serve to improve school conditions for students and teachers.

Students' fears also need to be dealt with. Their anxieties over gang activities and drug abuse are no less real than teachers', and their fear of embarrassment or humiliation in front of their peers often hinders their performance. Recognition of the fears is the first step; removal of the fears will take time but will pay off enormously.

9. *Break down barriers between departments.* Refer back to Figure 3.3, where we illustrated an educational system. What barriers exist in the system? A few are barriers between administrative functions and teaching, athletics and academics, counselors and teachers, and grade levels. This last set of barriers was tackled by a quality improvement study group under the tutelage of David Bayless and his associates; the teachers worked together to develop the Ishikawa chart seen in Figure 4.1.[31] With the recognition not only of the barriers themselves but of their causes, these teachers found themselves in a better position to remove the barriers.

What benefits do we expect from breaking down barriers? Increased cooperation between academic departments will greatly improve the quality of education. Collegiality between teachers is recognized as a strong factor in improving instruction,[32] and opportunities must be improved for teachers to share ideas across departmental lines. Correlation between subjects of study must also be improved, as it has at Mount Edgecumbe High School where, for example, student reports written for science (or other) classes are accepted as English homework.[33]

Students may be pleased to hear the suggestion that their teachers learn to work together, believing it may result in fewer or easier tests, but correlation and cooperation between departments may not necessarily make school easier by giving students fewer tests to study for or fewer papers to write. It will give students the chance to relate what they have learned in one class to what they are studying in another. Experiments in science will reinforce lessons in history; mathematical concepts will improve under-standing of social science. Students will learn that their subjects do reinforce each other, and the importance of their schoolwork will be more apparent.

Increased cooperation between other elements of the school system must be stressed. Cooperation between administra-tive functions such as purchasing, maintenance, and scheduling can smooth many roadblocks to quality. Improved understanding and coherence of action between school athletics, other extracur-ricular groups, and academics will greatly benefit students who are involved in outside pursuits. Anne Forester suggests large-scale projects that involve the majority of the school—"the study of astronomy, the building of a new playground, the celebration of a special event"—may be helpful in bringing everyone together, barriers down, in a united effort.[34]

10. *Eliminate slogans, exhortations, and targets for the students and teachers.* Promotional materials add nothing to the improvement of quality, and exhortations usually have little effect. As discussed with respect to industrial workers, slogans directed at students and teachers perpetuate the myth that poor school conditions or educational quality are entirely the stu-dents' and teachers' responsibilities.

While slogans such as "Just Say No" have a catchy ring and fit well on bumper stickers, the effectiveness of such promotional materials is questionable.[35] The resources spent on strictly promo-tional and exhortative materials could be used for providing better materials, training, or research which would be directly applied to the improvement processes in education and other areas.

93

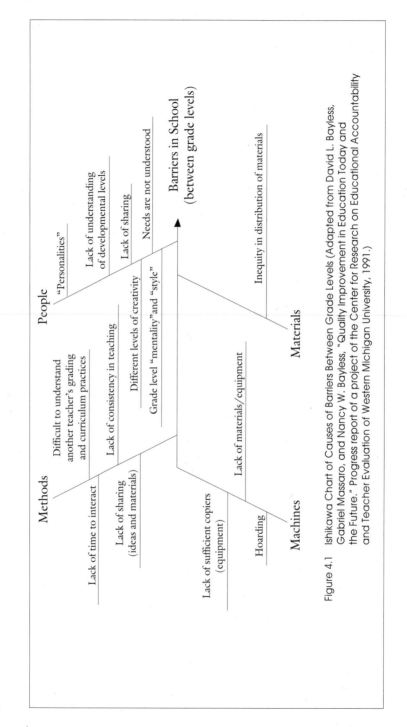

Figure 4.1 Ishikawa Chart of Causes of Barriers Between Grade Levels (Adapted from David L. Bayless, Gabriel Massaro, and Nancy W. Bayless, "Quality Improvement in Education Today and the Future." Progress report of a project of the Center for Research on Educational Accountability and Teacher Evaluation of Western Michigan University, 1991.)

11a. *Eliminate numerical quotas for teachers and students.* If a near-normal distribution does closely enough describe the student population (see Appendix C), the great majority of students operate within the system while some few will excel and some few will fail. Teachers must *not* be under any pressure to pass or fail all, or even a certain percentage, of their classes, or to give out a certain number of excellent marks. With constantly improving quality in education it will finally become evident that all but a very few of the student population are capable of completing their coursework, and most of the few who are not able to learn will be found to possess some type of disability (for example, dyslexia, dysphasia). In such an atmosphere, academic quotas become not only ludicrous but insulting.

Students, too, have "quotas" they pursue: the grading scale. A more arbitrary measure of performance was never invented. What is passing, and what is failing? Why 70 percent, or 60 percent, or 75 percent? Why not 50 percent, or 95 percent, or 100 percent? Where did these numbers come from, and what do they mean? Unless it can be shown that a given grade on a well-constructed test reliably measures what the student has learned, the number is meaningless. Typically grades are used as a gauge to judge performance that has been measured with only four or five items (including the weighty final exam). Performance is not tracked closely enough to notice when the student grasped, or missed, the key concept, and outside factors are rarely considered. This situation calls for leadership on the part of the teacher and an understanding of variation in reality.[36]

11b. *Eliminate numerical goals for people in administration.* As mentioned, arbitrarily set goals are meaningless in that they rarely understand the system or contain any plan of action, yet such goals are routinely used in the field of education. For example: reducing the rate of nongraduates to X percent in Y years, or increasing test scores by A points, or holding the budget to a B percent increase. The numbers do not matter; the goals are arbitrary and meaningless (see the sidebar on *National Education Goals*). Because some of these goals are mandated at a very high level, they can be difficult to ignore; however, four school districts in Wisconsin have been successful in eliminating some such goals.[37]

Another important arena in which administrators have been given quotas to live up to is the area of equal opportunity, which does not bode well for improvement of quality in education. The late philosopher Sidney Hook wrote:

> Although the term *quota* is carefully eschewed by those who have perverted the original meaning of affirmative action, in every area of public life today, especially in education, race and sex are regarded as relevant criteria in decisions affecting the admission, promotion, and reduction of personnel.[38]

Hook continues to point out that the quotas have "led in many areas to an abandonment of the quest for excellence on the ground that this leads to an invidious emphasis on the achievement of the elite."[39]

As mentioned in Chapter 2, it must be stressed that *goals, in and of themselves, are not bad*—every person and every organization needs goals to work toward, aims to achieve. The problem is that the goals are often set without reference to a plan of action to achieve the goals, then are used to measure performance. Goals that are rationally and responsibly set, and are used to provide a focus rather than to measure incremental performance, are positive and necessary. All too often, however, the goals are poorly determined.

Choosing numerical goals arbitrarily without knowing what the system is capable of doing sets those in charge of managing the system up to fail. When the goals are not met, explanations are demanded and careers threatened. Even if the goals are met, no one will know why or how or whether the figures have been creatively manipulated to protect those responsible. Administrators must not be given such arbitrary numerical goals because they will distract their attention from improving the quality of education. In addition, they are often made only to garner political favor with constituents who also do not understand reality.[40]

ᶻ❧ ᶻ❧

THE NATIONAL EDUCATION GOALS

In February 1990 the White House issued a nine-page paper entitled "National Goals for Education." The paper was the result of

96

the "education summit" held five months earlier between the president and the governors. The summit participants acknowledged that "sweeping, fundamental changes in our education system must be made"[41] and established a set of six national goals aimed at the year 2000, each of which is accompanied by a number of objectives. These goals have now been printed on posters and widely distributed (contrast this with point 10), despite the fact that they are largely arbitrary and meaningless.

The first goal is *by the year 2000, all children in America will start school ready to learn.* On the surface this seems innocuous enough; some might even call it laudable. But what does "ready to learn" mean? The stated objectives refer to health, nutrition, availability of preschool, and parental support. No plans are laid out by which any of the objectives, let alone the overall goal, may be achieved. As mentioned, this leads us to ask, "If it can be done without a plan, why has it not already been done?"

Goal two, *by the year 2000, the high school graduation rate will increase to at least 90 percent,* also begs questions. Where did this arbitrary figure come from? Why not 99, or 99.99 percent? This is a classic example of an arbitrary numerical goal set by management without any idea of what the system is capable of. How will those 90 percent be kept in classes they hate, with teachers they despise and grading practices they fear? Education today is working to capacity in this regard; the system itself must be changed before any significant improvements can be measured.

The third goal involves demonstrations of competence *in challenging subject matter* in schools in which *all students learn to use their minds well, so they may be prepared for responsible citizenship, further learning, and productive employment. . . .* This goal hints at the external customers of education, but it does not seek to determine their needs or build an education system that will meet those needs, nor does it indicate how competence is to be measured.

The fourth goal is *by the year 2000, U.S. students will be first in the world in science and mathematics achievement.* By now, I am sure you are able to formulate pointed questions about the validity and attainability of this goal.

The fifth and sixth goals deal with literacy and crime, respectively, and are no more realistic than the previous four. These goals tell us more about the dearth of educational leadership than they predict about educational improvements. If the leaders of education cannot give up these traditional management styles and management-by-objective approaches, there will be no educational transformation.

ᔿ   ᔿ

12. *Remove barriers that rob students and teachers of pride of workmanship.* Student assignments must be structured to reward ingenuity and industry and should be aimed at producing tangible results, for example, analytical papers, practical projects, homework. As stressed by Glasser and psychologist Alfie Kohn, group and team assignments should be given precedence over individual assignments to foster joy in learning as well as teamwork and cooperation.[42] Performance should not be measured to rank students or groups within the class; instead, assignments should make use of students' internal motivation and natural curiosity. This way, students can perceive their completed assignments positively, with pride of accomplishment and without fear of humiliation.

What gives the teacher pride of workmanship? Many intangibles, like the spark of understanding or enlightenment in students' eyes, or the enjoyment when students excel, or expressions of thanks from parents and students. Increased autonomy through professional status, emphasizing teaching rather than associated administrative duties, and the improved relations brought on by the education transformation will serve to increase the pride of workmanship of educators. Most powerful in this regard would be the abolition of annual performance appraisals, which stifle teamwork and innovation and cast a shroud of fear over schools.

13. *Institute a vigorous program of continued education and self-improvement for everyone.* All teachers and administrators must be given opportunities to continue their educations while teaching. Especially in highly technical fields, professional obsolescence cannot be allowed to compromise the quality of instruction. Every teacher, regardless of specialty, should be given the means to keep up with recent developments in their fields, as well as to study in

other fields if they choose. They must not, however, be forced or enticed to participate against their wishes; the current practice of tying increases in salary to the number of graduate credit hours taken must be ended (see Chapter 5).

School boards and administrators must work together with state agencies and local colleges and universities to provide classes, seminars, and workshops for teachers. Educators should be given ample opportunities—as well as financial aid—to pursue advanced degrees; this is not to say that they have been denied the opportunity in the past. Table 4.1 shows the breakdown of degrees held by educators as of 1983. Two things about this table are interesting. First, a large percentage of teachers in the United States pursue advanced degrees; this is more or less mandated by systems that reward teachers who earn higher degrees with higher salaries and require advanced courses to maintain certification. The advanced learning should translate into improved competence and teaching ability, and one might expect such teachers to enjoy an enhanced professional image. This is rarely the case, and in stark contrast only 3 percent of Japanese teachers pursue advanced degrees, but they are much more respected in their society.[43] Second, the percentage of high school teachers with advanced degrees was not that much greater than the number of elementary school teachers. While we may applaud the elementary teachers who advance their learning, high school teachers are expected to explore topics in much more depth than elementary school teachers and, in some cases, may benefit more from continued study in their subject areas. Of course, the data do not show whether the degrees are in subject areas or educational theory;

Table 4.1. Percentage of Public School Teachers by Degree, 1983

Degree	Elementary	Junior High	High School
Bachelors	51.4	47.2	42.9
Masters	44.7	47.6	49.2
Professional (six-year)	3.7	4.9	7.4
Doctorate	0.1	0.3	0.4

(Source: Statistical Abstract of the United States.)

nor do they show how the acquisition of advanced degrees is related to the number of years in teaching.

In addition to providing opportunities for teachers to attend advanced classes, administrators and school boards should encourage teachers to organize special classes in fields of particular interest. Funds may be set aside or specially raised to bring in notable lecturers; the public may even be invited, if the topic is of broad interest. Education managers must realize that *any* advanced education is beneficial, as long as it stimulates thought and personal development.

14. *Take action to accomplish the transformation and include everyone in the school in the effort.* The action should be well-considered, using all available techniques in a constant PDSA cycle to achieve never-ending improvement in education. Once the situation is understood and the path is clear, there is no excuse for not acting. It will require leadership from the top, hard work from everyone, and a firm resolve to see it through, but the benefit for the nation will be well worth the effort. Consideration of a strategy to guide the transformation is our next priority.

STRATEGY

Everything is difficult at first.
—Miyamoto Musashi, 1645

O nly a year after the National Commission on Excellence in Education released *A Nation at Risk*, the U.S. Department of Education was quick to report on the progress that had been achieved in education across the country. *The Nation Responds* reported on initiatives under consideration in the 50 states and the District of Columbia, some of which had already been adopted by states that recognized the crisis in education and acted accordingly prior to the Commission's activities. The initiatives covered a wide range from longer school days and tougher college admission requirements to career ladders for educators and teacher incentive pay.[1] However laudable some of the initiatives may have been (some were merely continuations of faulty practices already in existence), they were being studied and implemented in a very haphazard manner. Such is the nature of unguided local control.[2]

Comprehensive changes in education have been attempted before, with little success.[3] Must the quality transformation suffer the same fate? Past attempts have typically focused on changes to specific aspects of education, rather than the overall education process and system, and have often been the victims of political maneuverings. While specific elements of the quality emphasis in education may also fall prey to some politicizing, the principles of the transformation do not have to be lost. Additionally, the quality philosophy, starting with a carefully planned approach, will be both easier and more difficult to implement than past reforms because it proposes a radical cultural change. The acceptance of the need to change may come easily, but the overall change in perceptions and actions will take longer.

STRATEGIC DOCTRINE

We have already addressed the need for a transformation of education. The basic premise behind this development was that quality in education is a goal worth working toward with vigor and diligence. Once this premise was accepted, the search for practical methods of accomplishing the transformation began. This led to the philosophical foundations of the description of reality and the 14 Points, which are supported by the practical applications of planning and statistical methods (Appendix A). Now we are faced with the task of defining a strategy by which the transformation may be accomplished.

The move from theory into practice, especially in such a broad and complex field, is difficult at best. If quality in education is an important national aim, the strategy proposed here may provide a starting point for building the consensus necessary for promoting its never-ending improvement on a national, rather than strictly local, scale. This strategy begins with two basic assumptions. First, every organization with a stake in education, including external and internal customers, must be actively involved in the accomplishment of the transformation. Though some steps are aimed at specific elements, inputs from all elements are necessary for success. Our second assumption is that quality is a goal, not a state of existence (except as it is acceptably defined in operational terms). The effort to produce quality must continue without ceasing, beyond the completion of this proposed or any accepted strategy.

The strategy by which the education transformation may be accomplished involves introduction to and training in the quality philosophy, as well as practical implementations of particular aspects of the philosophy. The PDSA cycle is the key to the continuous improvement effort, and each stage in the strategy will involve its own cycle of planning, doing, studying, and action. Each of the steps must be carried through carefully, with emphasis on planning before any action is taken. Most of the steps in the transformation are themselves continuous efforts, where the PDSA cycle will be repeated endlessly.

A basic strategy for improvement of any endeavor can be gleaned from Deming's 14 Points. As has been pointed out in Chapter 2, the points may be arranged in a number of different ways to provide a framework for improvement. Such a framework is used as a basis for the educational transformation strategy, the steps of which are shown in Table 5.1. In the table, reference is made to the application of Deming's points, while the elements of the strategy are detailed in the following text. In addition, the strategy is presented graphically in Figure 5.1.

The final form of the strategy for education will undoubtedly be far different from what I will propose; I make no claim at omniscience and recognize that such is the fate of endeavors undertaken within the political arena. The aim, however, must remain the same: to accomplish the transformation of education in the United States and to instill an appreciation of and never-ending drive toward quality in education.

I have found it useful to apply Theodore R. Sizer's words of wisdom regarding curriculum reform to this exercise in strategy development: "Fascinating though the exercise of agenda-setting may be for academics,…[it] has limited utility. It is important, but never an end in itself. It is merely a point of departure."[4] Because practical implementation of the education transformation will involve choices and changes that cannot be predicted at the start, the strategy must be a guide rather than an instruction manual.

Recognition of the problem and acceptance of the quality philosophy is the first step, and must be accomplished soon. Recognition of the various problems of education is widespread; acceptance of the quality philosophy is a new variable in the equation. We have mentioned its acceptance and successful application in some schools, and more communities are working on

Table 5.1. Steps in the Education Transformation

Process Step	Predominant Level(s) of Activity
1. Recognition of the problem and acceptance of the quality philosophy (Point 2: Adopt the new philosophy) (Point 1: Develop and maintain constancy of purpose)	National, state, and local
2. Dissemination and adoption of the quality philosophy (Point 6: Institute training) (Point 7: Institute leadership) (Point 10: Eliminate slogans)	National, state, and local
3. Quality improvement organizations form (Point 9: Break down barriers) (Point 8: Drive out fear)	National, state, and local
4. Pilot projects (Point 12: Encourage pride of workmanship and accomplishment)	State and local
5. Development of standards (Point 11: Eliminate numerical goals) (Point 3: Eliminate mass inspection) (Point 13: Encourage self-improvement)	National and state
6. Adoption of long-term contracts (Point 4: Conduct business on the basis of quality)	State and local
7. (optional) National Teachers Corps formed	National

[Note: The entire strategy revolves around point 14 (involve everyone) and point 5 (improve constantly and forever).]

implementing quality ideas, but *national* acceptance is a long way off. With the quality movement gaining momentum among U.S. industries, corporations with quality improvement expertise may be enlisted to speed up the adoption of quality practices; this holds much promise for improvements in education, but industry and the government seem to have geared their activities more toward the results of education rather than its mechanisms.[5]

As mentioned, some states, communities, and schools are taking the lead, using the quality philosophy to improve their

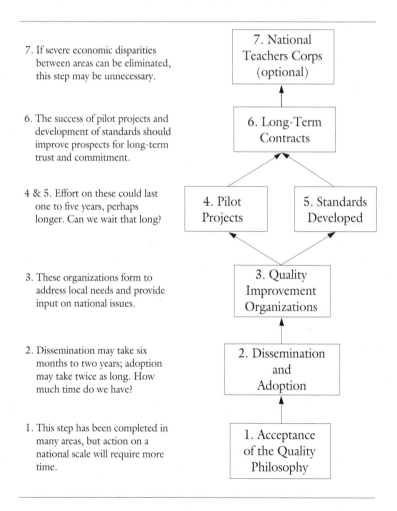

Figure 5.1 Transformation Strategy

educational environments—we will continue to discuss some of their successes—but acceptance of the quality philosophy must be national if education is to serve the needs of the whole country properly. Quality principles applied by separate state and local school boards are and will continue to be effective on that scale, but the problem our country faces is a national one. As a step toward solving the problems of our national education system, the quality emphasis has the potential to transform education on a much larger scale than has been previously attempted. Those in power on the national level may be skeptical, unwilling to admit that the quality paradigm presents powerful principles for improvement. The successes of state and local efforts may help sway national leaders to adopt the quality philosophy.

As part of national acceptance, the Federal Department of Education, the National Education Association, the American Association of School Administrators, and other prominent groups involved with education should include within their organizations executive councils or committees dedicated to the pursuit of quality. The sole purpose of these groups will be to facilitate the education transformation, communicating the vision and keeping the quality initiative moving with the aim of continuous improvement. Such councils must be large enough to encompass many different areas of expertise but small enough to be responsive to the need for change. To keep their activities from stagnating, these groups must foster creativity within their ranks and solicit innovative ideas from the outside.[6] With the proper training, coherence of action, and constancy of purpose, these groups could provide much of the impetus for the next step in the strategy.

Dissemination and adoption of the quality philosophy. Understanding and acceptance of the quality philosophy is essential to accomplish the education transformation successfully. Once the decision to act has been made, the first action must be a carefully planned and executed campaign that will reach through all levels of educational bureaucracy and teach everyone involved with the schools about the quality philosophy. Once training is in full swing, principals and superintendents who have a vision for improvement must begin putting the philosophy into practice.

State and local school boards should receive training alongside state and local education organizations. Most boards will not have to look far to find experts in the quality philosophy to conduct this training. Regional businesses that have adopted the philosophy may be able to provide assistance, as may university management and statistics departments. As with the industrial quality movement, no shortage of willing consultants will be available to conduct training, but boards are advised to use caution. First, beware those who are quick to agree or tell you only what you want to hear. Second, secure training that emphasizes the philosophy itself rather than only the analytical tools and techniques, lest you lose focus and look blindly for quick and easy solutions.

It must be made clear to all participants that the improvements we have in mind for education cannot be accomplished without a partnership between unions and management and between the private sector and the government. Unless all of the parties understand the need for and utility of the quality emphasis, they will not be willing partners in the education transformation. How long will it take to unite everyone in this effort? If the participants hold on to their limited viewpoints and continue the antagonistic relationships they have developed, it may take 10 to 20 years—but we do not have that much time to spare.

Following the idea that the philosophy should be disseminated downward through the organization, *educators* should start receiving training after the philosophy has been initially introduced to the state and local agencies. Their training will be accomplished by the boards of education and professional associations. Having been thoroughly trained in the philosophical base and familiarized with the statistical and analytical tools, superintendents, principals, and teachers' representatives will conduct orientation and training sessions in the quality philosophy for educators in their areas. Introducing the quality concepts this way will help calm local administrators' and teachers' fears about the philosophy; since they will be learning it from people to whom they can relate, they should find it easier to accept.

A danger in this approach is that errors will creep into the transmission of the philosophy, and be compounded by stepwise removal from the source.[7] Training coordinators would be well advised to invite consultants and experts from the national level (and from outside education) to augment the locally produced training program and assure the philosophy and methods are relayed properly.

Parent and student training should be undertaken by local school boards. By the time this step in the strategy is started, quality improvement organizations in state and local school boards should have been formed (see page 110). The local organizations should be planning to demonstrate the effectiveness of the quality philosophy through pilot projects involving all facets of the education process. These small-scale tests should spark interest in and help remove opposition to the quality effort (see pilot projects, page 111).

Through seminars involving student organizations, student bodies, and Parent-Teacher Associations, the quality emphasis should be formally presented to parents and students by their elected school board members and their principals and teachers. Whether the effort will take two months or two years or two decades is irrelevant; the idea is to rely on local educators and elected officials who are (we hope) trusted by the parents and students; thus informed, their support may be enlisted in the quality improvement process. Educators are again cautioned to solicit competent help from outside to ensure the philosophy is correctly transmitted.

&

Leaders must take action beyond simply providing training and seminars in the quality philosophy. Dissemination of the principles must be followed by their adoption in local schools. Teachers, parents, and students who learn about the philosophy will not be encouraged if superintendents and principals refuse to adopt the 14 Points in their everyday practice (for example, if they demonstrate inconsistency in their focus on quality, or if they make no efforts to allay fear or break down barriers). The local transformation is doomed if leaders fall back on their old management habits, such as managing by single data points instead of recognizing natural variation.

Adapting and adopting the quality principles in each school will require vision and commitment on the part of the leadership; the leader must be ready to withstand waves of criticism and fight through enormous inhibiting factors (see Chapter 7). One of the best choices an administrator can make who has a vision for change is to enlist the aid of local businesses, industries, colleges, and government agencies who are involved in the quality transformation. The quality movement has been marked by incredible amounts of cooperation and collaboration; almost everyone involved in transforming an organization is eager to share their experiences, frustrations, failures, and successes. Administrators who can tap into others' experiences, develop theories for adapting that experience to their own situation, and find expert guidance for their own transformation efforts will benefit two ways. First, the encouragement, information, and help they receive will greatly ease their burdens during the change; and second, the cooperation will greatly improve community relations.

One caveat is all too necessary. Administrative personnel, as much as teachers, students, or other participants in education, are constrained by the system within which they work. They may earnestly desire to make very specific changes but be powerless to do so. This frustration is common in every organization going through the transformation. Often middle managers who are not yet immersed in the paradigms of the organization see the need for change more clearly, but they are in no position to effect change. Administrators who find themselves in this position can approach it two ways. First, they can continue to improve the conditions in their local schools to the limit of their abilities. Second, they can find a sponsor or champion in the upper echelons of the system and ally themselves with that person. If they are successful in convincing the individual of the need for change and the proper mechanism for change, they will be able to use the sponsor's power and authority to push for more sweeping changes.

Quality improvement organizations will be formed at all levels once formal training in the quality philosophy has been started. Similar to the quality improvement councils or committees formed within national organizations, these groups will focus improvement efforts and keep the quality emphasis moving forward. Figure 5.2 shows a possible arrangement for these groups; they are linked together to provide a conduit for study, decision making, and implementation from bottom to top and top to bottom.

Boards of education. The industrial quality initiative involves teams of managers working together to effect the transformation, and the education initiative will also require the formation of quality organizations within existing state and local board of education structures. As with the previously mentioned quality management councils or committees, quality improvement organizations within boards of education must have enough members to assure that different departments are included but not be overburdened with excessive membership.

The quality improvement organizations, once formed, will guide the quality improvement process permanently. Representatives to the quality council (or whatever name suits the group) will oversee efforts to improve the quality of education in their districts and will, when situations arise, form ad-hoc committees to solve particular problems. As the improvement of quality is a

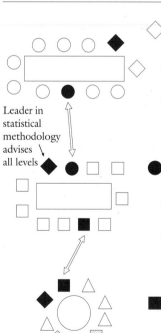

Leader in statistical methodology advises all levels

Executive Quality Council

Chaired by organizational leader

Members: functional area directors

- Develops, communicates organizational vision, constancy of purpose
- Formulates, directs policy for continuous pursuit of quality improvement

Quality Improvement Committee

Chaired by functional area director

Members: subordinate directors

- Identifies local problems, areas for improvement
- Approves, implements solutions and/or changes recommended by quality improvement teams

Quality Improvement Team

Chaired by subordinate director

Members: representatives of primary and affected areas

- Ad-hoc
- Addresses specific problems/issues
- Recommends solutions and/or changes

Figure 5.2 Quality Improvement Organizations

never-ending endeavor, these organizations and their activities continue indefinitely.

Schools (including support agencies, for example, Parent-Teacher Associations) will form their own local quality committees to address particular issues or needs. Such issues may include the selection of a vendor for the cafeteria lunch program, or a suggestion to broaden students' appreciation of history by sponsoring field trips to area historical sites, or an idea to involve local senior citizens in the education process. In addition to a formal quality organization, perhaps formed of the department heads and administrators of a school, grass-roots quality committees may form (shown in Figure 5.2 as quality improvement teams). Such groups, made up of volunteers with a common interest in studying elements of the philosophy or solving particular problems, would add greatly to the ongoing quality improvement process.

One excellent example of successful quality improvement organizations in a school district is Altoona, Pennsylvania. The Coalition of Altoona Professionals, created in 1988, helped the district management and the teachers' union organize two advisory committees (one for elementary and one for secondary schools), with building and grade-level teams at each school and district-wide special issue and subject teams. Each team has members representing different elements of the education population, and the teams provide a cross-feed of information across the district, focusing improvement efforts where most needed.[8] The experience in Altoona illustrates an important point: The design of quality improvement organizations is limited only by the imagination of the leaders and participants, but their success depends on the spirit of cooperation and collaboration within and across the teams.

Pilot projects. As the membership of the quality improvement teams is solidified and as quality principles are implemented in schools and classrooms, the local groups will select small-scale pilot projects that may be addressed using the quality philosophy. Using analytical and statistical tools like those in Appendix A, they will apply the PDSA cycle and study their processes, identify ways to improve them, implement the improvements, and analyze the results. Successful pilot projects may help build support for the quality initiative among skeptical teachers and administrators. This is covered in more detail in Chapter 7.

Standards. Several types of standards—applicable across the nation—need to be developed to complete the transformation of education. The first are curriculum standards; the second, teacher preparation and certification standards; and the third, educator professional development standards. Other additional standards may also be developed to provide guidance for such varied areas as accreditation, continuing education, school supply and service contracting, school day and school year length, and textbooks. These are discussed in detail in *National Standards* (page 113).

Encouragement and adoption of long-term contracts. Rewarding quality teachers, workers, and vendors with long-term contracts based on the quality of their performance and their continued improvement is integral to the ultimate transformation of education. It has two major implications.

The first part of this effort involves educational vendors. Long-term contracts, based on the quality of the vendors' products, bring the producers of educational materials into the quality transformation. Manufacturers of books, maps, visual aids, overhead projectors, school buses, athletic equipment, and other materials and equipment may all be encouraged to improve their quality, if they are secure in the knowledge that their continued improvement will be met with continued patronage. The results, improved profits and security for vendors and improved accountability of taxpayer money, are advantageous for everyone involved.

The second, and more important, portion of this effort involves educators themselves, and by extension, all workers in the school system. In the wake of teacher strikes that cripple school systems, it may be passé to mention this. In the section on standards we will discuss the requirement to provide educators with salaries that reflect their professionalism, dedication, and qualifications. In addition, contracts must provide teachers, administrators, and workers with job security. That security would, of course, be contingent upon maintenance and improvement of expertise (guided by professional development standards), and strict professional ethics (a teacher could, for instance, be removed for a breach of ethics as determined in relation to a code of professional conduct).

The development of new contracts must perforce involve unions, but care must be taken to include union leaders *throughout*

112

the transformation. Managers of education cannot wait to open a dialogue on improvement until this stage. The quality philosophy does not perpetuate an adversarial relationship between management and unions, it recognizes both parties as partners in the educational effort. This part of the strategy that involves contractual obligations is only a small part of the overall quality emphasis; unions representing teachers and other educational workers must be involved in the entire quality improvement process.

Development of a National Teachers Corps is an optional final step of the strategy. This is not to be confused with the Teacher Corps established in the 1960s or the Teach for America program started by Wendy Kopp in 1989.[9] This National Teachers Corps would supplement the income of educators who volunteer to relocate to areas that need teachers in their particular specialty, or to economically depressed or high cost-of-living areas. Such relocations would provide teachers to districts that might not otherwise be able to attract or afford them. These teachers' salaries could either be augmented by federal funds, or they could be enrolled as civil service employees (see *National Teachers Corps*, page 143).

NATIONAL STANDARDS

As mentioned previously, standards are required to guide the improvement of education nationwide. Just as industrial standards are symbols of cooperation with the aim of better serving all customers, educational standards for curriculum, teacher preparation, and professional development for educators can unite diverse elements with the aim of constantly improving the teaching and learning environment.

Curriculum Standards

If the U.S. educational system is to serve the nation as a whole, some set of comprehensive curriculum standards applicable to all public and private schools must be developed. These should be based on sound educational principles and designed to develop in young people the skills and knowledge needed after graduation. Districts and schools would structure their classes to meet the requirements; they could require more than the standardized curriculum if they so choose. The standards would form the foundation for the acceptance requirements of this country's colleges and universities, which would also be free to apply more restrictive standards. Of course, as William Glasser points out in his book *The Quality School*, simply standardizing curricula or making existing courses more challenging will not solve the problem of student motivation to do the work; as he has treated motivation and its improvement so well, I will not reproduce his efforts here.[10]

How will curriculum standards affect academic freedom and local control? Standards will provide guidance, not specific material; as such, they will have little adverse effect. Educators will still have academic freedom that "defends the rights of qualified teachers to investigate, discuss, publish, or teach the truth as they see it in the discipline of their competence, subject to no authority except the standards of professional ethics and inquiry."[11] Curriculum standards must not tell teachers *how* to teach their subjects, but instead must outline *what* subjects are to be taught and perhaps what elements of those subjects are considered most important. Teachers and school boards will have the final decision on how to implement the standards in their own unique learning environments.

Just such a curriculum standard is being established now in British Columbia. The Ministry of Education is working on radically new guidelines, concentrating first on elementary schools. "Instead of setting product goals, these new guides deal with broad developmental areas—Intellectual Development, Social Development, Social Responsibility, Emotional Development, Aesthetic and Artistic Development, and Physical Development. Specific skill building and subject knowledge acquisition is set against these process goals."[12] Similar broad guides will eventually be developed for secondary schools also.

With respect to the education transformation, development of these standards should come after dissemination of the quality philosophy. This allows school boards and administrators to begin quality training and local improvement efforts; they can then encourage their educators, who now have both theory and some experience, to submit suggestions to and comment on recommendations of a national curriculum commission. The commission, chaired at the highest level possible, must bring together representatives of all participants in the transformation, including educators, students, parents, industries, and the government to establish, review, and revise the curriculum standards. Like most of the parts of the transformation strategy, this is an ongoing effort; the standard curriculum will certainly be updated as time goes by.[13]

In fact, national standards in education already exist, although they are not explicitly called standards. They are the standardized college admission tests, the Scholastic Aptitude Test (SAT) and the American College Test (ACT). While neither is applicable across the entire United States, their presence is so pervasive and their influence so great that they are definitely the standard against which high school seniors and school systems are judged. These tests provide a benchmark against which admissions officers who do not understand variation rank incoming college freshmen, a benchmark that is only needed because the education system allows great disparities between the educational preparation of different young people. Despite their being used as "standards," the tests themselves do not provide much guidance for high school faculties who are planning courses of study for their students.

To improve this situation and provide for uniform treatment of academic subjects nationwide, curriculum standards that are applicable throughout the country are necessary. Such standards are not expected to ensure uniform achievement or uniform mastery among students; uniformity of that type is both unrealistic and undesirable. The standards will, however, ensure uniform opportunity and help ensure uniform quality of education. If our country is to remain relatively homogeneous and our people are to be capable of meaningful discourse with each other,[14] students in Maine must learn much the same things as students in Hawaii. The student in Oregon who wants to go to college in Florida must not be handicapped by the curriculum choices made by the local school board; likewise, the college admissions director in California must be assured that the freshman candidate from West Virginia is adequately prepared for a college education. These assurances cannot be provided by standardized tests, which are often poor indicators of future college performance—proof that quality cannot be inspected into education.

Elementary education. The first standards necessarily deal with elementary education, as that is the foundation upon which 115 all later education is built. Too much emphasis has been placed on secondary education recently because secondary education gets the headlines: our high school students are compared with other nations' much more frequently than our sixth graders. But as pointed out by many educators and researchers, the quality of elementary and preelementary (for example, in the home or in play school) education are keys to later success.[15]

It seems clear that the elementary curriculum and the efforts of elementary teachers cannot by themselves undo the damage children sustain from living in an intellectual malaise their first six years. In Appendix D we will discuss programs designed to compensate for the negative effects of poverty; such programs should be supported and strengthened. Other program ideas should also be explored. R. Earl Hadady, in his book *How Sick Is Uncle Sam?*, suggests that a federally sponsored preschool program for all poor children would help some of these children overcome the educational deficit they have been given.[16] This idea is certainly worthy of a pilot program, and other ideas must also be seriously considered if we are to find a solution to this problem.

While the easy answer is to make parents responsible for this, the simple factors of decaying family structure and severe socioeconomic pressure make many families unable to comply. Do we relegate their children to the cycle of poverty in the slums? No, but neither do we simply *give* them what we think they need. We give them tools and a world in which to use them.

The elementary curriculum itself seems to be structurally sound; it is designed to teach the Three R's and introduce children to the wonders afforded by other subjects. In teaching the Three R's, however, key improvements must be made if we are to defeat our twin enemies of illiteracy and innumeracy.

Children must practice reading, writing, and arithmetic to become proficient; there is no evidence that rote memorization of literary passages or mathematical rules gave eighteenth-century common-school students any great measure of proficiency. They knew enough to get by, and our schools have followed in their predecessors' footsteps, teaching our children how to get by. What has led to this? Diane Ravitch suggests that the problem

> lies not with the teacher, but with the experts who have told them for years that skills and processes are all that

matter. In this strange world of the overcredentialed but undereducated, content, knowledge, and context count for nothing. The children of this regime arrive in junior high schools and secondary schools knowing *how*, but not *why* or *what*.[17]

The first way to remedy this in teaching reading and writing is to reduce drastically the number of "readers" used by schools, replacing them with what we might call more "traditional" or "classic" fare, for example, fairy tales, children's novels, and historical stories. The children's sections of public libraries are filled with wide varieties of stories that spark children's imaginations and that make reading the joy and pleasure it should be; such books must be brought into the classroom. Despite evidence that the pseudoscience of establishing "reading levels" for children's books has been dreadfully misused, to the detriment of an entire generation of people, educational psychologists still have a strong foothold in the schoolbook publishing arena. As pointed out by child psychologists Bruno Bettelheim and Karen Zelan, part of the problem is that "neither children nor teachers buy textbooks: school boards and superintendents do."[18] It is hoped that the adoption of the quality philosophy will provide the means for correcting this problem.

A similar approach may be taken with regard to arithmetic teaching. The requirement that teachers pay homage to elementary mathematics texts can severely impair their ability to demonstrate to their students the utility and power of math. Too often, teachers are unable to make adjustments for differences between individual students in their rush to complete the textbooks. We must give elementary teachers (and, by extension, all teachers) the freedom to use whatever means they can to achieve their learning objectives, rather than holding them accountable to a textbook program.

An additional element of early education is exposure to music and the arts. While it may be tempting to cut cultural instruction when the prevailing emphasis seems to be on more intellectual pursuits, this would be a mistake of the highest order. In addition to exposing young people to their own and different cultures (thereby laying a foundation for acceptance and harmony), these subjects allow students the freedom of expression necessary for building strong self-esteem. It is vitally important to

remember that education is preparing people to interact successfully in society at large, both inside and outside the work environment; the arts are a vital part of fulfilling that requirement, and
concentrated exposure during the early school experience will
build the proper framework.

In short, elementary education must not only provide students with a modicum of skills but also encourage their creativity,
build their self-esteem, and pique their curiosity about future
learning. To accomplish that, we must do everything in our
power to enhance their joy in learning.

Secondary education. The proposed secondary curriculum is much more detailed than the broad brush given the elementary curriculum. At the risk of being overly ambitious (but
at least recognizing the risk[19]), I will consider secondary education as the combination of junior high school and high school
and will use the entire six-year span to build upon the solid educational base provided by a quality elementary education.[20]

Table 5.2 lists elements of the proposed curriculum for the
junior high and high school years. The curriculum elaborates on
the recommendations of the National Commission on Excellence
in Education.[21] We will add new requirements (such as physical
education) and make specific suggestions where the commission's
were vague. It assumes, of course, that students will enter junior
high school possessing the ability to read and write the English
language[22]; the ability to add, subtract, multiply, and divide, and
an understanding of simple mathematical concepts; some rudimentary knowledge of science; basic knowledge of our country's
history, customs, and relation to the rest of the world; and an
appreciation for (if not talent in) various art forms. Thus the elementary school foundation is critically important to the success of
the secondary curriculum.

English and literature. The English curriculum focuses on
the further development of reading and writing abilities and
seeks to introduce the student to many different forms of literature. We assume students will arrive at school with the ability to
read and write, especially once the elementary schools have
improved their programs. Students who are not equipped with
these basic skills will be given intensive coaching to improve their
skills before they can be expected to perform up to their potential
in the standard curriculum.

Table 5.2 Proposed Curriculum, Junior High Through High School

Required courses, to be taken each of the six years:
English and/or literature
Mathematics
Science
History and/or social science (see note A)
Physical education
Foreign language (three years minimum; see note B)

[Note A: The proposed subject matter requires that two units of social science be taken concurrently (see text).]

[Note B: These three years of foreign language should be effectively advanced study; elementary school students should be regularly exposed to foreign languages to build a basis for these classes.]

Elective courses, offered each year:
General electives, including music, art, photography, journalism, drama, typing, and so on.
Special electives, including advanced sciences, mathematics, literature, foreign languages, career-oriented courses, and so on.

Students will read short stories, essays, sermons, speeches, novels, plays, poetry, letters, criticism—practically everything. Most of the selections will be chosen by the student; teacher approval will only be required to ensure that a variety of selections are read. Some selections will be required of all students to establish common ground and cultural literacy. Textbooks will be seldom used, and literature studies will be supported by practice in composition. Students will write their own short stories, essays, speeches, poetry, letters, criticism, and research papers appropriate to their ages and maturity levels. Research papers that support work in other classes will be both acceptable and encouraged.

The curriculum's six years would consist of a balanced mix of American, English, and foreign literature designed to correspond with and reinforce other subjects being studied (see *Correlation,* page 123).

Mathematics. In order to build within students the skills and knowledge required of tomorrow's citizens and workers, the mathematics curriculum should be designed to lead them through a progression of abilities. Students who have only worked with discrete numbers will be carefully exposed to more abstract concepts such as word problems and the use of variables. This is a critical time in which the students' interest will either be held or lost; thus, emphasis on real-world applications must pervade the entire mathematics curriculum. In addition to being able to translate verbal problems into mathematical terms, students must be able to see the utility of algebraic formulas in solving everyday problems; this is much easier said than done, but may be helped by increasing collaboration among teachers and correlation between subjects (see *Correlation*, page 123).

Later years of the mathematics curriculum such as geometry and trigonometry must also be soundly based on applications. It is not enough for students to learn how Euclidean logic works (especially when it has significant weaknesses[23]). What does it teach us about our world? It is not enough for students to know what the sine, cosine, and tangent functions are. What do they do in real life? We cannot expect to hold students' attention if we cannot show that the concepts they are learning are useful.

At least one year of mathematics should consist of probabilities and statistics, possibly the most neglected areas of mathematics today. I was amazed when fully half of a graduate class I was taking did not know anything about probabilities—did not even know that probabilities are expressed in percentages! And most people accept newscasters' statistics without questioning where the numbers came from or what they really mean; of course it is easy to cloud any issue with statistics, but only because few people understand enough statistics to recognize the act. A large portion of this year should be spent teaching students how to produce useful data and interpret it, by allowing them to design and conduct experiments to investigate phenomena of personal interest.

At the last stage of the mathematics curriculum, students may be allowed to choose between two different classes, mathematical analysis or calculus. The mathematical analysis course would be designed for those students who have no immediate plans to pursue an undergraduate degree; it would consist of series of practical problems that allow students to use elements of their previous courses to reach the solutions. The calculus course, built for students who are planning to attend college, would introduce differential and integral calculus of one variable. As with all of the mathematics courses, calculus would also focus on applications. Both the applied mathematics and calculus courses would augment advanced science courses.

Science. The science curriculum also lasts six years. It should be designed to introduce students to the major branches of science and acquaint them with scientific principles and progress. The curriculum should follow a definite progression from basic to applied science.

Students should first tackle basic science, in which they are introduced to the scientific method and the rudiments of scientific inquiry. Course material will consist of laboratory experiments and demonstrations in several different scientific fields, studies of scientific discoveries and their impact on our modern world, and an early look at scientific ethics.

In schools equipped to do so, one year of the curriculum should be devoted to computer science. Students in this class will learn how computers work and how to work with them. The majority of this course will focus on computer applications, and in order for the computer science class to fit into the science curriculum, the applications should center around science. For example, students may learn to use the computer to write their laboratory and other reports (word processing), but they should also learn to use the computer to analyze data from experiments. Programming should be an integral part of the course; for example, students may learn to program the computer to solve algebraic equations, thus enhancing their study of algebra.

With a grounding in basic science and computer science, students should be ready to address a specific area of science, such as, biology, chemistry, or physics. The biological science course will introduce students to the wide range of life sciences, including biology, zoology, botany, and ecology. Given students' understanding of environmental problems, strong emphasis should be placed on the environment and our role in protecting and preserving our natural habitat. Students will take part in experiments and demonstrations, applying laboratory techniques they have previously acquired and using the computer to compare and analyze results.

In a similar manner, students would participate in chemistry and physics classes, where emphasis will be on student comprehension and application of scientific principles, rather than simply acquisition of tidbits of information. Chemistry students should learn how the science of chemistry has enhanced (and in some cases endangered) our lives and become acquainted with the difficulties as well as the triumphs of the science, instead of simply learning what the periodic chart looks like and the difference between aldehydes and ketones. Physics students should learn how physical laws govern the world in which we live, and how comprehension of those laws has led and can lead to significant breakthroughs, instead of merely memorizing that force equals mass times acceleration.[24]

The culmination of the science curriculum should be a year of applied science. Students would work in small groups (individual efforts would be highly discouraged) on self-chosen projects, applying the scientific principles they have learned in previous classes to solve complex problems. Their projects may be chosen from any of the other areas of science, such as computer science, biology, chemistry, or physics; students may, however, choose to explore some other field, such as astronomy or robotics.

History and social science. As noted in Table 5.2, this curriculum is the only one that covers seven years of material, two of which run concurrently. The curriculum consists of history, political science, economics, and humanities.

Two years should be spent studying U.S. history. One may cover U.S. history from the early discoverers and settlers up to the end of the Civil War, while the second covers the period between Reconstruction and the present. (These demarcations are tentative; there may be more appropriate ways to divide our country's history.) Both years will include studies of how our country has related to the rest of the world. To encourage collaboration between teachers and build a more coherent total curriculum, much of the source material for the history courses should also provide source material for the concurrent courses in literature (see *Correlation*, page 123).

One year should be devoted to world history. This class will divide its time between Eastern, Middle Eastern, and Western civilizations, looking at similarities and differences between cultures. Such a comparative course should greatly improve our abilities to relate to peoples different from ourselves. Like all of the history and social sciences classes, the world history class will include geography as a tool for improving comprehension of the course material.

In addition to world history, students should study a year of political science; this class will combine elements of a traditional civics course, in which students learn how our government works (and does not work), with in-depth comparisons of the world's different political systems. Course material should allow students to understand how different political systems have developed around the world; like the comparative studies in world history, this understanding will ultimately serve to reduce our U.S. ethno-centrism. Running concurrently with political science is a year of economics, which will address both macro- and micro-economics. By conducting these courses in the same year, students will learn about our political system as they learn about our economy, and as they learn about other political systems they learn about other economic systems as well. The course materials of these units, therefore, should closely parallel one another.

The social science curriculum also includes a year of sociology and anthropology, in which students examine the behavior and relationships of human beings in group situations (in both contemporary and historical settings). Complementing these studies is a year of psychology, in which students learn about individual human behavior.

Correlation. As far as possible, the courses students take should reinforce one another; ideally, concepts and ideas from each course would be applied in all others. Recall that building a quality education requires optimization of the entire system (Chapters 2 and 3); in a like manner, building a quality curriculum requires optimization of the whole.

For instance, required readings for American literature should support studies in U.S. history. Students may read and comment on Cotton Mather's sermons, the Declaration of Independence, the *Federalist Papers,* the Gettysburg Address, inaugural addresses, and so on. Required selections in English or foreign literature should support studies in other parts of the social sciences curriculum, for example, world history and political science. In all English courses, readings may be chosen that support studies in the mathematics and science curricula. (An example from Mount Edgecumbe High School has already been cited.)

Science and mathematics curricula quite naturally support one another as mathematical concepts are indispensable to serious scientific inquiry. Imagine the benefits students would receive who had the opportunity to seriously apply the abstract mathematical concepts they were learning in calculus to complex scientific problems they had chosen to study in applied science. Imagine the depth of understanding that would be engendered if students learning about social sciences could use and apply basic statistical theory they were learning in another class. The improvements in comprehension would be fantastic; that would be quality education.

Electives form an important part of the proposed curriculum. General electives could be taken by almost any student with the available time. For example, students who have completed their foreign language courses and are not taking more, students with an open hour of time in their schedule, or students who do not have to work a part-time job may all pursue electives. Some general electives might even extend into the evening hours or weekends, in the form of school athletics, service projects, or field trips. The list provided in Table 5.2 was, of course, far from complete; following R. Earl Hadady, at least one "elective" might be a seminar in marriage and parenthood, designed to give young people an in-depth look at the stresses of family life, with the aim of reducing the number of cruelty and neglect cases.[25] Of course, the availability of electives would hinge on the available facilities and financial support.

Special electives would be available for those students who desire a deeper intellectual experience in school; they may consist of subject matter study as noted in the table, or may be independent, interdisciplinary study of some type. Special seminars may even be arranged for interested students, for example, philosophy or religion seminars. Vocational electives fit into this category of special electives, also, and would consist of career-oriented courses designed to provide a wide range of skills for students entering the workforce after graduation. Unlike vocational programs in other countries, these would not lock students into one area of expertise.[26] One special elective students might be persuaded to take could be designed to give them community service experience.[27]

Note that Table 5.2 does not specify a course completion schedule for any of the curricula. Some courses may need to be taken in a particular order, such as algebra before calculus. The order is less critical for others; a student may choose to take chemistry before biology, or to take psychology before sociology, or to take both calculus and statistics in the same year. As Theodore R. Sizer advises, "All subject matter should be fuel for the travel to more subject matter. The details of every school curriculum must meet this test." I believe this proposal meets this criterion well enough, but Sizer continues: "There are few universal answers, though…. Master plans for cities, states, and the nation that standardize instruction are certain to be inefficient: no one set of procedures can conceivably serve most students well."[28] Any attempt to standardize *instruction,* to mandate that specific course items will be taught in specific ways, would be folly; this suggested curriculum does not so attempt. This proposal recommends national standards of what students should know at each level, that is, what measurable objectives should be set, but leaves decisions regarding instructional methods and curricular details in the hands of teachers (where such decisions belong). With regard to the order in which classes are taken, students should be allowed choices where appropriate; a little flexibility on the part of the administration and teachers may help keep the student interested in school.

Timing of school completion is not a paramount concern either. If a student completes the curriculum in six years, demonstrating mastery of the subjects, she should graduate.[29] But a student who has attended classes for six years should not graduate unless he can demonstrate mastery of the subjects. Why should a student be penalized if he takes seven years to master the subject matter? Students are different; we should find out why the student is having trouble and help correct the problem rather than stigmatizing any student for not grasping the course material in a specific amount of time. Some might argue that we are penalizing them by making them keep at it until they have mastered the material; I propose that we are really penalizing them when we allow them to graduate knowing that they have not reached their potential. Some students, especially in poorer areas of the country, work regular jobs to help their families meet expenses; they may have to take extra years of schoolwork to graduate to make up for the impact the jobs have on their learning environment.

In the same way, if a student can complete the curriculum in five years, or four, that student should graduate. The use of a series of pretests in the value-added approach will undoubtedly turn up some students who have entered classes knowing the concepts and the material. An interview with the instructor and perhaps a guidance counselor will be the final determinant of whether such a student should be allowed to take the next level class. These cases will be rare, however.

A novel approach to increasing options for students was described by David T. Kearns and Denis P. Doyle in *Winning the Brain Race*. They suggest that schools be open year-round, "permitting students to attend for as many days as they need to gain academic skills." In this way, students who grasp material quickly may spend time doing advanced coursework, helping other students, or working at a job. Students who have trouble with their classes would attend for as long as it took to master the material; conceivably, fewer students would remain and these students would have the benefit of increased attention from their teachers. The "flexible term" also includes provisions for increased time devoted to certain classes, such as, chemistry classes with laboratory periods.[30]

The idea of the flexible term calls into question one of the prevailing educational paradigms: the "standard" school of six or seven or eight periods with lunch and recess. Why must the educational experience be so constrained? It seems possible to arrange classes in a less rigid manner to better accommodate a more flexible curriculum. For instance, instead of holding chemistry class every day in 50-minute increments it might be more effective if held once a week for three hours (to allow for more in-depth experiments or demonstrations). In the same way, it might be more effective for history or English or drama to meet twice a week in two-hour blocks. (Admittedly, it may also prove less effective.) Such a schedule may be thought of as organic, with room to grow, develop, and change as the learning situation warrants. It may also enable teachers to combine their efforts for greater effect, for example, having a mathematics class and a science class meet together to work on cooperative projects involving concepts that are common to the two subject areas.

The question may now be raised about how many years of school will be mandatory. Should students be required to complete the entire curriculum, or would some shorter period of attendance be acceptable? If the curriculum elements are important, students should be required to demonstrate proficiency in them all; to allow students to leave school without studying a subject is tantamount to saying the subject is not important enough to be learned. On the other hand, if a student is determined that she does not wish to finish out the required curriculum, she should be allowed to leave so as not to become a disruptive factor or a distraction to the other students. As a suggestion for debate, I propose that completion of four years of this proposed curriculum (that is, tenth grade of high school) be the limit of compulsory education. Students who choose to leave school at this point may be given a certificate of completion of the compulsory period of education, but would not receive a diploma. Such students may wish to return to school after a year or two of work; they should be allowed to do so without prejudice.

ã

Compared to what is traditionally called the high school level, the proposed curriculum requires a great deal more course work than most U.S. schools. A 1985 survey of public schools tallied the average number of years of study required for high school graduation: English, 3.8; science, 1.8; mathematics, 1.9; social studies, 2.8. The English and social studies requirements came close to but the science and mathematics requirements fell far short of the recommendations found in *A Nation at Risk*. Private school requirements were much closer to the National Commission's recommendations.[31] In contrast, the proposed curriculum requires that English, mathematics, science, and social sciences be taken each year.

Two concerns with standardized curricula are its impacts on students who are especially capable and on those students who are not intellectually inclined. "Gifted and talented" students will be considered in detail in Appendix D. Concern over students who may struggle with the curriculum is prevalent in countries such as Japan, where the standardized curriculum is fast-paced, difficult, and leads to comprehensive tests for advancement.[32] The argument is that standardized curricula leave too little room for the slow student or the student whose household situation is not conducive to academic pursuits; the result is often inordinate amounts of stress on the student.

No doubt standardized curricula are difficult. They should not, however, be impossible for any but the dullest student. Most students, with concerted effort and the support of teachers who are dedicated to making learning a joyful experience, will be able to master the skills and concepts such curricula would teach. All students deserve to be challenged by their learning opportunities: if learning is not a challenge, how can it be worthwhile?

ैंं

The difficulty of the curriculum may also be a vehicle by which another often neglected but highly valued skill may be taught: teamwork, too often called cheating in school situations.[33] One recent movement in education is pushing for more cooperative learning experiences. The potential for study and work groups to encourage and help each other with assignments is incredible, and is covered in detail in William Glasser's *Control Theory in the Classroom;* however, some approaches to team learning are perpetuating competition in schools.

In the quest for academic excellence, some cooperative learning programs mix internal and external motivators for the students. These programs rely on the students' innate desire to do good work and contribute to the group effort, and allow them to pool their talents to produce a better product than they could alone; the negative impact comes from the institutionalized use of external rewards (for example, prizes, certificates, or parties) for some of the teams.[34] Some cooperative learning programs actively encourage tournaments and competition between the learning teams.[35] What happens to a young graduate or nongraduate who has been consistently rewarded with special incentives for working on a team when teamwork is no longer rewarded, but rather expected (as on the job)? Worse, what happens when a learning team "loses?" Will not one of the members be blamed, his performance ridiculed and self-esteem shattered by the very people with whom he is supposed to cooperate? As we have discussed in previous chapters, competition for grades or other recognition have no place in institutions where we should be building up all students' abilities and self-worth.

ᎧᎭ

The promulgation of a standard curriculum also helps solve the problem of competitive grading. In order to be promoted to the next class under a standardized curriculum, students would demonstrate a modicum of proficiency in a subject, and their instructors would be reasonably sure they are able to handle the next level of material. Students measure their achievements against themselves and what they need to work effectively at the next level, rather than against one another.

This mastery approach requires that students at each level demonstrate proficiency sufficient to begin the next class. This requires sets of standards for what students should know prior to entering a grade, standards that must be carefully set, taking into account the capabilities of the educational system as well as the students. It may seem that some subjects lend themselves to this—mathematics and science—and that other, less concrete subjects are less amenable to this approach. However, social sciences and English courses are also made up of sets of concepts and pieces of knowledge that make sense to teach in some specific order—for example, Greek civilization before Roman.

It may also seem that this approach requires a massive effort to measure each student's abilities before they move to the next class, but recall the discussions on inspection from Chapters 2 and 3. Certainly teachers will often evaluate where their students are in their understanding of the material; but these must be considered process measurements, not final *go/no-go* inspections. As process measurements, they must be designed to give the teachers useful information for changing the teaching and learning process to better meet the students' interests and present level of understanding; the aim is continuous improvement of the process to ensure that the outcome is acceptable.

By adopting the standardized curriculum, education will fulfill its purpose of leading students systematically through the development of definite abilities and/or knowledge. This development will be tailored throughout the educational career to guide the student in progression from basic to applied knowledge, from concrete to conceptual thinking. By adopting the new rationale behind progression, students will not be unnecessarily embarrassed by comparison with their peers. Grade progression will become obsolete, as grade levels are not the base unit of the curriculum. The connection of progression to demonstrated mastery over a period of time, based on a realistic curriculum and teaching plan, will give students a sense of control over their own educational destiny, and enhance their joy in learning.

ે▲

The previous discussion on curricula notwithstanding, the question we need to ask ourselves is not "What should we teach (in terms of subjects and courses) to prepare students for life?" To ask the question in that manner is to assume the learning process stops once an individual ceases to be a student, that is, leaves school. The question assumes that the curriculum is capable of providing students with all they need to pursue their ambitions. In fact, as stated previously, learning and development continue long after school is out. The learning may be individual or institutional, and certainly different people choose to pursue different levels of education, but the learning process is not limited to the confines of the campus.

The question is better phrased, "What should we offer (in terms of learning experiences) to engage students and prompt their continued learning throughout life?" By asking the question this way, we step beyond the traditional boundaries of strictly defined courses. This outlook enables us to develop programs that use students' interests, cultures, and aspirations to capture their imaginations and stimulate their development. We begin to lead students into life-long learning; we begin to offer quality education.

ે▲

The **postsecondary** curriculum is beyond the scope of this work, but it too is undergoing changes. One of the movements in higher education is for increased accountability, part of which involves schools stating explicitly what students must know and be able to perform in order to graduate. Several accreditation organizations are requiring colleges and universities to state clear and measurable learning objectives for their classes and degree programs, in effect to guarantee that graduates of the programs meet some minimum criteria.[36] The reader can undoubtedly realize what a dangerous trend this is, as it could potentially limit professors' academic freedom and require perpetuation of the stereotyping of grades.

As the transformation in education grows, colleges and universities will be faced with the need to address their own approach to instruction and the needs of students as larger numbers of more uniformly prepared students emerge from secondary schools.[37] Students from Mount Edgecumbe High School, for example, where the quality philosophy has been working for several years, have expressed disappointment over the poor learning environments they find in colleges.[38]

Before the classroom instructor is affected, however, admissions counselors will be faced with the problem of choosing what students to admit to the institutions. If improved learning processes in secondary schools produce more students who are capable and enthusiastic about learning, and better understanding of theory of variation and theory of knowledge results in less reliance on standardized admissions tests, admissions counselors may return to written essays and personal interviews to evaluate candidates. While these also provide little evidence on which to predict a candidate's success, it may prove worthwhile to evaluate candidates on their attitude toward learning and reasons for attending a school and selecting a field of study.

In addition to sending better prepared high school graduates to college, the educational transformation is being applied to higher education to improve its products and services. Many colleges and universities are turning to the quality philosophy for ways to improve their operations and enhance their competitiveness. Some are including the quality philosophy in management or related courses, but few are actively trying to apply the philosophy to optimize their academic endeavors.[39]

National Teacher Training and Certification Standards

"The teaching profession is in sad shape. The way teachers are selected and trained must change if schools are to perform better." 131

So wrote Gerald Dorfman and Paul Hanna in an article entitled "Can Education Be Reformed?"[40]

This area has been the subject of much discussion and debate in recent years. Standards in this area are intended to guide colleges and universities in designing curricula for potential teacher candidates. This effort will not necessarily involve developing original standards; each state already has standards. It may be possible to adapt the existing state requirements to form a comprehensive set of national training and certification standards.

The same way employers and colleges must know that new employees and students from different areas of the country have mastered certain skills and obtained a body of useful knowledge, a board of education in New York must be assured that a teacher candidate from Arizona is qualified in the subject to be taught. Present state certification requirements, while often quite comprehensive, differ enough from state to state to make situations like this quite difficult. This often forces teachers who relocate to take additional courses or tests, either before starting to teach or during their first year.

When the educational crisis was first widely perceived, differences in the quality of teacher education prompted the adoption of certification testing nationwide. By 1987, 45 states had begun competency testing programs for initial certification of teachers, though few states had adopted the National Teacher Exam.[41] Certification testing is misguided: if teacher education and preparation were of uniform high quality, such testing would be unnecessary. This point has been discussed with respect to student testing, for example, the SAT. (It is interesting to note that a prominent teaching education reform group, the Holmes Group, proposed not one but at least three tests for initial teacher certification![42])

Producing quality teachers certainly depends on having quality candidates entering colleges of education. As stated by Dennis Lawton, "It is important to do everything possible to improve the initial training of teachers, but it is even more important to look at problems of recruitment."[43] While this viewpoint has merit, providing qualified teachers also depends on developing to the utmost the candidates at hand. Large and prestigious colleges and universities have been able to select candidates early who show promise, but many smaller and poorer institutions have not had that luxury. In attempts to boost enrollment to qualify for increased financial support, they "admit some applicants whose capabilities do not assure competence as future teachers."[44] The following questions may appropriately be asked: whose capabilities ever assure competence in any future endeavor? How can we know?

Enhanced professional status of teachers and improved compensation should attract many capable teacher candidates who might otherwise go into the private sector. (The current Teach for America program, in which top college and university graduates are spending two years as teachers before embarking on their chosen careers, was in fact organized to overcome this poor perception of teaching.[45]) National standards governing education preparation requirements and providing adequate resources for teacher education should help assure more uniformly high quality instructors. The education transformation will also feed itself by assuring that all students entering the university—including those who will be teachers—are of uniformly high quality.

So how should teachers be prepared? Mastery in the subject area must be the first requisite for teacher certification even before the ability to teach. Mathematics teachers must be mathematicians, chemistry teachers chemists, and history teachers historians. Elementary education may require teachers who have mastered pedagogy, but the specialties of secondary education require that instructors be scholars in their subjects.[46] Secondary school teachers should major in their subject area and minor in education, rather than obtaining their degree in pedagogy (even with respect to a selected area). Restructuring of education curricula will be necessary to produce these scholar-teachers. This will open the door for professionals in other fields to enter the teaching profession, and it has implications for professional development as well.

While it is certainly true that "providing prospective teachers with strong subject matter knowledge does not equip them with the understanding or skill necessary to teach that knowledge to someone else,"[47] it is equally true that knowing how to teach does not automatically mean one knows what to teach. Educators who know what to teach, by being scholars in their fields, can be taught *how* to teach; the importance of being a scholar first cannot be overstated.[48] What pedagogical principles teachers need to know should be learned more through practice than

133

through study; some have suggested that the education degree itself be eliminated.[49] Some amount of educational theory is certainly helpful, but student teaching is the obvious medium for practical acquisition of teaching skills. In addition to student teaching, all new teachers should work as apprentices to established teachers during their early careers (see *National Professional Development Standards for Educators,* below). And all teachers should learn to apply quality principles.

Certification standards will continue to be used by the teaching profession to assure that new teachers are fully qualified. Educational achievements (such as level of degree completed), some period of practical service as a teacher, and the recommendation of established educators will be the predominant factors determining eligibility. Whether special examinations will continue to be used remains to be seen, though uniform preparation under the quality philosophy should make them superfluous.

In order to be accepted as truly national standards, however, extensive coordination with teachers' organizations, colleges of education, and state boards of education will be required in order to reach a consensus. The time spent in such coordination will be rewarded, however, with a body of educators of uniform high quality. As with other efforts, this one involves continuous reappraisal of the standards with respect to educational research and teacher requirements.

National Professional Development Standards for Educators

Professional development standards follow naturally after development and acceptance of teacher training and certification standards. Like all professions, initial training for teachers is not enough; our educators must know that their continued professional development is desirable and will be fully supported. All educators and administrators must be encouraged to participate in seminars and advanced courses both in their specialty areas and in other areas of personal or professional interest; however, this must be more than rewarding teachers with more pay according to the number of advanced course credits they hold. To guide this process, standards similar to those concerning certification must be developed for professional development. This effort provides the framework for establishing permanent contracts with educators (the next step in the transformation).

Professional status of educators, especially secondary school teachers, was not questioned or challenged in the early days of the institution, perhaps because the high school was philosophically closer to the college than to the common school. Robert L. Church writes:

> Before 1900 a good many people served both as college professors and high school teachers at different times in their careers, even moving from college teaching to secondary teaching or administration without demonstrable loss in status or self-esteem. High school teachers were often called professors, and before 1900 presented papers at meetings of the scholarly organizations dedicated to academic research.[50]

The incredible rise in secondary school populations in the early twentieth century made it increasingly difficult for teachers to participate in such outside activities. Today, when most teachers are responsible for instructing over 150 students every day and have limited time to prepare their lessons and review their students' papers, discussions of professional development for educators must address the simple fact that teachers do not have time to spare.

Few would argue against the premise that advanced professional development for educators is a good thing. Teachers, however, are justified in asking, "What do we have to give up to participate?" It would be self-defeating to ask teachers to give up their lesson planning time or some other academically oriented activity to participate in career development; first we must reduce the administrative burdens on teachers and reduce their student loads. Reducing administrivia will be accomplished through application of some of the quality principles; reducing the student load requires more teachers, pure and simple. Bringing in more teachers requires more money, not just more money to pay an increased number of teachers the same meager salaries, but higher salaries as well, to attract more qualified candidates and make the teaching profession competitive with other professions.

Many of the recent educational reforms have addressed professional and career development for educators and administrators; many states have adopted "career ladders" or similar professional development structures for their teachers and principals.[51] Tabling for a moment the issue of teacher salaries, consider Figure

5.3, which shows a proposed Professional Development Plan for educators.

The first level is the *apprentice teacher*, or intern. She has a bachelors degree in her subject area and meets the basic requirements for certification as a teacher, but must work for a period of time (perhaps one to three years) under the tutelage of at least a master teacher. The length of the apprenticeship will be determined by a committee of teachers and administrators at the local level, using recommendations from the mentor and others involved (that is, other teachers). Previous work experience or advanced degrees may serve to shorten the apprenticeship, opening the way for other established professionals to enter the teaching field without substantial penalty (as many states are now allowing).

After the apprenticeship, the individual is a fully certified *teacher*, with more freedom in classroom management and lesson

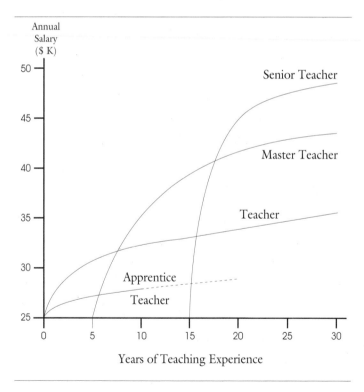

Figure 5.3 Proposed Professional Development Plan
for Educators

planning and more responsibility in institutional decision making. During his term as a teacher, he should complete one of two special development options. One option is to obtain an advanced degree in his original subject area or perhaps a related field, for example, a history teacher earns a degree in sociology, or a physics teacher a degree in mathematics. The other option is to work outside the education system for a year or two; this period of service with industry or government would provide the professional teacher with valuable insight into the world outside academia, as well as opening the door for exchange programs through which corporate or civil service employees can bring their practical experience into the classroom.

After a period of service as a teacher (perhaps 10 to 15 years) and completion of one of the special development options, the individual is not automatically promoted to *master teacher.* That decision is based on the recommendation of senior and master teachers in his school system, since the master teacher has the special responsibility of being a mentor to new apprentice teachers. Master teachers should complete their second special development option before being considered for promotion to *senior teacher.*

The senior teacher is the pinnacle of the teaching profession in this model. She will usually be a department head and will have counseling and mentoring responsibilities for a number of teachers and master teachers. Professional development must not stop for senior teachers, however; they should have opportunities to pursue independent research or advanced degrees and may even be granted paid sabbaticals for personal renewal or study.

Now back to the question of pay—often a difficult subject as teachers have traditionally been underpaid as well as underappreciated. The 1987 average salary for all teachers was a little over $26,000, but this figure is misleading: as an average, it includes new teachers as well as those who have been teaching for 40 years or more, and includes teachers from poor urban areas with those from the more affluent suburbs.[52] The projected average starting salary in 1992–1993 for new teachers with bachelors degrees was less than $23,000; for chemical engineers and computer scientists with bachelors degrees the projected average starting salaries were over $41,000 and $35,000 respectively.[53] The *Y*-axis of Figure 5.3 shows annual salary. A starting salary of $25,000 was chosen (arbitrarily, to be sure) as a way of rewarding teachers who are experts in their subjects and making the teaching profession more attractive to college freshmen and graduates who would otherwise pursue more lucrative professions in the private sector. Following the quality philosophy, however, we cannot rely solely on monetary incentive to attract and hold teachers; we must make their profession one that is worth pursuing for other reasons as well.

The same professional development plan is proposed as a basic plan for *principals*. During service as a teacher, the individual who wants to become a principal (or who has been identified as a potential principal candidate) would either obtain an advanced degree in management or attend a special training institute. Instead of being selected as a master teacher, the candidate would apply for a vice principal position. She would serve as a vice principal for a period of time (perhaps five to ten years) before being eligible for a principal position. This does not preclude a master or senior teacher from moving over to become a vice principal, nor does it keep a vice principal or principal from getting back into the classroom.

Nota bene: These proposals for professional development progression and annual salaries are only meant to foster discussion and serious consideration of the professional development issue. They are *not* presented as final solutions.

Other Standards

The variety of areas in which standardization could lead to improved quality and equity in education is astounding. One example is the length of the school day and year. It has long been recognized that "time on task" is an important factor in the effectiveness of instruction.[54] A national standard governing the length of the school day might be beneficial by giving teachers throughout the country the same opportunities for instruction and planning. A nationally standard school year of 210 days or more would also increase educational opportunities and allow for easier transitions from grade to grade.[55] The effectiveness of lengthening the school day and year will be limited, however, if it is not accompanied by other changes. "State legislatures have taken up this recommendation with particular zeal because it is easily susceptible to rapid implementation and review by law. By itself this measure is unlikely to produce much because more time spent in an unproductive school environment will not be beneficial."[56] If the school experience is unpleasant, adding additional days will not make it less so.

Some degree of standardization could be used to stop the declining quality of textbooks. The importance of well-written, challenging textbooks cannot be overstressed, but as reading abilities among young people have declined so has the challenge level of their texts. Even in the earliest grades, books should not coddle the student.[57] The standardized curriculum should generally help improve textbook quality by giving authors and publishers clearer guidelines within which to work.

&

To make any of these national standards enforceable through rule of law would be both unnecessary and oppressive—it might even be unconstitutional, considering the Tenth Amendment (powers not granted to the federal government by the Constitution are reserved for the individual states). Here another industrial example may prove helpful. National educational standards could be developed along the lines of industrial standards promulgated by a number of standard-setting bodies. Such standards are accepted by industry without being forced on them, though some have been used as the basis for legal requirements.[58] It has been recently suggested, for example, that industrial quality standards (and the criteria for industrial quality awards) be adopted by the education system.

& &

QUALITY STANDARDS AND AWARDS CRITERIA

The search for guidance in implementing quality improvements has led some to favor adoption of existing industrial quality guidelines by educational systems. Proponents of this method often suggest either adoption of the 9000 series standards of the International Standards Organization (known as ISO 9000 standards) or use of the criteria for the Malcolm Baldrige National Quality Award (mentioned briefly in Chapter 1).

The ISO 9000 standards were published in 1987, and registration to the standards is becoming a prerequisite for businesses competing in the world market, especially the European market. As they exist now, the ISO 9000 standards and their U.S. counterparts, the American National Standards Institute/American Society for Quality Control (ANSI/ASQC) Q90 series, are primarily aimed at manufacturing industries; while their use by service industries is possible, ISO and ASQC are still working on standards specific to the service sector.[159]

The ISO 9001–9003 standards deal with contractually specified delivery of products or services and are meant to provide the consumer some assurance that the provider has adequate systems in place to continue to meet specifications. Note that the standards (and registration to them) cannot guarantee a product or service *will* meet specifications, only that systems are in place that *should* result in a product or service meeting customer requirements.[60] The fourth standard, ISO 9004, is designed to help organizations create and evaluate their own "quality management system."[61]

Where the ISO 9000 and related standards are largely concerned with the field of quality assurance, that is, measuring conformance to specifications, the Malcolm Baldrige Award criteria take a more holistic view of an organization. The Baldrige Award criteria look at areas outside traditional quality control, such as leadership, human resources, strategic quality plans, and customer satisfaction. In addition, while the Baldrige Award is concerned with the continuous improvement of quality, ISO 9000 is not.[62]

ISO and education. The impetus to use ISO 9000 standards in education, like the drive to use them in industry, comes from Europe, especially Great Britain (the ISO 9000 standards themselves were adapted from standards of the British Standards Institute).

For education, the ISO 9000 standards manifest themselves as the guidelines for Medallion Schools, that is, schools awarded the ISO Medallion "after a complete review...certifies the school to be in compliance with the requirements."[63] In some cases pursuit of the Medallion is proposed because of its relative ease: its requirements are less involved than the Baldrige criteria, and it does not require the same level of thoughtful commitment involved in adopting Deming's quality philosophy.[64]

Baldrige. The Baldrige Award does not yet have an education category, though one has been proposed and at least two states, New York and Minnesota, have quality awards similar to the Baldrige Award that look at education as well as industry.[65] Especially in higher education, interest in the Baldrige Award criteria is growing.

Some colleges and universities beginning to pursue quality improvement are already using the Baldrige criteria; some are using them because the criteria afford them a quick and convenient model to plan or measure improvement, while others appear to want to pursue the expected academic version of the award. An academic Baldrige Award was recently endorsed before a U.S. House of Representatives subcommittee, aimed at improving the quality of undergraduate engineering education.[66] As with the ISO 9000 standards, a primary factor in using the criteria as a basis for improving quality is its concreteness, its reduction of quality management principles into specific categories and requirements. (Readers who have been frustrated by my reluctance to offer concrete instructions may relate to the desire for a step-by-step, fill-in-the-blank approach; I warned you in the Introduction that this was not a "how-to" book, but an adaptation of quality management theory to the problems of education.)

Possible pitfalls. If a category of the Baldrige Award opens up for education, many schools will undoubtedly compete for the award, aware of the prestige such a prize would bring to their campuses. Some will pursue the award even though they will probably not win it, the way some Japanese companies pursue the Deming Prize, to enjoy the benefits the initial quality improvement effort will bring (see Chapter 1). Those that selectively adapt (not copy) the criteria, making it part of a comprehensive improvement effort, should see surges in their measures of quality. While this makes such an approach attractive, they should be aware of potential problems.

Adoption of quality standards or quality award criteria as guidelines for improvement efforts is tempting, especially as it seems a quick way to realize the benefits of quality improvement without having to learn any new theory of leadership and management. Might this not be one more case of trying to get something for nothing? It seems (both for maximum benefit and in keeping with theory of knowledge) that theory should be the basis for any policies, procedures, or criteria, not vice versa. How tempting it is for schools (or any organizations) to latch onto some general standard and claim "Now we have quality" when they really have only a facade of quality (more possible with ISO 9000 than Baldrige).

Additional problems exist with standards and awards criteria. First, registration to standards or competition for awards depends on producing and maintaining careful and complete documentation, only part of which is useful in quality improvement. Recall that earlier we introduced the value-added concept. Veteran quality consultant Peter Scholtes calls unnecessary paperwork and other activities "cost-added," because they add cost and nothing else.[67] Second, some of the criteria appear to support traditional management practices (for example, merit pay, performance measurement) which the quality philosophy invalidates.

Finally, standards and awards concentrate attention on comparison with outside agencies instead of on the needs of the customer(s). The gauge of success becomes how well we perform in the eyes of the standard-setting agency or awards committee or in relation to our competition (benchmarking), when it should be how delighted our customers are with our products and services. This preoccupation with outside comparisons can lead to copying precisely what others are doing without understanding why their methods are successful; this is usually not completely satisfactory. The statement from Johnston County School District in North Carolina is appropriate: "You will not be able to come to Johnston County to see or copy our approach. Each district must study, learn and design their [sic] own approach to suit their community."[68]

ଶଛ   ଶଛ

The educational standards discussed in this section would be most effective if accepted by schools and school systems rather than being forced on them. The process by which these standards (voluntary or mandatory) are developed will be long and tedious; while we may be confident the results will be positive, whether we have much leisure with which to work is doubtful.

NATIONAL TEACHERS CORPS

As mentioned, the National Teachers Corps is an optional final step to the transformation strategy. The idea behind the corps is twofold. First, the National Teachers Corps would consist of volunteers who relocate to supplement the teaching staffs of poor schools or districts, since they are often unable to afford to hire enough teachers to reduce their class sizes. Such districts often cannot attract teachers in specialty fields; corps volunteers could also fill these positions.

Second, the corps may be able to equalize the compensation of teachers in different parts of the nation. Teachers who make little money but live in high cost-of-living areas could join in the same way as the volunteers mentioned previously. All teachers enrolled in the program would qualify for adjustments to their pay, to enable them to continue teaching where they are needed. The adjustments could perhaps be paid out of federal funds, perhaps out of contributions from local businesses (discussed in detail in the next chapter).

Salary adjustments provided by this program would have the effect of bringing new teachers into and keeping qualified teachers in what might otherwise be undesirable assignments. Poor areas no longer paying as much for teacher salaries could put some of their savings into maintenance and repair of old facilities or purchase of new equipment (such as computers or laboratory supplies). If the program was adopted nationwide and supported by federal funding, the participating teachers might even by considered federal employees, with concomitant benefits.

The biggest benefit of this program would be to help school districts that have a shortage of teachers in certain areas, for example, mathematics and science. This is not an isolated problem: "Over half of the public and private high school principals surveyed in 1985–86 reported that their schools had trouble hiring fully qualified teachers in physics, chemistry, computer science, mathematics, and foreign languages."[69] Whether this program would prove to be bane or benison is impossible to tell at this stage. This is an effort that seems tailor-made to a small pilot program to evaluate its effectiveness.

❧

The strategy and the transformation naturally include activities at both the national and local levels. At the national level the quality philosophy must be used to formulate broad policies and guidelines, which themselves are not static but must be continually improved in the quality effort. The policies, along with the tools and training in the quality paradigm, can then be put in the hands of local authorities who will control the adoption of the philosophy.

I cannot stress enough that the overall *results* of the education transformation will certainly not be seen according to any timetable we devise. We may notice some students who are more eager to learn, some others who are happy that they no longer have to compete with their friends. We may notice teachers whose enthusiasm had waned regaining the confidence and esteem they once had, some others who are simply thankful to be recognized with more autonomy. These are only indications, not measures of the success or failure of the transformation. In the words of Robert M. Hutchins, "A program that begins at the age of six or seven cannot be expected to show 'results' for at least ten years. And, since the real test is what the students are in later life, an educational system can claim to have succeeded in its own terms only after a quarter of a century."[70] Or more.

ROLES AND RESPONSIBILITIES

Therefore the general who in advancing does not seek personal fame, and in withdrawing is not concerned with avoiding punishment, but whose only purpose is to protect the people and promote the best interests of his sovereign, is the precious jewel of the state.

—Sun Tzu, c. 400 B.C.

The process of transforming education in the United States will take time, resources, leadership, and commitment on the part of everyone—individually and corporately—involved in the education system. That commitment will be characterized by constancy of purpose toward continuous improvement, new understanding of participants' roles in the system, and acceptance of responsibility by all parties.

The key to successful transformation will lie in the type of leaders who can be developed within the education system. It will not be enough for one or two leaders to accept the quality philosophy or apply its tenets; everyone within the establishment has the potential to lead, to be proactive in the positive and continuous   145 change process. This has been the basic assumption underlying the transformation in many areas, such as the Johnston County School District in North Carolina.[1] This chapter and the rest of the book will more closely examine the necessary elements of building this leadership base.

As seen in previous chapters, a key to accomplishing successful transformation is constancy of purpose in improving the overall system. This of course requires deep understanding of the system; considering the nature of the educational system, it seems safe to assume the required understanding of the system can only be based on intimate knowledge of the myriad human interactions that dominate the system. These interactions and relationships among the participants form the foundation for every process within education. If the transformation is to succeed not only in constantly improving education but in strengthening these relationships, it is imperative that each group understands the other groups' roles as well as their own. To that end, let us now examine some of these roles more closely.

ADMINISTRATORS

By administrators we mean those who lead and manage schools and educational systems, including both principals and superintendents. They have as much—if not more—responsibility for the success or failure of the system as anyone. Research has shown, for example, that principals who have a clear vision for the success of their school, work to communicate that vision, and facilitate their teachers' and other administrators' efforts to make the vision reality are highly successful in improving quality in their schools. Constant improvement in quality is already a theme for many of these principals.[2] Roland S. Barth notes that

> principals who are successful in unlocking the talents of their teachers seem to hold...that every teacher possesses strengths and insights of value to others...and that teachers have a great capacity to stimulate professional growth and effective practice in their colleagues.[3]

These principals have discovered that a major part of effective leadership involves empowerment and trust. Those who would become leaders rather than managers of their schools must likewise sharpen their leadership skills, learn to trust their teachers and other workers, and use their power to improve the systems within which their people work. Above all, they must "go beyond pronouncement and blessing" and get involved and immersed in the change process.[4] We will discuss this development process further in the Conclusion.

As guides of the transformation, administrators and other leaders have several distinct responsibilities. They must keep in constant touch with educational customers (internal and external), monitoring their perceptions of the services they are receiving and anticipating their future needs. They must work diligently to uncover the root causes of shortfalls in the delivery of service and take appropriate action to improve quality at every opportunity.[5] "At every opportunity" takes on special significance as the transformation leader knows opportunities for improvement never end.[6]

As part of the improvement process in education, principals and other administrators must find ways to reduce the frequency of intrusions into teachers' preparation and class times, which, as Theodore R. Sizer puts it, "signal the low priority that routine teaching may hold, and…certainly puzzle students who on one occasion observe the school casually canceling some classess…and on another severely admonishing individuals not to miss any classes."[7] To increase class time spent on productive study and learning, teachers' administrative duties must be minimized to give them more time to concentrate on planning and teaching, and fair and equitable means of effective discipline must be utilized to minimize class disruptions.

The shifting of the administrative burden away from teachers will require either less administration or more administrative assistants, clerks, and secretaries. Most school administration and staff functions are presumably necessary, but the quality improvement tools and techniques can be applied to streamline administrative functions and find new ways to accomplish the same ends. For those functions that must continue, attracting more administrative help will be difficult, because administrative salaries in the education system are no more competitive with those outside education than are teachers'. To augment paid staff, schools for some time have used students as office runners and unpaid clerks; this practice will almost certainly continue. Such positions could also easily become paid positions reserved for students who, for 147 economic reasons, would otherwise leave school. This would provide the means for such students to finish their secondary education and relieve some of the burden on teachers.

Disciplining children and young people has become increasingly difficult in recent years. The time of "two days or two licks"[8] seems to be long gone, and the prevalence of drugs and gang activities on campuses makes it and other, less physical discipline methods seem almost too pacific. Corporal punishment, while sometimes an effective deterrent against mild offenses, is certainly not enough to deter misbehavior by students who are practically hardened criminals; at any rate, it will probably not be reintroduced any time soon. When parents who spank their children in public are in danger of being turned in to the Department of Health and Human Services for suspected child abuse, teachers and principals who are not the children's parents will certainly not be allowed to spank as a punishment. Even if in loco parentis were still in fashion, it would be difficult to implement.

In addition to dealing with these very real problems, administrators must support teachers' professional development and encourage them to take advantage of learning and self-improvement opportunities. They should avail themselves of the opportunities also, especially principals who are trying to set an example for their teachers. Like everyone under the quality philosophy, administrators must be free to express their ideas and opinions without fear of reprisal or censure. Relations with school boards and local interest groups must be focused on the continuous improvement of quality and the long-term future, and principals and other administrators must work diligently to solicit and develop support for their schools and programs in their communities.

EDUCATORS

Teaching should be among the most noble of professions, but we saw in Chapters 3 and 5 that it is often considered less than a profession. As part of the overall transformation, public officials as well as citizens in general must learn how important teaching is to the strength and vitality of this or any nation. Few other professions serve to prepare for the present and the future as teaching does; if teachers were compensated according to some measure of their students' success (for example, how much their students earn over their lifetimes), they would be the highest paid professionals in the country.

Teachers and others who work with young people have both a great challenge and a great responsibility: they not only inform, but they influence. By influence we mean the effect a teacher or other significant adult has on the development of the student's attitudes and outlooks. Veteran youthworker Jim Burns writes of a simple experiment that illustrates this. Compare how difficult it is to think of five speeches or sermons or lectures that significantly influenced your life with how easy it is to think of five people who have greatly influenced your life.[9] This demonstration was used on me when I started youth work; interestingly, even when I thought of something someone said that had a profound impact on me, I was first thinking of the person.

The personal role cannot be discounted. Most people make their significant life decisions—for example, what career to choose, when and whom to marry—while they are still young; teachers must realize that their influence over those decisions may be for good or for ill (see Appendix C). Society must recognize the powerful influence significant adults play in the lives of young people, and be prepared to support and affirm those adults whose influence is particularly important.

Teachers, as well as administrators and other participants in the educational system, must learn about reality as presented in Chapters 2 and 3. They must especially be able to recognize and understand variation and to apply the theories of knowledge and psychology in their efforts; if they are to become leaders of the transformation, they must understand the intricate workings of their systems, also. Statistical techniques that will help them to better control classroom participation, disruptions, and other factors must be made accessible to all teachers, as must open forums for sharing information about special situations (both problems and solutions) and effective teaching techniques. Teachers must be continually encouraged to cross departmental lines and participate in reinforcing one another's efforts.

The value-added concept of learning should become an integral part of lesson planning and student evaluation. Teachers must learn to assess their students' abilities realistically by clearly stating measurable learning objectives for each class, and tailor their approach to the development and strengthening of all students' abilities. In doing so, teachers must be free to experiment and innovate to find ways to reach their students. As one factor, they must search for and share concrete examples of the usefulness of their lessons, so students will better appreciate the subject matter. Algebra must become more than tricky manipulation of numbers and figures; Hemingway must be more than a writer who committed suicide.

Under the quality philosophy, value-added will apply equally to the teachers themselves. They must constantly stay abreast of new developments in their fields, and as such must be given ample opportunities to attend (or present) seminars and classes as well as to do special research. In addition to keeping up in their own areas of expertise, teachers must have access to the latest research in cognition and pedagogy. They should also be encouraged to attend classes and seminars in nonrelated subjects, perhaps even to the point of obtaining advanced degrees in new areas.

The move is finally afoot in this country to view teaching as it should be viewed, as a profession rather than a vocation; the quality emphasis only adds to the movement. The career ladders under consideration in many states for teachers and administrators are extremely important and should lead to some comprehensive professional development plan. Educators must know that there is room for recognition and advancement in their chosen profession. Localities must covenant with educators to support them in every way (for example, monetarily and professionally) in exchange for the quality instruction and leadership they have to offer.

STUDENTS

The primary job (so to speak) of the student is to learn, to participate in the educational process as the recipient of knowledge. This is neither a static nor a mundane task and is affected by many things. Health, extracurricular activities, emotional balance, family harmony, and other factors may either improve or detract from the educational experience.

Motivation is one of the key factors in education and one of the most complex. We have already discussed the necessity of students knowing why their education is important; one professor of education has in fact defined educational motivation as "the ability of the learner to see the applied value of the lesson to be learned."[10] By stressing cooperation and coordination between departments that will demonstrate the interrelatedness of the different subjects in the school curriculum—as suggested in the previous chapter—the quality transformation should make it easier for teachers to show students how the pieces of their education fit together into a coherent whole. The transformation of schools would also remove the external motivation of grades and replace it with the internal motivation and joy of learning that are natural to all people. When learning is a pleasure, rather than a burden, students will thrive and their education will be more effective.

Positively impacting the student population will take more than simply revising curricula and improving sharing between academic disciplines. As stated by educational researcher Torsten Husen, "The school must be able to give teenagers the opportunity to take part in meaningful tasks where they are made to feel productive in the broad sense and to play pertinent roles in the adult community."[11] That is, students must put into practice the principles they learn in school, their motivation fed by applications of their learning.

Many of the extracurricular activities schools offer fill this need, especially those associated with adult civic groups; the quality improvement organizations in the schools themselves will also give students opportunities to take leadership roles and make a positive difference. Work in the Chicago public school system has shown that when students are given appropriate training they develop and use remarkable leadership skills. Students there have begun to take active roles in school reform, using their perspective as the primary internal customer of education to suggest improvements and work toward solutions.

ᘛᕱ   ᘛᕱ

EXPERIENCE IN EMPOWERING STUDENT LEADERS [12]
(contributed by Gary Goldman)

Team-building and the quality concept have shown that participative management and a trained, collaborative team of people closest to the actual work being accomplished produces greater productivity, quality products, and increased customer satisfaction. This very common sense approach, with innovations suited to the educational environment and quality education as its goal, has been pioneered in the Chicago-area school system.

In the school setting, the people closest to the issues and challenges of producing educational excellence are the students. They know full well what the problems and solutions are in raising student motivation and achievement. When are the adult stockholders of education—the parents, teachers, and administrators—going to realize they need to listen to and involve students in school improvement? In Chicago, adults are listening and students are getting involved and trying to change their roles as they change their schools.

High schools. In 1990 student representatives to local school councils (LSCs) formed a coalition and invested in leadership training from quality consultants. After the training, one student remarked, "Now I will be heard at the LSC meetings." The coalition then created seven student quality action teams to work on such areas as student/teacher partnerships, curriculum and materials, school policies, and student leadership. Using the Quality Student Leadership Process, the students went through three phases of training: interpersonal and leadership skills, team-building, and action planning. The resulting student teams have been empowered to bring new ideas and solutions to their schools, helping raise morale and bring renewal to education.

High school student leaders in Sturgis, Michigan, learned about the concept of paradigms and worked to identify old and new paradigms about the way the school looked at students, their roles, and their relationships with staff. The students then met with faculty and parents to create a new paradigm of adult/student teams for school improvement. The mission they created declared: "All students can learn. It is everyone's job to see that it is done."

Elementary schools. We cannot begin too early giving students opportunities for thinking critically and solving problems in their own environments. Such experience will serve them and their schools well throughout their entire school career and beyond.

One district with 44 elementary schools implemented a seven-week student leadership program. The students learned about planning and goal-setting, then outlined plans and identified goals for their home schools. They also interviewed staff and administrators at the district level to explore what makes a good leader. The district superintendent concluded that the students were now ready "to assume a role consistent with the student empowerment intent of the Chicago Reform Act." This effort will soon be expanded to include all stockholder groups: district personnel, local school councils, teachers, administrators, students, parents, and the entire community. The program is designed to be a model for developing cooperative quality teams in other communities.

At-risk settings. The environment in at-risk settings is not usually conducive to quality and excellence, but that can be changed. Teaching staffs at a juvenile detention center in Chicago and at San Quentin Prison near San Francisco recently went through team-building training; at both institutions, the participants created relevant and inspiring mission statements and formed quality teams to address priority issues. As a result, the mood of the institutions has changed. Both are permeated with a renewed sense that "things can be different," and this new attitude is filtering down to the students.

Involving and encouraging students. We need to show a willingness to trust young people to choose the issues and concerns they want to address, the methods and approaches they want to use, and the outcomes and objectives they want to achieve. Instead of being passive recipients of our good intentions, they must be active players in their schools and communities, testing their knowledge and determination—sometimes "failing," sometimes going where others fear to tread.

True education must be a process that allows students to discover their innate talents and encourages rather than discourages creative thinking and new ideas. It starts with teachers approaching their students in such a way that trust is established. The student is able to make mistakes without fear of retribution, realizing that mistakes and how we deal with them are themselves part of the education process.

This kind of attitude brings a different climate into the classroom and school. Learning becomes a natural event that springs from the willingness of people to relate to each other with caring and compassion, instead of a mechanical process of just giving and receiving information. For most of us, such an attitude would have made all the difference in the world in our own school experience: to feel we were being invited to be ourselves, to learn with our teachers and classmates, and to be listened to as young people who had worthwhile ideas and could help other students find greater fulfillment and achievement. Today, we have the obligation to enter our learning organizations and share with students, teachers, parents and administrators a new way to motivate, involve, and celebrate the opportunities of schools filled with enthusiastic people sharing in a partnership of growing and trust.

&a &a

Extracurricular activities, mentioned briefly with respect to developing leadership potential, are an important part of the education experience. Students must be encouraged to participate in sports and club activities that build camaraderie, teamwork, and self-confidence. Two extremes must be avoided, however. On one end are those students who do not play any sports or participate in any clubs. They may or may not work after school, but their overall activity level in and out of school is low. The other extreme consists of those students who try to participate in everything: clubs, sports, and jobs, both in and out of school. Most of the student population exists between these two extremes, but how can the groups at the extremes be reached?

Outside activities are essential to student development in a holistic sense. Extracurricular activities give structure to students' lives and help them develop discipline. Too many activities, however, can be a significant source of stress in the lives of young people. Performance in school or in some of the activities may suffer, tempting parents and teachers to intervene. Teachers and parents must be cautioned, however, against arbitrarily restricting students' activities; it may be better to let the student learn his limitations.[13]

On the other hand, too few activities, especially after-school activities, are cited as factors contributing to delinquency, hooliganism, and drug use among young people. Certainly the modern phenomenon of latchkey children (predominantly but not exclusively affecting elementary schoolchildren), who have little to do after school except watch television, does nothing to alleviate the problems of youth. One suggestion to curb this problem is to keep the school building open until dusk, the way some youth centers are open for student activities in the afternoon. Students would be free to remain in the building, reading or playing organized sports or working on projects of personal interest, instead of spending their time in idle pursuits at home or on the streets.

It may not be an historical truism, but it seems that the sins of the fathers are quite often visited upon the children. In Edwardian England the problems of society were visited upon the children of the day, and the children's sorry state was perceived as indicative of future troubled times. This was the crucible from which was forged the British Boy Scouts, an unparalleled success among youth movements.[14] Today's scouting and other programs offer productive activities for young people that supplement the educational programs of the schools. In all extracurricular activities the focus on productive action is paramount, because through service projects and similar activities students learn to work effectively in groups and define for themselves an important role in the community.

The quality transformation will also allow schools to do something at which they have never succeeded in the past. By focusing on the future needs of all customers, with one of the most important customers being the student, education will be able to adapt to the changing needs of the evolving teenage culture. Students 10, 15, 20, or 50 years from now will be drastically different from those today, but the continuous improvement in quality will allow education to be sensitive to those differences.

PARENTS

That parental participation in the education of young people is important is rarely disputed. It can be one of the most decisive factors in preparing young people for their school experiences.[15] When we view education as a complete system, as in Figure 3.2, we see parents as one of the key suppliers of the schools. Their participation, and the resulting disposition of the children they send to school, has been severely affected by modern socioeconomic factors.

The numbers of single-parent and double-income house-holds has been rapidly increasing in this country. This makes it extremely difficult to foster increased participation of parents in the education process. Traditional Parent-Teacher Associations will have to adapt to new family structures, for example, providing baby-sitting so single parents can attend meetings or holding mul-tiple meetings to accommodate conflicting schedules. Under the quality philosophy, teachers and administrators will explore new alternatives to enhance parental participation and input, in line with Deming's sixth point. It will not be easy. The reality that the "traditional" family is now a minority signals the need for change in the way schools interact with parents.[16]

Parents do have a profound influence on the educational achievements of their children. But while they may want to encourage their children's academic endeavors, parents must be careful not to impose their own goals on their children.[17] Instead, they must be prepared to help their children identify the goals appropriate to them. This is the premise behind the biblical injunction to "Train up a child in the way he should go" (Proverbs 22:6). The operative word in this proverb is not "should," which implies the imposition of one right course of action over other, wrong courses. The operative word is "he," which implies the selection of a personal course, one that matches the disposition of the young person.[18] Focusing on what is right *for the child* assures that "when he is old he will not turn from it."

How do parents assure that their children are able to recog-nize and strive for what is right for them? One way is to strength-en their children's self-esteem. Self-esteem and self-assurance are driving forces in our lives and help determine if we are static or dynamic. Young people's self-esteem is built first and foremost on the opinions of their parents and plays a major role in their emo-tional well-being and their educational achievements.[19]

≈

As part of our discussion of parental roles, please permit me a digression on the subject of parental choice.

A recent trend in U.S. education, which capitalizes on the parental desire to be involved with their child's education, is the emphasis on choice. Under the guise of a democratic ideal, the current trends in choice have relied mainly on parental emotions and carefully built political and media support to advance to national attention. Basically, the choice movement allows parents to choose what public school their children will attend (within limits set by law); the choice is often based on a particular emphasis at the school (for example, performing arts or science and technology) or the perception of the school's quality.[20] This is not the choice to send one's children to a private school instead of public school; this is the choice to send your children to a particular public school over some other school. On the surface, choice is a good idea, as it follows the proverb just discussed; it has garnered tremendous popular support, but has some troubling implications.

Rather than improve the entire system of education, choice allows parents to place their children in what they perceive to be the "best" schools. These schools fill up quickly, and, in the competition, other schools—those that are not favorably perceived by those making the choice—decline. When enrollment falls at the schools that are less desirable, quick fixes and desperate measures like principal or teacher replacement are applied, often amid threats of school closure.[21] The atmosphere of tension and fear this creates is far from conducive to school improvement. The chances for a poor school or a new school to rise to the level of a good, established school are limited, as their reputations are almost self-fulfilling prophecies. This has been a source of consternation in Japan, where all high schools are routinely ranked against each other, and in the United States, where many poor schools continue to get poorer.[22]

Choice fosters a spirit of competition between schools that goes far beyond the athletic field; they compete for students and the share of educational funding the students bring with them.[23] The increased funds available to the schools are a prime component of the choice concept, despite the admission by former Secretary of Education William Bennett that increased education funding did not necessarily correlate with improvements in education.[24] If more money has not been successful in bringing about improvements in the past, why should we assume it will be this time? Certainly those schools that receive less money will not be able to implement significant improvements. This is a case where theory of knowledge (as discussed in Chapters 2 and 3) requires   157 amendment or abandonment of the theory, because of its failure to explain experience.

While athletic events may provide healthy releases of energy and build teamwork and a corporate spirit within the school, allowing community spirit and solidarity to continue, this new competition serves only to divide students and communities into small, specialized groups. Of lesser concern only because it seems less likely, placing students in artificially limited environments with other students who have exactly (or nearly) the same desires, aspirations, and abilities may not develop in them the ability or willingness to work together with people with whom they have little in common. Were this to play out, it would bode ill for their futures when they will have to interact with people who have not been immersed in the specialized worlds of science or the arts.

While improving schools on the surface—many schools report marked increases in reading abilities among their students, for example[25]—choice will eventually lead to a reduction in the overall quality of education. Consider the consequences: the choice program is so successful at pulling students into "desirable" schools that the undesirable schools close. Their enrollment has fallen below a level at which teachers, staff, and facilities can be maintained. *Where do their students go?* They can only go into the desirable schools, where, until the financial plans are laid for expansion and hiring to accommodate the greater numbers, they will tax the facilities and increase both the student-teacher ratios and the amount of educational resources paying for transportation rather than instruction. Unless constrained by local ordinance, they will duplicate in the new schools the conditions they just left (and if they are constrained, there is choice only for a few). *Where do their teachers go?* If they are not specialized they may not be hired by the desirable schools; if they are, those schools may not have the classroom space to accept them.

Even if the undesirable schools do not close, their dwindling enrollments will still mean they receive fewer education dollars, their facilities will fall into disrepair, and they will be forced to make do with inferior and out-of-date educational materials. Only those students who could not (because of constraints on their choice) or would not go into the desirable schools will be left—what psychological price will they pay? Many good teachers will leave in droves, enticed by opportunities in better schools or better pay outside the education system, to be replaced by incompetents. Once this new crisis is recognized, massive amounts of money and time will be needed to repair the damage. The reader who believes this is merely a theoretical discussion should read Jonathan Kozol's *Savage Inequalities*.

જીત

It is entirely possible that schools that improve through application of the quality philosophy may become schools of "choice."

A variant on choice in public schools is the proposal to move education back into the private sector, presumably through a system of schools similar to nineteenth-century academies (see Appendix B). This would be financed through a system of vouchers; parents who did not wish their children to attend public school would receive education vouchers equivalent to some predetermined sum. The sum would probably be calculated based on the average amount of money spent per child in the public school system; the rationale is that since these children are not participating in the public schools, the money that would be spent on them is superfluous. The vouchers would be redeemable for tuition at private schools.[26]

The assumption that an accurate figure for dollars spent per child in the public school system may be calculated hinges on the availability of an operational definition of what costs are to be included. Will the costs include only instructional and administrative staff salaries, or also the wages of custodians, cooks, and maintenance personnel? Are vocational and academic tracks considered together? Are revenues from lab fees subtracted? Are transportation costs included? Are costs of athletic equipment and revenues from ticket sales both on the balance sheet? Without a clear explanation of how such numbers are determined, any figures presented are meaningless, any "reasonable" estimates inherently questionable.

Recall our previous assertion that the most important figures in any endeavor are unknown and unknowable.[27] How many students will pull out of the school system? How many students will be left with the remains of the public schools? How few students may a school have before it must be closed, and what

159

becomes of those students in that event? None of these questions have easy answers.

Whatever the method, choice between public schools or subsidized choice of private schools through vouchers, the overemphasis on parental choice means that *overall* quality will be ultimately sacrificed. The public school choice movement is a placebo, not a solution. This is not to say that parents do not have the right to influence how their children are educated; indeed, parents have the right and with it the responsibility to participate in their children's education. Choosing to move children to another public school is certainly easier than working to improve conditions at their present school, and given the discussion of the U.S. fall from economic preeminence (Chapter 1) seems to mirror "corporate America's" search for easy and immediate solutions to deep-rooted problems. It may be better for the current programs of choice to be thought of as experiments, pilot programs that will be examined to determine the long-range effectiveness of the choice movement. It is hoped they will answer some of the nagging questions and provide reasonable solutions.

ã.

Conceptually close to the choice programs is the current movement in home schooling. Many parents, some for religious reasons, are choosing to provide an elementary education for their children. (Some are providing their secondary education as well.) Usually one of the parents stays home with the children and structures learning experiences for them throughout the day. By home schooling, parents have interpreted their responsibility for their children's education in very personal terms and strive to provide the instruction and nurturing their children need.

The home-schooling phenomenon can be thought of as parental choice teamed with parental commitment. The choice these parents make, to keep their children out of public schools, is well within their rights and harms no one; the current public school choice movement has the potential to harm a great many children, as shown previously. That home schooling is somehow bad for children has not been demonstrated. The basic foundation for successful education has always been laid in the home.

Why must education stop there and become the exclusive domain of structured schools? The security and self-esteem that home schooling builds into children may well offset any lack of expertise their parents have in certain skill areas, and social skills may easily be built by including home-schooled children in group activities such as church youth groups, Sunday schools, or even cooperative efforts with other home-schooling families.[28]

Home schooling, private schools, and parochial schools are examples of choice that do not take resources out of the remaining public schools. As such, they are preferable to the choice and voucher proposals that effectively penalize a proportion of the student population. While not all families have the time, patience, and talents to home school, or the money to send their children to private school (even if church-sponsored), at least these options do not take away educational opportunities from other youth.

Recognition of home schooling (and other alternatives to public schools) as part of a larger education system is important to building an optimized system for the education of all the country's young people. Children who have been schooled at home invariably enter a more structured school at some time; few parents have the resources to expose their children to chemistry laboratories or other advanced learning activities. While private schools and established parochial schools can more easily support enrollment through high school graduation, many newer schools do not have the faculty or the facilities to provide secondary education; their students may have to matriculate into public schools, also. And even if the student completes high school in the private arena, the total education system includes higher learning as well. To optimize the opportunities for these young people and assure they are ready for new learning at each successive stage, leaders of the education system must provide guidance to the principals of private schools as well as parents who have chosen to home school. The solution is not to force parents into any required educational program but to provide them with accurate, timely information that allows them to make their decisions wisely to their children's benefit.

&.

To recap, parental involvement in education is essential. The role of parents in their children's education has always been recog- 161 nized as powerful, especially in the education of very young children. Parental support of extracurricular activities, participation in fundraising or other support activities, and encouragement of teachers is vitally important to improving the quality of education. Even when parents cannot help a school monetarily, they can participate in the life of the school by grilling hamburgers for a field day or pitching in to clean the school grounds.[29] With the large number of single-parent and other nontraditional households in the United States, it will be difficult to coax parents back into partnerships with schools; however, the benefits of doing so will be well worth the effort.

COLLEGES AND UNIVERSITIES

As discussed briefly in the previous chapter, institutions of higher education will almost be forced to make changes if the quality philosophy permeates very deeply into elementary and secondary education. Colleges and universities will find incoming freshmen better prepared, more motivated, and much more uniform in their capabilities; this will improve prospects for starting every student's college career on a positive academic note. The main problem this raises is in admissions, where the lack of easy differentiation (possible before with standardized test results) will make it difficult to select from the large pool of motivated and prepared candidates.

Certainly the college entrance process will be drastically changed by the education transformation, but the changes will heighten the opportunities for students as individuals rather than nameless social security numbers. As mentioned, perhaps colleges will return to the practice of administering entrance examinations (though it seems such single data points may also be contrary to the quality philosophy). Perhaps instead of trying to measure students' proficiency in verbal or quantitative skills, colleges will spend more time ascertaining whose academic desires can be most closely matched with degree programs they offer. Many prestigious universities are able to do this now; they can afford to be selective. Improvements in student preparation and exposure of students to quality concepts should make selectivity secondary to the services each school can offer prospective students.[30]

In addition to changes colleges and universities will have to go through, they have the potential to become leading agencies in the transformation process. Several prominent institutions are beginning to adopt quality principles in their operations, though generally two-year and technical community colleges have been more aggressive in quality improvements than four-year colleges and universities. Many community colleges are not only improving their operations, but they are serving as headquarters for quality enhancement activities in their communities.[31]

In our discussion of higher education, we must remember that colleges and universities play a much larger role than simply teaching and conferring degrees. The quality emphasis has potential to improve their roles of research and service as well. Advanced research as part of graduate or postgraduate studies is a hallmark of higher education, and the centers of excellence formed by many universities give them extraordinary potential for furthering our knowledge of the world and ourselves. As for service, many institutions have long traditions of service to their states and the nation, notably land-grant universities. Research and service readily lend themselves to applications of the quality philosophy, especially as they are more closely related to the commercial industries where the quality approach is already proven.

COMMUNITIES

The support of the entire community is vital to the strength of the education improvement effort. Our communities are diverse and offer a wide range of talents that can help the transformation succeed. We have previously mentioned the many communities pioneering quality improvement across the nation. Their cooperative efforts are bringing together local government, businesses, industries, and schools to share their successes and setbacks in transforming their areas.

Even where quality improvement does not yet encompass the entire community, many businesses and industries have entered into partnerships with the schools. They recognize that improving education is one key to improving their corporate future. Schools and corporations are working together with the aim of constantly improving the quality of education and service throughout the community. Notable among these partnerships are 3M and Independent School District 832 in Mahtomedi, Minnesota, the Lehigh Valley Business–Education Partnership in Pennsylvania, and the George Stone Center for vocational training in Pensacola, Florida.[32]

In this continuing effort, businesses may bring their experience with the quality philosophy to schools, sharing their successes and lessons learned, training teachers and staff members in quality tools. To widen their influence, local industry may sponsor special seminars or classes open to the community, hire disadvantaged youth part-time (with the understanding that they will continue their education), or sponsor outside activities for students. Industries may invite classes to tour facilities or participate with vocational curriculum developers to establish effective and flexible vocational classes.

In Chapter 5 we discussed the difficulty some schools and districts have bringing in teachers in certain subjects, or paying teachers enough to live reasonably in high cost-of-living areas. These became factors in proposing the National Teachers Corps to supplement teacher incomes in certain areas. We briefly mentioned the proposition that industries help subsidize teachers' salaries, creating in elementary and secondary schools the equivalent of endowed professorships. Some possible connections are obvious: technical firms endowing chemistry, physics, and mathematics teachers; newspapers and other media firms endowing English and journalism teachers; automobile dealers and shops endowing auto shop teachers. Others may not be obvious: doctors', dentists', and chiropractors' groups endowing biology, health, and physical education teachers; local civic groups endowing history teachers; small businesses endowing economics teachers. Besides a sizable tax deduction for the participating companies, the districts and schools would have extra money to spend on materials, equipment, maintenance, or retiring debt.

જ

In addition to pushing the transformation itself, communities can make other contributions to education. Local community institutions such as churches, civic groups, and community centers can support the work of schools by addressing pertinent social issues

164

from their specific points of view. The input these organizations give to the values education of the schools will keep the education current and provide acceptability criteria for elements of the values curriculum (Appendix C).

All communities must recognize that changes in their schools will not happen overnight; they must be willing to support the proposals of the quality initiative with their time and effort as well as their money, but more importantly they must have patience. Until the processes are in control, community leaders must refrain from managing their systems by single data points. Once control has been achieved (see Appendix A), leaders like you may turn attention to identifying areas for improvement, bringing educators together with the rest of the community in the continuous improvement of quality.

GOVERNMENT

This will not be a treatise on the proper role of government in a free society but a short look at the role of government in promoting quality in education. That role has been and will continue to be hotly debated.

Education in the United States has been historically characterized by a decentralized system that is locally controlled (see Appendix B), though recently state governments have greatly expanded their activities in education.[33] Few commentators today wish to see local control abolished. The National Commission on Excellence in Education upheld state and local governments as having the "primary responsibility for financing and governing" education, while relegating to the federal government special programs for the "gifted and talented," socioeconomically disadvantaged, handicapped, and minorities.[34] While appealing to those jurisdictions that will struggle to maintain their control and can afford to provide quality education, this proposition does not recognize the incredible inequities that exist today in public education financing. Simply put, states with large tax bases (for example, California and New York) would seem to have an advantage over smaller, less affluent states (for example, Montana and Mississippi). Even within states, more affluent localities have advantages in hiring teachers and building facilities than other

165

communities.[35] Local control cannot resolve these inequities; it exacerbates them.

The aim in the educational quality initiative is to provide a uniformly high quality education for all students throughout the United States. In order to achieve this, regional and local inequalities in funding, facilities, and teachers must be eliminated. This should not be achieved by penalizing the affluent excessively, but augmenting the needy will require some input from those who can afford it. While this seems a clear place where the federal government may assert itself and fulfill its responsibility, other avenues such as corporate partnerships and sponsorships must be considered. Altruism is not the motive in this approach; the goal is equity, and altruism is the means of achieving that goal.

The National Commission's recommendation that the federal government not interfere with local or state initiatives, but work only to identify items of national interest, is incompatible with providing a quality education to students across the nation. State and local interests are national interests, and vice versa. The U.S. Department of Education cannot continue as an unobtrusive spectator in an ivory tower of educational purity; it must come down into the trenches of educational practice and help state and local boards of education adopt and apply the principles of the quality philosophy. If quality education is a national resource, the federal government must assume a leadership role and usher in the quality age, despite the restrictions of the Tenth Amendment.

Adoption of the quality philosophy by and improvement of the operations and services of the Department of Education will be necessary to solidify this leadership role. Presumably, the adoption of quality principles by all agencies of the federal government (see Chapter 1) will accomplish this. Beyond improving quality within the education department, training in the quality philosophy and quality improvement tools must be provided to teachers' organizations and state boards of education while plans for achieving equity in educational opportunity are laid. As presented in the previous chapter, the transformation strategy calls for broad plans and recognition of national priorities by all levels of education.

As part of the quality initiative, the federal government must understand education as a far-reaching system which, working properly, can solidify the future of the nation. The entire system, beyond the narrow limits of the formal education process, must be considered (see Figure 3.3). As such, preparation for being educated is not only a key to optimizing the system; it is also an investment. Programs such as Head Start, which provide educational opportunities for disadvantaged children, must be continued (and expanded where possible). In some areas it may be desirable for the federal government to establish preschools for socioeconomically deprived children, to give them proper preparation for entering school.[36] At least two states, Missouri and Minnesota, have expanded on Head Start; these states are educating parents of preschool children on proven parenting techniques and providing a support structure that has been well received.[37]

The roles of state and local governments must change radically for the overall education system to be fully optimized. Instead of formulating their own agendas for education, state and local boards of education will move to interpreting and applying the national agenda. They must relate their educational resources to the national priorities, and structure their planning to achieve the priorities as nearly as possible. Where budget shortfalls necessitate a compromise, localities must use the available resources judiciously and look elsewhere (for example, to the federal government or corporate partners) for additional resources to augment their own.[38]

In addition to implementing plans to achieve the national educational priorities, state and local agencies will have both the opportunity and the responsibility to comment on and suggest changes to the priorities. Those priorities that are either unrealistic because of limited resources or irrational because they serve no need will be debated, and the ideas and opinions of those who are working to reach the goals will be necessary to improving them. This must be a cooperative project, undertaken in a spirit of professionalism and trust, in which school districts feel comfortable and confident presenting their views (especially dissenting views) to state and national agencies.

LEADERSHIP ROLES

In our discussion of the roles and responsibilities of the parties involved in transforming education, it may not have been clear that members of the different groups must assume leadership

167

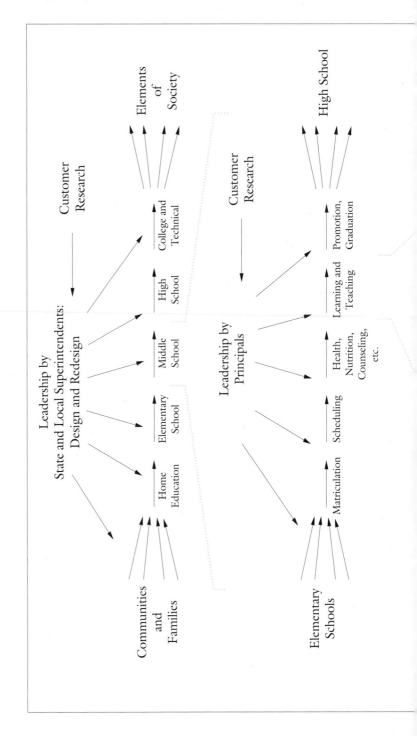

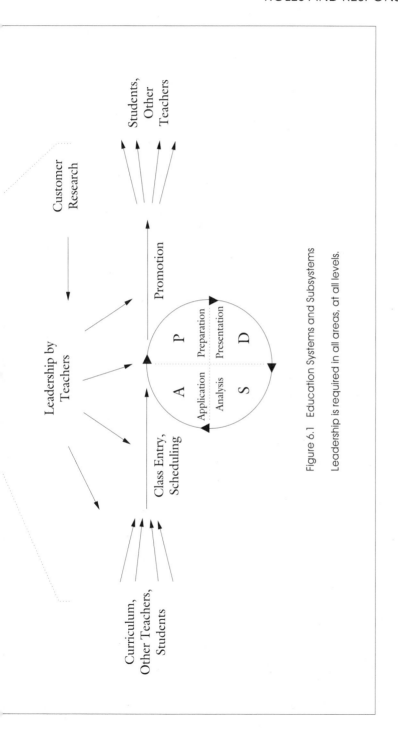

Figure 6.1 Education Systems and Subsystems

Leadership is required in all areas, at all levels.

roles in the education system. Principals' and superintendents' leadership roles are clear; others are more difficult to grasp. Each group—administrators, teachers, students, parents, universities, communities, and the government—has a distinct part to play, but their roles cannot be passive if they are to advance the transformation process and add to the continuous improvement effort.

The differences in leadership roles may be visualized using Figure 6.1, in which selected subsystems of the overall education system are pictured. The overall system is pictured at the top, with subsystems expanded below it; each is shown in a simplified version of Figure 3.3.

At the bottom of Figure 6.1 is an oversimplified representation of the learning process using the PDSA cycle, as discussed in Chapter 4. Here the primary customers are the students and the teachers who will work with them next; the current teacher has the leadership responsibility to optimize and continually improve this system.

Moving upward and outward from the bottom of Figure 6.1, the reader should be able to visualize the different leadership roles needed from each of the education partners. For example, students not only have leadership roles among other students, each individually should optimize their personal approach to the learning process, with the aim of continually improving their learning habits. Also, parents should optimize the home environment for effective, joyful learning appropriate to their children's developmental levels. You may find it helpful to sketch out system flowcharts of the different subsystems to gain a better understanding of the need for and difficulty of optimization.

❧

In considering the theory of management and leadership discussed in this book and the empowerment of leaders within the education system, it would be improper not to consider some possible difficulties in bringing about this transformation. They are the subject of the next chapter.

PROBLEMS AND PROSPECTS

The superior man makes the difficulty to be overcome his first interest; success comes only later.

—*Confucius*

To begin and continue the transformation effectively, leaders must be acutely aware of the problems they may face. The education transformation will certainly not be effective overnight, and it will not happen at all without stress. The transformation entails a significant cultural change, a complete upheaval of the common perception of education. The very nature of the transformation guarantees problems, in that it challenges the deeply rooted paradigms of both the present educational practitioners and the political leadership. It is hoped that the promise of better education will be strong enough to weather the storms of change. This chapter is intended to examine possible problems associated with executing the transformation. I do not mean to imply that transformation is impossible, only that it will not be easy—for the leaders or the participants.[1]

CHANGE AS AN INSTITUTION

Progress may be a comfortable disease, as proposed by e.e. cummings, but the changes progress brings can be anything but comfortable, especially considering that all change is not progress. Change can be a stimulus to strong emotions, especially when it is sudden and unexpected, and leaders of the transformation must be prepared to deal with these. (This is one reason to exercise caution and move slowly, to alleviate this problem; however, the present situation may call for more immediate action.) Unexpected changes may be precipitated by crises or perceived crises, and the *perception* (that is, how the changes are seen and understood) is at least as important as the reality.[2] Both individuals and institutions must find effective ways to cope with and manage the changes they encounter.

Coping with change often involves situations that are beyond our control but with which we are intimately involved. For instance, we are rarely prepared for sudden change—it comes as a shock, like the death of a loved one or some other traumatic experience. Some people may be able to function normally while coping with the situation; others may be nearly paralyzed. Predicting how fast people will make it through the crisis and its aftermath is practically impossible; helping them process through the emotions is an important area of counseling.[3] As mentioned previously, the changes proposed for the transformation should not be sudden or traumatic, but they will still elicit strong responses in the participants; reminding all of the players of the significant amount of control they have over how the changes affect them may help them cope with the pressures of the change.

Changes within our control to help or hinder may be easier to deal with emotionally, but they may also give us additional problems. The quality transformation is such a change, being largely a cultural shift, a new paradigm of what education can and should be. In his book on paradigms and paradigm shifts, Joel Barker discusses the reactions of people who are part of the "prevailing paradigm community" to the innovations presented by the "paradigm shifter." When presented with the ideas, concepts, or methods of the new paradigm, their reaction can range from incredulous ("That's impossible!") to sarcastic ("Okay, back to reality") to derisive ("You always were weird") to defensive

("Who are you to tell us we're wrong?"). (The reader may now freely admit such a reaction, secure in the knowledge that it has been expected.) From the perspective of the accepted paradigm, these reactions are perfectly understandable; the success of the old paradigm blinds people to the value in the new idea.[4] How the participants manifest their reactions will be important to the success of the transformation; while some will approve of and work for the change, some will sulk, some will balk, and some will actively work against the change.

Understanding the possible reactions of people to change, leaders cannot afford to let changes create trauma in their organizations. They cannot have parts of their organization paralyzed by anxiety over a change, nor can they allow a small contingent to sabotage the change. They must manage the change, displaying some sort of control—if not over the change itself, at least over their personal reactions to it. One of the best ways to manage change in an organization is to encourage members' participation in the change effort. The leader assumes the role of teacher and coach, explaining the need for the change and helping the members evaluate alternatives and develop approaches to the change.[5] This participative approach is ideally suited to the education transformation.

If you choose to implement the education transformation, you will undoubtedly encounter resistance. Some will resist because their personal empires are threatened. Some will resist because it is their nature to resist anything innovative that they did not develop. Most who resist will do so because the education transformation challenges their paradigms about education (as discussed previously). As leaders in the transformation effort, you face perhaps the hardest task of management: changing the attitudes and behaviors of groups of people, not just individuals.[6] You must convince a "critical mass"[7] of people that the transformation is necessary, educate them about reality and guide their efforts to improve quality. Many obstacles stand in your way.

INHIBITORS TO CHANGE[8]

Some resistance to the education transformation will come from all participant groups: administrators, teachers, students, parents, and government. Each group has developed significant cultural paradigms about what to expect and how to proceed. While some members will embrace the change, others will mildly resist it, and still another segment will resist it vehemently (as pointed out by Juran; see *Leadership for Change,* page, 183). It will require almost a leap of faith for some reluctant members to follow the transformation, and while their resistance to such a radical change is understandable, it must still be overcome.[9]

Inhibitors for Administrators

Administrators are and will continue to be the front-line managers of the education system. In addition to having the responsibility for implementing the transformation, they will be charged with carrying on the quest for endless improvement in the quality of education. It is an awesome challenge, and they will encounter especially difficult problems as leaders of the transformation process.

Administrators, along with government agencies and school boards, may be so caught up in day-to-day activities that they fail to plan for the long term. Because of their positions as managers of districts and schools, some may overemphasize nonquality issues, like budget targets and tenure. If they are overly excited about the transformation, they may rush the process without providing adequate training on new responsibilities to their people. If they set up training but do not personally get involved, it may send mixed signals to their people and hurt the effort (even more dangerous would be their use of additional training as a form of punishment or a reaction to problems).[10]

Some administrators, anxious to apply the principles in the classroom, may neglect other key players like maintenance supervisors and purchasing agents. Some who have been steeped in traditional, adversarial relationships may be reluctant to include unions in the transformation.

The position of administrators, including principals, in the education hierarchy may itself inhibit their acceptance of change. Some may be reluctant to change because of fear that their positions or authority may be jeopardized. The tenure of a superintendent or principal in any one place is typically short (less than five years), which will itself be an inhibitor to systemic change. Because of it, leaders may feel their attempts at implementing change will be disregarded or actively opposed by those who will outlive them in the organization.

Isolation from teachers and students may cause some to miss signals that fear and anxiety are alive in the organization. They may believe fear has been removed and perhaps not see the need to plan for new fears that may arise because of the quality initiative (like their own fear mentioned previously). Isolation may also make administrators reluctant to implement suggestions from teachers and other participants; they may even refuse to acknowledge the feedback they receive from internal and external customers.

Administrators may have an alternate problem if they try to implement certain elements of the education transformation too soon. They may introduce statistical techniques before the philosophical foundation has been built or emphasize the statistics to the exclusion of all else. It would also be dangerous for them to try to apply the statistical methods without proper training by and guidance of a competent statistician.[11]

Finally, some administrators may try to hang on to the current performance appraisal system or current systems of merit pay. (In many cases they may be powerless to remove them, but some may defend these practices and fight to keep them.) By continuing to reward and punish their employees without regard for the capabilities of the systems the people work in, these administrators will stifle the quality improvement process.[12]

Inhibitors for Teachers

Teachers are charged with working within the educational system to give their students opportunities to learn and develop. As the transformation of education continues, they will see the larger system changing around them and may be immersed in fear and anxiety unless their management involves them in the changes.

Some of the fears that may inhibit teachers' participation in the transformation are obvious. Some may fear new standards for certification and professional development, believing that the standards endanger, rather than solidify, their positions. Some teachers may be reluctant to participate in career development and continued education because they are afraid of failing in the attempt; perhaps in a worse position are others who feel obligated to participate when they really do not want to. Some may not actively participate in improvement efforts for fear of censure by their peers or segments of the administration, or out of belief that the quality philosophy has nothing to do with them.

175

Some teachers may have grown so accustomed to the adversarial relationship between unions and management that they fear the quality initiative is a new attempt by management to exploit them. Close relations with teachers' unions from the moment the transformation process is started will be necessary to allay this fear. Management must recognize that these problems, created over many years, will not be solved overnight.

If teachers hear management ask for quality while pushing quantity or some other measure, the quality transformation is doomed.[13] How many previous reforms were doomed to failure because management proposed goals that could not be met? How many teachers (and administrators, and students) have been humiliated by these efforts? How many educators today are working feverishly toward "national goals" that are no more than pie-in-the-sky?

Other factors may inhibit teachers to a lesser degree. Some few may not be sensitive to feedback from their customers, that is, students and other teachers. Some may not be willing to cross departmental lines—for example, teachers who are intimidated by mathematics may be reluctant to include mathematical applications or analyses in their classes.[14] They may not want to use the quality tools in their classes; perhaps they are intimidated by the statistical methods.[15] These factors cannot be ignored. Every effort must be made to coach reluctant teachers through the changes and bring them completely into the quality effort. The transformation cannot be accomplished without them.

Inhibitors for Students

It appears the student population that will be most affected by the change will be the current middle and high school group; having spent several years in the system, their perceptions of school will have to change radically. In light of this, one of the primary inhibitors to the change process involves not students themselves, but the adults who work with them. Quite often, adults simply cannot relate to teenagers.

In Appendix B we will briefly discuss the development of teenagers as a separate cultural group. Though that process began almost 50 years ago, U.S. education has yet to catch up with the rate of change of modern teenage culture. This is largely because the culture today's teachers grew up in is drastically different from that of today's students. One example of this is shown in a comparison of the top offenses in public schools over a 40-year gap (Table 7.1).[16]

Lest the reader be lulled into thinking the 1980 offenses in the table occurred only in inner-city schools or problem schools, those items marked with asterisks were evident in only *one year* at the author's alma mater: Winyah High School, student population approximately 900, located in Georgetown, South Carolina, a bustling metropolis of 12,000. While there is no asterisk by bombings, the school did experience several bomb threats and in 1981 was largely destroyed by arson (it does not exist today). The presence of somewhat sophisticated problems at even small schools in social backwaters is and should be suitably shocking. As stated by veteran youthworkers Mike Yaconelli and Jim Burns:

> Today, high-school students live in a world so different from any previous generation's that comparisons are almost impossible.... Although the external structure of the high-school years appears to be the same, the world of today's high school student is radically different from that of other generations. It is not just that the high-school environment has changed; it has become a totally different experience.[17]

It is no wonder that educators and adults in general have trouble relating to today's youth.

To give up on contemporary youth would be premature, however. Teenagers in this generation certainly have as much or more potential as their counterparts of previous generations, but they are caught in the stress and turmoil of our modern society. While Daniel J. Boorstin laments, "Perhaps the nation would never recover from its idealization of adolescence, its new tendency to treat 'youth' as a separate right-entitled entity, a new American estate within the Union."[18] Jim Burns explains it this way:

> The young people that you and I work with today are different from those of any previous generation. They are smarter, better-looking, and filled with greater potential than people of any other time in history. This same teenager is filled with more stress, anxiety, and pressure than teens of any previous generation.[19]

Nurturing these students is a special art, one that we must cultivate within our entire society (including all arenas, for example, media, families, and communities, as well as schools) if we are to guarantee our children a place in the world. A commitment to quality in education can help us tap into the energy of youth; education does not operate in a vacuum but, along with other influences, can certainly help students reach their potential.

Part of the revolution in education will include innovative solutions to the problems facing students and teachers. Problems such as gang activities, drug use, and teenage pregnancy have been attacked from many directions, and the educational community has often been enlisted in efforts to solve them. While these problems do not simply go away, effective improvements in education can provide a solid foundation on which young people can build the self-esteem necessary to conquer these problems and to achieve productive and fulfilling lives.

One problem of youth that will not be completely solved by the education transformation, but will affect its success, is the failure of many young people to plan for their futures. Young people exist in an incredibly intense world of immediacy and often do not perceive the need to make future plans. Even when they do

Table 7.1 Top Offenses in Public Schools, 1940 and 1980
(Note: These are not arranged in any particular order.)

1940	1980
Running in the hallways	Robbery
Chewing gum in class	Assault *
Wearing improper clothing (included a shirttail out)	Personal theft *
	Burglary *
Making noise	Drug abuse *
Not putting paper in wastebaskets	Arson *
	Bombings
	Alcohol abuse *
	Carrying weapons *
	Absenteeism
	Vandalism *
	Murder
	Extortion

(From Jim Burns, *The Youth Builder: Today's Resource for Relational Youth Ministry.* Eugene, Oregon: Harvest House Publishers, 1988.)

make plans, they may not recognize school's utility in bringing those plans to fruition and enabling them to reach their goals. Like other participants in the transformation, students' focus on the short term will hamper efforts to improve quality,[20] and teachers, parents, and administrators must take on the responsibility of helping students understand the relevance of their education.

ॐ

With regard to the quality philosophy itself, one of the first inhibitors to student acceptance may be their rejection of the industrial, or systems, model of education. Because of their short-term emphasis, some students may find it hard to accept the fact that they are being prepared for a future of social interaction, work, and continued learning. Many of the young people I have worked with recognize the need for work but believe deep down that it is something they will not have to do, that someone or something will relieve them of the burden of labor and provide for them the rest of their lives.[21]

Another major inhibitor to student involvement in the transformation process may be their fear that improved quality in education will mean more work for them. This will be overcome only by undoing another paradigm and changing the perception of education from a tedious task to a joyful experience. Quality education may indeed require more effort, but it will also provide more pride and more fulfillment.

A final factor that may affect student participation in the quality initiative is the shift from reliance on external motivation to nurturing and allowing internal motivation to lead students to learn. Many youth today are so locked into external motivators that they often do not want to learn what will not be on the test.[22] It will take time for the culture to change, for students to accept and enjoy learning for learning's sake.

Inhibitors for Parents

Parents play a pivotal role in the total education experience of their children, and like the other partners they also face many obstacles on the road to quality. Some parents may not understand their place in the education system or recognize the importance of their participation in the process, especially in their children's early development. Some parents will understand but will not have enough time to devote to the improvement process. Some few will actually be unwilling to put forth any effort, believing that the schools should handle it all (the population of this last group is thankfully quite small).

Parents who grew up in the school system as it is now may not recognize its problems; like others in the system, their paradigm of what school is (or should be) may cloud their vision. For instance, they may continue to emphasize grades over improvement, even when the value-added approach and measures of subject mastery are used in the schools.

Parental guidance can be pivotal in shaping children for the future, as discussed in the previous chapter. Sometimes, though, guidance can be haphazardly applied, as when parents unwittingly transfer their own goals and ambitions onto their children; while this is done out of a desire for the child's success, it places a great deal of unnecessary pressure on the student.[23] An additional danger of transference is that the parents' fears (for example, of failure, of relationships) may also be transferred to the child.

Some parents are at times reluctant to discipline their children, and similarly reluctant to monitor their children's participation in school, church, or civic activities. Because it is socially acceptable for young people to display their natural teenage rebellion openly, these timid parents often try to avoid the rebellion by placating their children. "Peace in our time" is no more a reality in the family than it was in Chamberlain's Europe: appeasement of teenagers does not work. Young people need consistent discipline and authority figures in their lives to provide them with a secure environment for growing up.[24] The discipline issue carries over into student participation in activities outside of school. Parents who are inconsistent with discipline may not be prepared to help their children find a balance among their activities, for example, between homework and sports or work and play. Of course, many adults do not have this balance themselves: how can we teach what we do not know?

Inhibitors for Government

State and federal governments may themselves develop strong inhibitors to the transformation. Perhaps because of their stifling bureaucracies, their inhibitors may be more pervasive. Over-emphasis on politicized policy statements, inattention to educators and industry, words without action, and continuing reliance on arbitrary numerical goals are just a few of the possible problems of governmental involvement.

Perhaps the most insidious obstacle of the state and federal governments will be the temptation to bureaucratize the transformation, to control it so tightly that they strangle it. Because bureaucracy lives and dies by policy, agencies that succumb to the temptation may establish strict policies rather than a far-reaching, compelling vision for education; their policies may become the be-all and end-all of the transformation effort, instead of simply tools for achieving the vision. Educational policy cannot be thought of as sacrosanct or it will stagnate, and the rest of education with it—policy must be secondary to vision in establishing constancy of purpose and a common aim. Policies, while important, are not paramount; they must be continually updated and improved in relation to a clear vision, as guides to and examples of the quality philosophy.[25]

Zeal to take a leadership role in the transformation may itself cause problems. Government agencies may move so fast that they effectively ignore the suggestions of educators, corporate representatives, and other interested parties as they allocate funds, enact legislation, or propose standards. Again because of the prevailing adversarial paradigm, they may fail to enlist teachers' organizations in the quality effort. The government may also continue to rely on well-intentioned but largely arbitrary and meaningless goals, like the "national goals" we discussed in Chapter 4.

It may be difficult for some local and state boards of education to recognize the problems of education as national rather than local priorities; others may recognize the problems at the national level but not at their own. These boards will find it difficult to accept the premise that national standards and a national curriculum are necessary. This results from an insistence that their geographically distinct regions have needs that overshadow the needs of the country as a whole; they forget that the strength of the nation influences the strength of the states as much or moreso than the reverse.

Another problem, and one likely to be encountered, is the inability or failure of government agencies to plan for the far future. Often political entities spend so much time trying to solve the problems of the present—to garner and maintain support among constituents—that they neglect to plan for the problems of the future. The political arena itself often weighs against cooperative efforts: bipartisan agreements on fundamental issues are rare and practically unheard of on controversial issues. Organizational (rather than temporal) farsightedness may also plague upper levels of bureaucracy: by looking so intently at problems and conditions in the lower echelons of the school system, it may not recognize that its own internal functions also require constant improvement.

The final inhibitor to change in governmental agencies and services may be the hardest to overcome: the political process itself. Because political action committees and lobbyists often manipulate governmental processes for their own gain, it is extremely difficult to implement effective reform. Even the president, pledged to improve the education system, will be harangued and harassed in the attempt. "We still do not trust our leaders....We run the risk that interest-group rivalry will produce policies targeting the lowest common denominator or no change at all. If reform is achieved at one moment, it is likely to come under vigorous attack at the next."[26]

Other Inhibitors

We have previously discussed the tendency among us to place blame for the failures of our institutions. This is one of the inhibitors to change that affects all participants. Teachers must resist the urge to deride students' inattentiveness and laziness. Parents and the media must not hold teachers entirely responsible for school performance. Everyone is working within the system. The effort expended in placing blame could be better spent improving the system.

Another inhibitor to the changes involved in the quality effort also applies to every participant. It is at once the most pervasive and the most subtle, and is what Deming calls "hope for instant pudding."[27] Participants in the education transformation must not be encouraged to expect immediate results, because immediate results (especially immediately favorable results) will simply not materialize. The strategy presented in Chapter 5, if adopted and implemented today, would not be accomplished soon. It would take *years* for all of the pieces to be put in place, and the overall results of the transformation would not be seen for years after that. Of course, quick adoption of quality principles will result in improvements in local schools over the short haul, but it will take a long time to effect a cultural change throughout the education establishment. The length of time will depend on those who lead the effort; but, regardless of the final schedule, quality in education will not be achieved in the blink of an eye.

LEADERSHIP FOR CHANGE

It should be obvious from the preceding discussion that leaders in the educational community must deal effectively with many problems and obstacles to succeed in the transformation. Not all managers will agree that the quality philosophy is the key to immediate and continuing improvement in education, and we have discussed various ways in which members of the educational community may (inadvertently or not) inhibit its progress.

Many attempts have been made to improve education in recent years, and may themselves affect the transformation. The success or failure of "reforms" and improvement attempts with which they are familiar will color people's perceptions of the quality philosophy and this transformation. Some will be enthusiastic, eager to explore the possibilities of improvement. Others will be more cautious, admitting that improvement is necessary, but wary of implementing broad measures until their effectiveness is proven. A third group will completely avoid participating in the change, despite every attempt to convince them; Juran cautions that this group should be approached last by those leaders advocating change and improvement.[28]

In Chapter 5, pilot programs were included as part of the transformation strategy. Pilot programs are small-scale demonstrations of improvement methods; their successes can convince the majority of cautious onlookers that the improvements are viable and deserve their support. Once the philosophy is understood by the participants and adoption of quality principles is underway, pilot programs are a logical step to solidify the transformation and the new quality culture. It will take a number of successful pilot programs, spanning every sector of education across the nation, to

183

prove to wary educators that the quality philosophy is the key to continuous improvement—some are already underway, led by educators with the courage and foresight to change. We have discussed early results from Mount Edgecumbe High School and the efforts of several school districts, but their programs continue and others follow suit, adapting the philosophy to their own unique circumstances. How long will these pilot programs take? No one can predict exactly how long: two, five, ten years perhaps. It will take time to convince more people to participate in the quality improvement effort, but we must use our available time wisely.

One potential timesaver is the use of lessons learned from previous improvement efforts, but it is not without its drawbacks. Lessons learned are used throughout industry and government to share information about a wide variety of topics. Juran points out two important merits of lessons learned: (1) they catalog the prior experience of many people in a form that can be used by almost anyone, and (2) they may be used many times over.[29] A number of reports on educational reforms could conceivably be used as lessons learned, for example, *The Nation Responds* and *Reaching for Excellence*. This approach has two main problems. First, most of the current lessons learned are either negative or use methods inimical to the quality philosophy. Second, an overwhelming number of reform movements are included in these reports; where do we start? And despite the availability and use of lessons learned, carefully selected and well-designed pilot programs will still be necessary to demonstrate the effectiveness of the overall philosophy.

Once the philosophy is accepted and work has begun, leaders must find ways to work through problems and avoid obstacles as they move toward quality. To maintain constancy of purpose, the quality effort must not get bogged down in fire-fighting and turf battles. Because so many different groups are involved—teachers, students, administrators, and parents—it will be extremely difficult to deal effectively with each group's particular problems. Principals and other mid-level administrators who have close and intense contact with each group will be hardest hit, their diplomatic abilities sorely tested.

The leader with insight and knowledge does have at least one advantage in transforming her respective area. By recognizing and understanding the anxieties and problems of each group, she can exchange her coaching role (teaching and encouraging others about the change process) for the role of counselor to help everyone through the perceived crisis. Unfortunately, many managers are afraid to open a dialogue with troubled people, but addressing their fears honestly and dealing with their problems openly is often the best way to resolve them.[30] As seen, the obstacles and inhibitors to the transformation are largely manifestations of the groups' fears; the prudent leader can help her people remove the roadblocks to cooperative success.

The basic fears may be removed or at least reduced through the education of participants; this is why introductory education and dissemination of the quality philosophy to all levels is such an important step of the transformation strategy. After the initial education, you as leaders of the transformation must turn your attention to the mechanics of the change, such as, putting in place policies and procedures consistent with the quality philosophy. Part of this change requires leaders to empower teachers, administrators, and other players, providing them with substantial investments of information, resources, and support. In turn, the empowered participants will respond with their own innovative solutions to deeply rooted problems.

These three items—information, resources, and support—are necessary elements of innovation; obviously, they are the responsibility of leadership and management to provide.[31] Much of the required information (for example, raw data, specific technical knowledge, an appreciation of reality) will, however, have been provided in the introductions to the philosophy. Additional classes and seminars on quality tools, statistical methods, and team-building will add to the information base—faculty and students who are involved in the transformation will probably clamor for more training.[32] Resources for the transformation will come through traditional channels as well as outside (for example, through corporate sponsorships). School boards and administrators should encourage innovation by making at least small amounts of money available for pilot programs, especially programs that begin as suggestions from teachers or students. Investing money in their projects is a sure sign that their inputs are valued and their efforts needed. Financial resources are not the only ones required, however; teachers and administrators will need time and materials to accomplish parts of the transformation.

Support of the effort, the third element of innovation, will be invested in participants by voters, corporate leaders, civic leaders, and superiors, who lend legitimacy to the quality revolution.

The final factor in overcoming the inhibitors and accomplishing the transformation of education is to emphasize the use of teams. Only dedicated teams of educators, administrators, and other participants working together on specific issues will be able to address all aspects of the issues and reach acceptable solutions. Leadership in team-building will be required to overcome barriers between team members and allow them to express not only their ideas and opinions but also their fears and frustrations. Only the concerted efforts of teams at every level of the education system can hope to overcome the obstacles to quality improvement and achieve the goals of the transformation, but like the rest of the transformation simply instituting teams will not be sufficient. The teams must be guided; for the transformation to succeed, everyone's efforts must be combined into an optimized whole, working toward a common aim. Success will require leaders with courage and vision.

OF LEADERS AND THE FUTURE

Where are the Jeffersons and Lincolns of today? The answer, I am convinced, is that they are among us. Out there in the settings with which we are all familiar are the unawakened leaders, feeling no overpowering call to lead and hardly aware of the potential within.

—John W. Gardner, On Leadership

Leaders through history have cultivated a mystique to surround their function; if we are to raise up leaders for the transformation, we must break this mystique. One of the earliest mysteries of leadership was whether it was an inborn trait or a learned skill. In the past, leadership was considered to be a gift, not an ability, but many social scientists today agree that leadership involves the mastery of skills which can be learned. This implies that leadership can be taught; however, simply teaching an individual a few basic skills will not make him a leader. Strong leadership ability comes about as a result of dedicated study of leadership theory coupled with practical experience, whether it involves leading armies or countries or, in this case, schools. If you 187 are determined to lead the education transformation in your school or community, you must master the basics of leadership and practice them in your own life; then you will be able to build your vision of the future into reality.

A LEADERSHIP PRIMER

Generally, leadership refers to the process by which an individual—the leader—exerts some amount of influence over a group of people, motivating them to work toward a goal or goals. The influence a leader exerts may be directed in a variety of ways. For example, a leader who practices behaviorist motivation will use the promise of reward or the threat of punishment as a motivator, while a leader who treats her people with respect as human beings with freedom of choice may convince her followers through force of reason that a goal is worth achieving, and that they should rely on their own motivation. This latter approach is more reliable and effective in the long run and has been addressed several times so far.

In that leaders exert influence of one type or another, leadership is closely tied to power, for all leaders have a certain amount of power over the people they lead. The leader's power may be based on position in the organization (as the principal in a school), personal magnetism, or expertise (which the principal presumably possesses, also). This combination of power sources enables the leader to deal with a wider variety of people; exclusive reliance on any single source of power tends to weaken the leader's position by alienating some members of the organization. Leaders who conscientiously apply their power to advance the interests of the entire group (rather than their own interests) can earn from their followers referent power, in which the members of the organization identify strongly with the leader, earnestly desiring to please him or be like him.

Power is a primary aspect of leadership that sets the leader apart from the manager. Management is associated with administration, with setting things in their proper places, and as such is a static discipline. Leadership, however, is dynamic, associated with a motive force pushing or pulling a group or organization toward its goals. Leaders use their power to propel the group toward its aims and keep it from stagnating, but fear of Lord Acton's assertion that "power corrupts" can make them wield their power only tentatively. In fact, Lord Acton is often only partially quoted and actually observed, "Power corrupts, and absolute power tends to corrupt absolutely."[1] By avoiding the definitive he provided an outlet for the person of strong will and good character to wield power without being corrupted by it.

An inordinate fear of power may be one reason why many individuals seem to prefer managing to leading and why, as a result, "many of our institutions are reasonably well managed, but poorly led."[2] This unfortunately includes our schools, which need strong leaders who are not afraid to use their power to propel them toward quality education. Every organization and every school needs a leader who "captures the hearts of the people and awakens their enthusiasm."[3]

Despite the fact that leadership as a concept is difficult to define, many sociologists, psychologists, and leaders have attempted to do so and have identified a number of traits or skills that leaders typically possess.[4] This theory is incomplete in that it is not capable of directly correlating traits with leadership potential and does not define traits consistently or clearly. It can, however, be useful in placing leaders in categories for better understanding.

Four of the leadership attributes that are usually identified are character, communication skill, decisiveness, and knowledge. Character, not a well-defined quality, is considered to be a unique combination of other attributes, including, to some extent, courage, the willingness to accept blame and share rewards, adaptability to changing circumstances, humility, responsibility, sincerity, self-control, and wisdom. Communication skill is more easily understood. Leaders must be able to communicate effectively to and with their followers, whether explaining what the aim is, discovering how the system elements work together, or providing deeper insight into the reasons behind particular courses of action.

Leaders must be prepared to make timely decisions, often with little or no information. Finally, as we have seen in theory of knowledge, knowledge implies something other than simply intelligence. An intelligent individual without theory that explains the group's past successes or failures, analyzes current situations and strengths, and predicts success with reasonable probability will not be able to lead the group effectively.

As all individuals are different, leaders develop these attributes in different ways, but all use them to guide the organization toward its aims. It would do no good for someone to try and develop each skill to its utmost. First, they are complementary and support one another. Second, no matter how well-developed these qualities may be, the strength of the leader's position is also related to his followers' *perception* of the qualities. To pull together a diverse group (whose individual perceptions may be influenced by very different things), a leader must become at various times a coach, spokesman, figurehead, and counselor—whatever may be necessary to achieve the aims of the group.

As a coach, the leader tracks the efforts of the team or organization and identifies potential problem areas both inside and outside the group. Her efforts then turn to solving those problems, not haphazardly but carefully and methodically. Problems inside the group often involve resolving conflicts between members or moving people to jobs more suited to their talents; thus, effective leaders must know their followers intimately, taking "into account the abilities and limitations of [the workers], circulating among them and asking nothing unreasonable."[5] Problems outside the group may require removing a set of obstacles that stand in the way of the group's success; with respect to the education transformation, this removal of inhibitors was discussed in the previous chapter.

As spokesmen, leaders send many messages to their followers. Leaders communicate the vision of the group and report on progress toward the group's aims. With their messages, leaders focus the group's attention on pressing issues,[6] empowering the group to find innovative approaches and solutions wherever possible. Communicating clearly and directly to the group allows the leader to "[raise] their spirits in times of trouble, [inspire] them at moments of crisis," and thank them for a job well done.[7] In order to be effective, a leader's communication must above all be reliable and sincere. "When orders are consistently trustworthy …the relationship of a commander with [the] troops is satisfactory."[8] So too the relationship of a superintendent or principal with faculty members and students.

Whether they like it or not, leaders are figureheads. Leaders set an example the group will either want to follow or avoid and should strive to present a good example to the group as much as possible. One of the ways in which the leader's example determines the group's performance is the leader's attitude toward the work at hand; by showing enthusiasm or disdain for the tasks to be accomplished, the leader can either improve or hinder the group's performance. "He teaches not by speech but by accomplishment."[9]

Leaders, by working closely with their followers, act often as counselors (this too was addressed in the last chapter). The rationale behind this function of a leader is twofold. First, personnel with problems or perceived problems may degrade the performance of the group; to keep the group's performance on track, the leader must solve (or at least attempt to solve) the problem. Second, and more importantly, if people think their leader is insensitive to their problems their willingness to perform will decline; to promote and maintain harmony in the group, the leader must be concerned with the people and their welfare. The leader "should know their morale and spirit, and encourage them when necessary."[10]

LEADERSHIP DEVELOPMENT: FROM THEORY TO PRACTICE

Based on the leadership theory we have discussed, it is possible to identify attributes a leader should develop and skills a leader should master. It is an entirely different thing to predict who, on the basis of development and mastery, will become leaders. John W. Gardner, in his excellent book *On Leadership*, points out that "the individual's hereditary gifts, however notable, leave the issue of future leadership performance undecided, to be settled by later events and influences."[11] Just as teachers may recognize a student's potential to excel, one can recognize an individual's potential to become a leader, but potential without opportunity is simply untapped potential.

Research on leadership has shown that the ability to lead is developed through practice.[12] Unless individuals are given the chance to lead, they will not develop as leaders. Thus, while skill training is important, only the *experience of being a leader* will solidify a person's ability to lead. This follows directly from theory of knowledge: once a theory has been formulated or learned, it is proven or disproven by experience. Experience leads to refine-ment of the theory or concept but will not itself provide a basis for the theory.

The need for experience to test theory and the need for improved leadership among young people are two reasons why the quality emphasis in education stresses group interaction and group activities; through opportunities to lead, young people will improve leadership skills and attributes. The benefit of this was pointed out by Thomas Jefferson as

> the incalculable advantage of training up able counselors to administer the affairs of our country in all its depart-ments, legislative, executive and judiciary, and to bear their proper share in the councils of our national govern-ment; nothing more than education advancing the pros-perity, the power, and the happiness of a nation.[13]

To realize these benefits requires that our students learn and accept their leadership roles and work diligently to master leader-ship theory.

Because leadership development involves more than the acquisition of a few skills, requiring instead the continued effort of studying and leading, the number of people who develop into leaders is relatively small. It is not that the process of becoming a leader is too difficult, it is simply that most people—unless their leadership potential is pointed out and developed through oppor-tunities to lead—will not strive for the self-improvement necessary to develop as a leader. Newton's First Law states it in physical terms: a body at rest tends to remain at rest.

For you hoping to lead the transformation or to teach stu-dents about leadership this point is of paramount importance. The primary focus of any leadership development program has to be *learning* leadership, rather than *teaching* leadership. Moreso than any academic subject, the development of leadership abilities relies heavily on internal motivation; the burden is placed on the prospective leader more than the teacher.

Leadership development, therefore, is a process that entails far more than learning a few basic skills and principles. This book and others present theory of leadership consisting of principles to be applied; if readers choose not to apply the theory, it is a will-o'-the-wisp, immaterial and fleeting. The superintendent or prin-cipal who would develop as a leader must be prepared to study the theory and continually strengthen and sharpen her skills through the practice of leadership. While leadership may be studied, it must be practiced to develop fully. The process requires intense motivation that must come from within the person seeking to be a leader.

Finally, the process of leadership development does not end. Leadership, like quality, is not a thing to be achieved but a goal to be worked toward. Working to develop as a leader teaches individuals to better handle themselves; from that ability they learn to better handle others. "Today is victory over yourself of yesterday; tomorrow is your victory over [others]."[14] Through this conscious effort, largely self-motivated, true leaders are developed and empowered to change their worlds.

LEADERSHIP FOR THE FUTURE

For years we have lied to young people, telling them they are the future of our country and our society.[15] How can they build the future when we give them nothing with which to build it? All we do is to hand over the responsibility; with it we give them social, political, fiscal, and environmental garbage. And we give them no training; the future is a model kit we present to our young people, but the pieces are broken and they have no instructions.

We can no longer abdicate our responsibility, claiming that our young people will make the future. It is all too clear that we control the systems with which the future will be built; we must be the leaders *today* who prepare and launch the future. Whether the future is full of promise or woe for our young people is entirely up to us. We must accept our responsibility and continuously improve the systems we control to build the best possible future for ourselves and for them.

The first system we must understand and improve is our system of education, because education ultimately touches every area of our society. If we can provide our young people with the tools and the knowledge to succeed, if we can instill in them a love for knowledge and a desire for continued learning, if we can build within them the skills required for effective leadership, we can be sure at least that the future will be in good hands when we finally turn it over to them.

We cannot, however, focus so completely on education that we lose sight of the other things we will also pass on. Facing these looming issues is difficult and dealing effectively with them will be even harder, but we cannot shy away from the task. The future is ours to make or break.

If we fail in the attempt, perhaps our children will remember that we tried and carry on our efforts to ultimate success. But if we close our eyes and turn our backs, if we fail to even try, may they remember us with contempt. The teacher said, "For everything there is a season, and a time for every matter under heaven."[16]

The season for change is upon us.

QUALITY TOOLS AND TECHNIQUES

B eyond the theoretical principles presented in Chapters 2 and 4, the quality philosophy involves the use of many tools and techniques to measure and plan the continuous improvement of quality, seven of which are presented here. Some of these tools originated as statistical process control instruments and require knowledge of statistical concepts to master. Others are conceptually obvious.

Please do not be alarmed or intimidated by this section. Detailed knowledge of the mechanics of the techniques is not necessary to understanding what they accomplish. I know just enough statistics to get myself in trouble—and may thereby offend you who are more statistically fluent—but I understand the basic principles behind them. Notwithstanding that some of these quality management tools are easily adapted to educational processes, others do require more detailed knowledge of statistical methods and some conceptual leaps to facilitate their use. Educators are strongly urged to seek the guidance of a competent statistician before putting the statistical techniques to use. Some administrators with mathematics backgrounds and some mathematics and science teachers may even choose to study applied statistics and the quality philosophy in order to use the methods effectively.

Flow diagrams. Perhaps the most powerful tool for analyzing processes and systems is the flow diagram. Flow diagrams allow the visualization and understanding of any process, and form a vital part of Juran's quality planning road map (see Chapter 2). An example flow diagram of supermarket shopping is shown in Figure A.1; please note that no attempt at completeness has been made in this example.

By presenting the process steps in an easily understood format, flow diagrams provide valuable information to those who manage systems, those who work within the systems, and their customers. Often the exercise of putting together a flow diagram will lead to recognition of redundant activities or questionable practices. Here a work atmosphere free of fear (Deming's point 8)

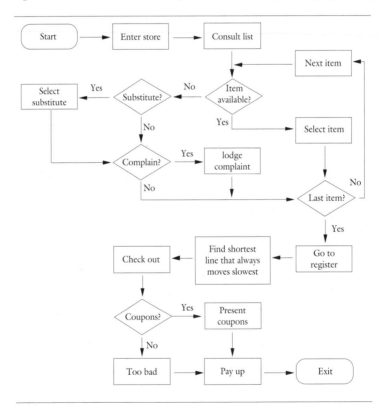

Figure A.1 Flow Diagram Example

will allow employees and managers to be candid enough to ask, "Why are we doing that?" and allow those in control to admit that the process should be changed.

Flow diagrams are particularly useful in describing the steps of a process to people unfamiliar with it. They may be used to introduce new or unusual facets of the educational system to school board members or the public at large. Such improved understanding could help both board members and voters in their decision-making process.[1]

Flow diagrams are also powerful tools for studying processes that are often repeated. Examples of repetitive processes that may be studied using this tool are the processing of various types of paperwork, steps in ordering materials or approving new textbooks, and steps in selecting and training new teachers.

Flow diagrams may also be utilized by teachers in planning, to arrange the parts of a course or lesson for logical presentation. They may be applied in the process of planning curricula, allowing the placement of courses to correspond with factors such as teacher and facility availability, student maturity, and the transition from concrete to conceptual thinking.[2] For example, Mount Edgecumbe High School teachers and students worked together to flowchart some of their school activities and objectives and used the information to restructure the learning environment.[3] The biggest use of flow charting may be in the classroom, where the charts can be used to teach analytical and problem-solving skills.

Ishikawa charts. Designed by Ishikawa in 1943 and also called a fishbone or cause-and-effect diagram, the Ishikawa chart (Figure A.2) is useful in identifying the elements that go into an outcome and observing relationships between the inputs.[4]

The outcome is placed at the head of the chart. It may be either a manufactured product, a service, or a problem that is plaguing the organization. The major and minor factors that affect the outcome are then placed behind the head. Usually factors are grouped according to categories, such as environmental factors or human factors, as seen in the Ishikawa diagram of inputs to learning in Chapter 3.

The Ishikawa chart can often be used by management to discover patterns among the various causes; these may in turn lead to effective improvement ideas. Synergistic relationships between

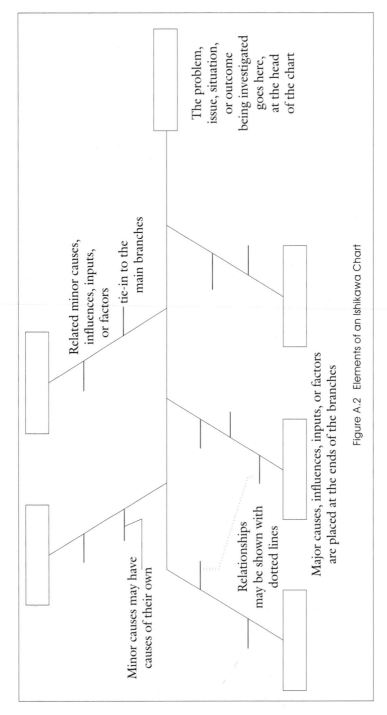

The problem, issue, situation, or outcome being investigated goes here, at the head of the chart

Related minor causes, influences, inputs, or factors

tie-in to the main branches

Minor causes may have causes of their own

Relationships may be shown with dotted lines

Major causes, influences, inputs, or factors are placed at the ends of the branches

Figure A.2   Elements of an Ishikawa Chart

causes that may amplify their effects may be seen and given closer attention by management.

Ishikawa charts allow the analysis of various inputs into specific problems or situations. Ishikawa charts may be used to study the factors affecting such social problems as illicit drug use, gang violence, and teenage pregnancy, with the aim to determine what positive effects the school system can hope to achieve. (Used in this manner, this tool would undoubtedly show that schools cannot solve all of society's ills. Ideally, politicians would acknowledge that fact and stop heaping more burdens on education than it can bear.)

More practical uses of the Ishikawa chart in education are as an aid in lesson and curriculum planning that differentiates between major and minor parts of a larger topic (for example, the fall of Rome or the mechanism of heat transfer). Ishikawa charts may be used by teachers to explore and explain the combinations of inputs to events or problems (for example, the factors influencing experimental errors and results in chemistry, or the events that contributed to the beginning of the Civil War). When the inputs are seen graphically, relationships between them can be more easily grasped and a better idea of the whole obtained. Students, teachers, and bureaucrats may finally recognize that our world is far too complicated to be reduced to simple models and easy answers.

Run charts and control charts. A run chart is a plot of data taken over time. The data are simply plotted in the order in which they are taken, as shown in Figure A.3. (The *Y*-axis of the run chart represents some measurement; it is unlabeled in the figure to illustrate the versatility of this tool.) Whatever measure of process performance is required by management can be plotted on a run chart, for example, percent defective, maintenance downtime, purchase order processing time, worker absenteeism. By keeping track of the performance of the process over time and recognizing the variability of the process, managers and workers can understand their processes better and find ways to improve them.

The control chart was Shewhart's great contribution to quality analysis (see Chapter 1). Shewhart recognized that every process has some natural variation associated with it; the control chart tracks its variability, measures how well the process is in statistical control, and allows the visualization of the effects of special causes of variation.[5]

The concept of statistical control is vitally important. Any process that is repeated a number of times will produce different results; this is the variability Shewhart recognized. Some processes may produce results that are very close to one another, while others produce results that fluctuate wildly. The results depend on the capability of the process.

Measures of the central tendency of the process (usually the arithmetic average or mean) and the dispersion of the results (for example, the standard deviation) can be used to determine if

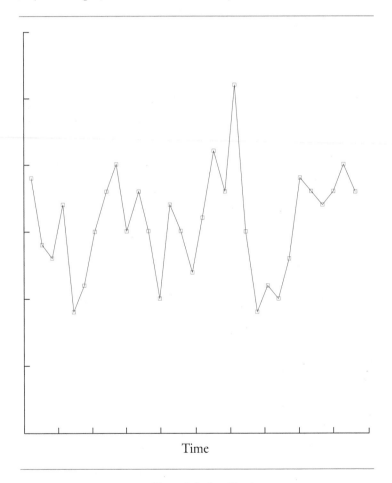

Time

Figure A.3 Run Chart
The Y-axis is intentionally unlabeled to
demonstrate the run chart's versatility.

the process is in statistical control. If the process is indeed in statistical control, reliable predictions can be made about the future outcomes of the process; otherwise, any predictions are pure conjecture and made without knowledge. While even predictions based on statistical control cannot be definite (considering Murphy's Law), they can be made with confidence based on the known capability of the system.[6]

If the outcomes of a process are in statistical control, then control limits for the process may be placed at plus or minus 3 sigma (a measure of the dispersion of the data, for example, an estimate of the standard deviation) of the mean.[7] It is not absolutely necessary that the distribution be Gaussian; in all likelihood it will not, but this is not a cause for alarm. More important than testing the distribution to see how well it fits the normal curve is analyzing the data to find if it is useful for prediction.[8] Applying the 3-sigma limits to a run chart produces a control chart that shows graphically whether a process is in statistical control. Figure A.4 shows a control chart based on the attributes data plotted in Figure A.3.

As seen in Figure A.4, all the data points are between the control limits and appear to be randomly distributed, forming a system that is in statistical control. Such a system may be expected to remain in control until it is acted on by some outside factor. This points out a previously mentioned concept developed by Shewhart, that of common versus special causes of variation. Common causes of variation are those subtle differences between process runs that result in variation within the statistical limits. Special causes, however, result in aberrations such as points outside the limits, or continuous runs above or below the mean or in a particular direction. The task of management is to identify special causes of process variation when they occur—correcting them if they are bad or learning more about them if they are good—and to shrink the overall variation in the process.

Two parts of the control chart shown in Figure A.4 are of particular interest, but not for the reasons you might think: the point nearest the upper control limit and the series of six points at the right that are all above the mean. First, the single point near the upper control limit is *not* an anomaly. Many "single data point managers" would become alarmed at this point that is so far above the others, but their concern would be unwarranted.[9]

The point is within the control limits and is within the capabilities of the process. If the point had been outside the control limits, it should have piqued the interest of the workers and managers, because it would be assumed that some special cause entered the process at that time to produce the outcome outside the statistical limits.

Second, the run of six consecutive values above the mean

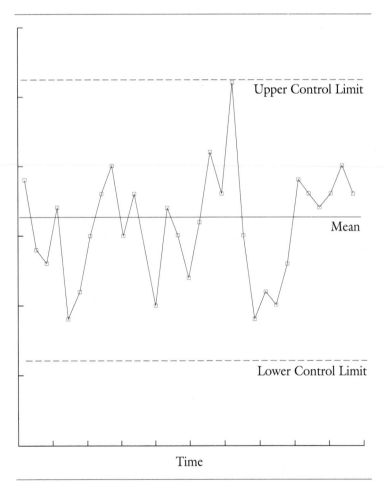

Figure A.4 Control Chart
Plotted using the data from Figure A.3.

$$\begin{matrix} \text{UCL} \\ \text{LCL} \end{matrix} = n\bar{p} \pm 3 \sqrt{n\bar{p}\,(1-\bar{p})}$$

may also be mistakenly attributed to a special cause. Six points all above (or below) the mean, or marching in the same direction, may not indicate a special cause. If the system is still in control, the next value will probably fall on the other side of the mean or in the opposite direction. If, however, seven or more consecutive values fall on the same side of the mean, or in the same direction, this may indicate that some special cause has thrown the process off. There are more indicators of special causes outlined in the *Statistical Quality Control Handbook* published by AT&T.[10] Once a special cause is indicated by the chart, it must be identified and corrected if management wants to return the process to its original capability or continue to improve it.

The control chart is a marvelous tool, but it is not perfect. The chart cannot guarantee that any point represents a special or common cause; a point outside the control limits may be due to a common cause, and a point inside the result of a special cause. Dr. Shewhart designed the chart as a management tool to reduce tampering and the losses from acting on one type of cause as if it were the other.[11]

ع‌ا

In discussing control charts and the concept of statistical control, a few words must be said about the difference between enumerative and analytic studies. Enumerative studies count items or evaluate things; most educational statistics are based on enumerative studies.[12] Examples of enumerative studies in education are estimates of the number of nongraduates in an area and results from standardized tests. Analytic studies, however, are made to discover causes behind phenomena; instead of counting the number of nongraduates in an area, an analytic study would try to discern why there were so many (or so few).[13]

Testing and grading in school are enumerative, not analytic. Their purpose is to find out how many questions a student answered incorrectly, not why the student missed the questions. In enumerative studies, action is taken on the frame that defines the study: a student passes or fails the test. Analytic studies, on the other hand, provide a basis for action on the cause system. Information from such a study would be used to modify the teaching and learning process to produce more desirable results in the future.[14] Educators must learn the difference between enumerative and analytic studies to complete the education transformation.

કàત

Run charts and control charts are particularly powerful tools and may be used in many ways to better understand the processes of education. Tracking things over time provides much more information than relying on a few discrete data points, as pointed out previously. Run charts can track absenteeism, classroom interruptions, effective teaching time, student time-on-task, and expenditures for services, materials, and maintenance. At Mount Edgecumbe High School, students used run charts to keep track of and improve their study habits (they were surprised to find that they did not study as much as they claimed).[15]

Much damage may be done if the training of teachers and administrators is not conducted by persons familiar with statistical theory. Statistical studies performed by laypersons without the guidance of competent statisticians usually produce results that are questionable at best.[16] Leaders of the transformation are advised to secure the services of an expert in statistics when the quality improvement efforts begin.

In the classroom, run charts may be used to track student performance only in certain situations. Recall that run charts are continuous plots of measurement against time: what is being measured? If students are expected only to learn discrete items such as the name of the sixteenth president or basic multiplication skills (that is, only knowledge-level learning is desired), evaluation of their progress and mastery could entail collection of measurements that would be suited to a run chart (recognizing that other immeasurable quantities, such as motivation, boredom, personal problems, and illness are included in every measured value). This is the main difference between points 6 and 13 of Deming's 14 Points. Point 6 refers to the learning of skills (the cognitive equivalent of knowledge-level learning), while point 13 refers to comprehension-level learning. The first is amenable to evaluation by statistical methods; the second is not.

Once enough data about a student's acquisition of knowledge-level material or a certain skill are gathered, control limits may be plotted to determine if the processes are in statistical control.[17] If the measurements turn out to be in control, reasonable predictions of future performance can be made and aberrations can be more easily discovered; if not, steps may be taken to get the processes under control. Comprehension and application of concepts, however, cannot be discretely measured and so do not lend themselves to statistical analysis. Any measurement would assume that the issues and concepts involved concrete, black-and-white questions and answers. Typically, higher cognitive levels of learning do not have clearly right and wrong answers; students are learning to think beyond what the teacher has presented, addressing and solving new problems. In these cases, the student's approach to the problem and what she gets out of it are more important than categorizing her answers as right or wrong.

In cases where it is applicable, the use of run and control charts in classroom evaluation may prove helpful. Subjects such as basic mathematics (that is, mathematics skills rather than theory) and spelling seem open to evaluation by statistical control. If criterion-referenced testing is used in these subjects, the percentage of errors may be a good indicator of whether the student has mastered the subject matter.

Given the application is appropriate and enough measurements made to plot a chart, some useful information may be generated. If the process measurements are reasonable indicators of student cognition, and they demonstrate statistical control as evidenced by the control chart, it may be said that he has mastered the subject matter and is ready to move on. If one or two points come close to the control limits but are still within them, neither he nor his teacher should panic; the student's performance is still under control.

If a trend is evident on the chart, it may indicate either that the student is moving up the learning curve (that is, getting better at applying the skills) or that her performance is getting worse. In the former case, the student has not reached a level of mastery; in the latter, it may be safe to assume that some factor is causing the change. She may have missed a key concept, or require glasses, or be going through a personal crisis that is affecting her ability to concentrate. The data will point to the time when the problem began, giving the teacher a good starting point for uncovering the cause. With the chart in hand, the teacher may approach the 205 situation confident that a problem exists; without the data, any such conclusion would be pure conjecture.

The quick answer to this charge is, "Of course such a downward trend would be noticed." How? With the benefit of hindsight, we see that the records are full of cases where trends were apparent after some tragedy, such as an attempted suicide.

What about a student for whom the process measurements are in control, but his learning does not seem to be acceptable for promotion to the next class? Here may be a case where the student has a special need, or simply learns some material more slowly than others, or learns best in a different way. The nature of systems in statistical control is that they remain in control until something changes in the system. The change may come from outside or inside the system, and it throws the system out of control. What his teacher must do is investigate what will enhance his learning and change the learning system (see Figure 6.1) to fit his needs. (This concept will be useful in discussing "gifted and talented" programs in Appendix C.)

Another situation involves systems in chaos. If the process measurements show no statistical control, no reasonable predictions can be made of the future process results. The system must be brought into statistical control; the manager's (teacher's) job is to do so. How? By studying the process and developing a theory of the causes of the system's wild performance, then systematically working to bring stability to the process. Guidance from an expert statistician is invaluable in all these cases.

છ

Several times I have mentioned the need for enough data. Meaningful charts of process measurements cannot be plotted if they are only taken once or twice in a given time period. Using our earlier example of learning simple mathematical skills, if measurements were only made two or three times in a semester we could not expect to build a meaningful chart; yet often the number of evaluations is quite low. Teachers may choose, of course, to use homework assignments, pop quizzes, and many other measures to gauge mastery, but there must be enough data to plot. A wealth of information may be gleaned from properly plotted run and control charts, information that would be lost without them. How many students might have been saved from suicide or other destructive behavior if a teacher had noticed a measurement going out of control and investigated the situation?

What feedback may be given to a student from these data? Obviously, if the "graded" work is given back to the students, they will almost immediately compare their grades. This is exactly the situation we want to avoid (see Chapter 4). Especially in the early days of the transformation, students who are used to the external motivators of grades will feel the need to know (immediately) how they are doing. One possible solution is simply to withhold information until a trend is established, then to explain what the chart indicates about their learning or their study habits. This would allow teachers to more closely tailor their approaches to their students' needs, and a chart that shows good control or improvement should add to students' self-esteem. [One undesirable (but widely practiced) feedback technique should be particularly avoided: explaining the performance of the class as a whole (the average, the questions missed most, and so on). This almost inevitably disintegrates into comparisons and competition between students.]

&. &.

I have been lucky enough to teach mostly small, comprehension- or application-level classes. My students write papers and take essay and short-answer quizzes, or they demonstrate the skills they have learned. In the former, because of the open-ended nature of the material, I simply cannot mark any answer completely wrong. Instead I write comments that challenge my students to think about their answers in more depth or indicate whether they need more study or personal consultation on a concept. I admit that in the beginning they are surprised to receive papers that do not have discrete letter or number grades on them. (In the latter, the students are usually well aware when they have mastered the skills.)

&. &.

Two additional points need to be made. First, measuring anything is a tricky business, especially measuring student mastery. Nothing that is measured has a true value; the only meaning of a measured value is given by the operational definition of how it is measured.[18] Unless teacher and student agree on the operational definition, there will be difficulty; this may be reduced (but not entirely alleviated) by setting clear, measurable objectives and using criterion-referenced evaluations of student performance.[19] Second (and as mentioned earlier), if a student's performance is chaotic, that is, evaluation of his skills mastery shows no control and no trends, steps must be taken to bring his performance into control before any further assessment can be made. The student may have a learning disability, or require glasses, or not be ready for the course material. Management and guidance of this student is completely different from a student whose performance exhibits control,[20] because the student's future performance cannot be predicted with any confidence. The teacher cannot recommend that the student be advanced to the next class and cannot gauge her own teaching effectiveness if the student's performance is not consistent.

Scatter diagrams. These diagrams simply plot two variables against one another. When the variables are carefully chosen to represent factors that may be related to one another, these diagrams are useful in visualizing the relationship between them.[21] Note the three different scatter diagrams in Figure A.5. The first indicates near complete variability; no predictions are possible about the variable Y given any value of X. The second and third indicate that the two variables are linearly related; positively in the second and negatively in the third.

Scatter diagrams, then, can be helpful in visualizing educational correlations. There may be a correlation between the percentage of questions a student misses and the number of questions on the test: some students cannot take long tests. (Consider the implications of this in taking standardized tests like the SAT.) There may be a correlation between the number of administrative interruptions and the age or experience level of the teacher: young or novice teachers may be saddled with more extra duties, a decided disadvantage at a time when they should be learning all they can about teaching. There may be a correlation between absenteeism and student age, or classes taken, or extracurriculars. Without the data, no correlations will be found; however, extreme caution must be taken to avoid discovering a

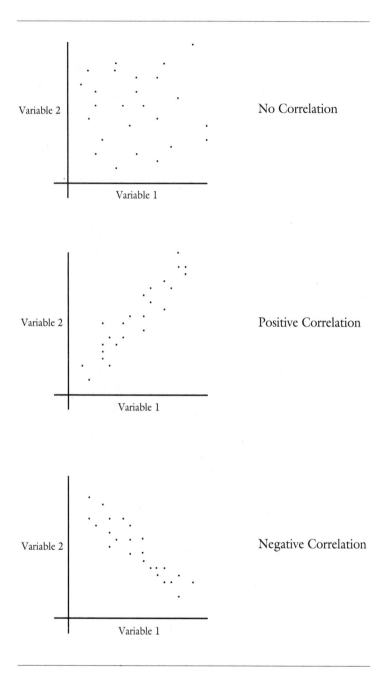

Figure A.5 Scatter Diagram Examples

correlation where none exists, like between vandalism and school board voter turnout.[22]

Histograms and Pareto diagrams. Histograms are plots of the frequency with which measured values occur. Especially if large numbers of samples are taken, it may be cumbersome to show all of the data on a chart (though this may be taken care of by use of an $\bar{x}$-R chart when measuring variables).[23] The histogram makes the presentation of data easier by breaking the data down into discrete ranges. Once the ranges have been determined, the frequency—the number of times or the percentage of the time that a value falls in the range—is plotted. When the frequencies are plotted as bar charts they can give an indication of the type of distribution of the variable. Deming points out that care must be used in analyzing histograms: the order in which the data were taken may be important and cannot be shown on a histogram.[24] Figure A.6 shows an example of a histogram.

Pareto diagrams take the frequency information that might be arranged in a histogram and arrange it in order of decreasing frequency. The Pareto principle (sometimes known as the Juran principle)[25] states that a "vital few" of the variables are responsible for most of the responses; most of us are familiar with this as the *20–80* rule (20 percent of the people do 80 percent of the work). Table A.1 is a hypothetical record of injuries sustained by an organization's workforce in a year; in Figure A.7 the frequencies of the

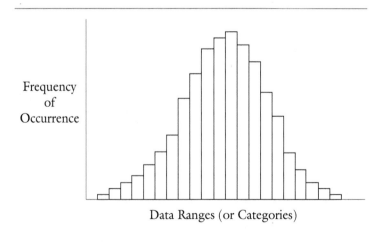

Data Ranges (or Categories)

Figure A.6 Histogram Example

injuries are shown on a Pareto diagram. Here the vital few defect types that occurred most frequently are readily visible.

It is easy to see how these two tools may be used in managing the educational process, histograms to visualize distributions and Pareto diagrams to easily identify and communicate the vital few. Recall that a Pareto diagram was used in Chapter 3 to identify the customers of education; they have many more possible uses in schools and school boards. Reasons for absences, student involvement in extracurricular activities, disciplinary problems, school and community demographics, and destinations of graduates are only a few possible applications.

Many more analytical and decision-making tools are available for adaptation to education. Techniques such as force-field analysis, breakthrough planning, nominal group technique, brainstorming, and others all have applicability to educational improvement. My purpose, however, was not to exhaust the possibilities but to introduce a few basic tools. You are encouraged to explore other options that may benefit you in transforming your school.

A final caution: While quality improvement tools have definite applications in education, they cannot be allowed to become ends in themselves. You are cautioned against applying these tools and techniques before understanding and accepting the philosophy behind them. A comprehensive effort to improve quality in every

Table A.1 Hypothetical Injury Record

Injury Type	Number	Percentage	Cumulative Percentage
Hand/Wrist	17	48.57	48.57
Back	8	22.86	71.43
Head/Neck	3	8.57	80.00
Foot/Ankle	3	8.57	88.57
Leg/Knee	2	5.71	94.28
Eye	1	2.86	97.14
Arm/Elbow	1	2.86	100.00
Total	*35*	*100.00*	

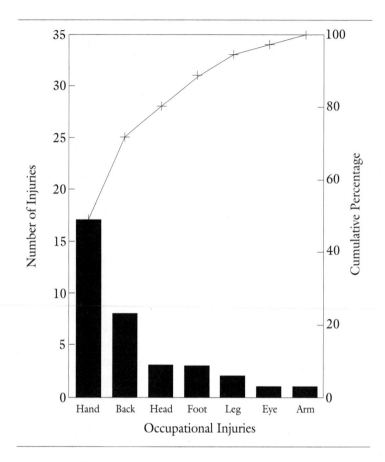

Figure A.7   Pareto Diagram Example
Displays the "vital few" injury types,
where the greatest gains may be made.

aspect of education, that is, a change in the educational culture, must be the first priority.

AN EDUCATION PRIMER— A QUALITY SHIFT?

In considering how quality relates to education, it may be helpful to examine briefly how we got where we are in education. By developing a thorough understanding of the problem, alternative solutions may be explored; in addition, cogent commentary on current U.S. education virtually requires that we understand how it came to be.

Understand that we look at education through the eyes of history to comprehend its problems more fully, not to examine causes and place blame for the problems. Doubtless some causes may be uncovered, but the only value in identifying them is to understand their application in the present and predict their impact on the future. George Santayana said, "Those who forget the past are condemned to repeat it," but to this we now add a corollary: those who glorify the past are condemned to live in it forever.

ৰ

From the time of the earliest colonies, education in America has reflected the communities it served. Colonies in the New World were widely separated from each other, often ideologically as well as geographically. From Puritan New England to Quaker Pennsylvania to planter Virginia, each different colonial society built the educational system that served its needs best, but the first settlers were forced to pay more attention to the hard work of meeting their daily needs than to setting up educational institutions. The realities of colonial life required the participation of all members of the colony in the basic work of survival; because the early colonies were largely agrarian, children were enlisted to help with everything from husbandry to harvesting. As settlements gradually became more stable, however, the education of youth became an important issue, especially in New England.

The strict Puritan emphasis on the Bible virtually guaranteed that schools would develop to teach citizens how to read; unless they knew what was in the Bible, they could not be expected to live by it. As early as 1642 the Massachusetts Bay Colony passed a law requiring the leaders of each community to make certain that children learned to read and write; the law was upheld by the colony's general court five years later.[1] Education in New England was deliberately structured to take advantage of, and to instill, the values of Puritan society. This is an important lesson of early education.

Outside New England education was less systematic. The plantations of the South were vast and widely spaced, and southern cities were not as rich or densely populated as cities in the North. Schools could not be supported by the populace, and many wealthy landowners in Virginia and Carolina chose to send their children to boarding school in England. In Britain they learned to be proper gentlemen and ladies, building the sense of gentility that pervades Southern society even today.[2] In contrast, the Quakers in Pennsylvania and New Jersey, an eminently practical people, relied on the experience of living and working in their own towns and shops to educate their children.[3] Their emphasis on experience over formal instruction would eventually return to

214 U.S. education early in the twentieth century.

The Puritan emphasis on education had a far more wide-reaching influence on the development of early American education than any other group's. Their education did not focus on producing gentility or an aristocratic class, nor did it neglect formal training in favor of glorified experience. It simply produced good citizens, a purpose that would stay affixed to public education years later.[4]

ê

For all of the effort put into New England elementary education, often it was not enough to secure the opportunities of the New World for its citizens. The city populations supported a large number of free-enterprise specialty schools or "private venture schools." These taught subjects such as applied mathematics to students going into particular fields, such as bookkeeping, navigation, banking, or trading.[5] Many young people also learned trades through apprenticeships, which combined instruction in reading, writing, and arithmetic (the Three R's) with the specific skills of the chosen trade. The specialty schools may be thought of as equivalent in spirit to today's technical colleges and apprenticeships as akin to modern vocational education.

The early American school system was generally poorly defined; education was sporadic. In some areas, especially those served by district schools, classes might not be convened for an entire year. Even when in session the school year was often very short, and teachers may have had no credentials or experience. In short, according to educational historian Robert L. Church, "the course of study was so unorganized, teachers so poorly trained, and schoolhouses so primitive that it was difficult to find a course of study to guide."[6] These humble beginnings, however, laid the foundation for the universal education to come.

In the wake of the Revolution, the former colonies prepared their new government under the Articles of Confederation. The Articles did not mention education at all, differentiating the American Revolution from other revolutions in which the reconstruction of education was a major factor in preserving revolutionary ideals.[7] Intellectual pursuits under the Articles did not cease altogether, however; as reported by Edmund S. Morgan, "There was an astonishing production of historical writing, verse, painting,

215

and even schoolbooks dedicated to magnifying America. New scientific societies were begun....The Americans were already embarked on their tireless...campaign to improve themselves and the world."[8]

After the political debacle of the Articles of Confederation, the Constitution of the United States was written and adopted, but like its predecessor it lacked any article about, section on, or indeed any mention of education. It was generally left up to the states to provide education for their citizens through the provision of the Tenth Amendment. Throughout the early national period many comprehensive educational plans for the country were prepared, but none were adopted.[9] Congress' lack of foresight, in not giving some national structure to education in this country, would plague efforts to provide equity in education later.

ၨ

The Industrial Revolution hit the United States early in the textiles industry; out of textiles and other, later industries, a true working class evolved. Improvements in transportation, starting with the steamboat and continuing through the railroad era, brought the nation closer together. Besides making the nation more homogeneous, improved transportation and growing industrialization gave workers new opportunities by increasing the amount and types of work available. A national plan of education might have helped workers make easier transitions to new job opportunities by giving them the most transferable skill: the ability to learn effectively. According to historian Daniel J. Boorstin, "As the machinery of production became larger, more complicated, more tightly integrated, more expensive, and more rigid, working men were expected to be more alert and more teachable. Open minds were more valuable than trained hands."[10] A national education system stressing the acquisition of learning skills, however, did not exist (and has yet to be created).

Industrialization pulled workers together into densely populated urban centers, but another force conspired against homogeneity in this country. The vast numbers of immigrants who provided the labor pool for industrial expansion certainly learned English and worked hard to realize their dreams of freedom and prosperity, but they remained culturally aloof, clinging to the traditions they had brought with them. They settled in distinct areas, where each group preserved their national or racial heritage and avoided contact with, and understanding of, each other's. U.S. cities were incredibly varied; the country was not a melting pot, but a cornucopia.[11]

Despite conflicting influences toward homogeneity and pluralism, education did not languish during the late eighteenth and early nineteenth centuries. During this period, the most important educational institutions were the academies. Mostly private, the academies were favored by students who needed education beyond elementary school but would not be attending the universities; these young people did not require the strictly intellectual education offered by the college preparatory schools of the day.[12] Part of the success of the academies may have been due to the decrepit condition of the public schools (or district schools) of the time. Education reformer Horace Mann wrote in 1842 of the disparity between the way children were packed into tiny schoolhouses while farmer's hogs enjoyed neat, spacious barns. Six years later it was reported that only a little over half of the schoolhouses in Connecticut had outhouses, while of the remainder over 40 percent had no facilities whatsoever.[13] With these revelations the *common school* movement begun in the 1830s gained momentum.

The common school movement's goals were simple. First, common schools would provide free (that is, not supported by direct payment but rather by general levy) elementary education, though such education was reserved for only white children. Second, it would focus effort on training professional teachers; third, it would bring local schools under state control. Church suggests that the movement "is better understood as a means of raising attendance at elementary schools so that those common schools could achieve their major goals of teaching common values to all children," rather than simply a drive to create free schools; the "common values" would support and improve the economy by creating more cooperative industrial workers.[14] Little was done to answer the most vehement complaints and improve the general condition of the schools' physical plants, but the government- and teacher-led campaign eventually succeeded in establishing free and public schools to replace the academies. The new public education system maintained its reliance on local control (albeit local governmental rather than parental control), while at the same time other nations made moves toward centralizing their education systems.[15]

The nineteenth century saw another educational innovation besides the common school movement. The growing sentiment that working class people should have better educational opportunities led to a public forum in which ideas could be freely exchanged and to which anyone was welcome: the lyceum. Local lyceums sponsored lectures on a wide variety of subjects and brought in speakers from many parts of the country. Ralph Waldo Emerson, for example, was a popular lyceum lecturer.[16]

Despite the new interest in and support of public education, it was a long time before education for all segments of the populace became the rule rather than the exception. Late in the nineteenth century the National Commission on Education formed a committee (known as the Committee of Ten) which proposed a curriculum that would afford equitable educational opportunities for everyone.[17] Women and minorities, however, were still left out of, or forgotten by, the education system (despite the fact that women's educational opportunities, especially as regards higher education, were much improved over colonial times[18]). In the South particularly, blacks were left out of public education for many years, and even those schools they attended did not provide adequate facilities and equipment.[19] The result of this educational neglect was noted by Boorstin: "While there are no reliable statistics, we have reason to believe that illiteracy in the South was more widespread than elsewhere in the nation: the great majority of Negroes were illiterate, and so were a far larger proportion of the whites than in the North."[20]

❧

Early in this century U.S. secondary educational institutions were almost completely reorganized. The junior high school was introduced as a transition between elementary and high school. As the high school matured, it became the middle ground in education and almost reached the status of a college for the masses.[21] This reorganization was the final step in the movement of education from private to public control or, to use a less favorable phrase, the socialization of education.[22]

As the high school's appeal became more universal, its focus shifted away from education in the intellectual sense toward social utility; high school educators shifted their allegiance from colleges and universities to common schools.[23] In 1918 the National Education Association (NEA) stated the *Cardinal Principles* for the high school, given here in alphabetical order: Citizenship, Command of fundamental processes, Ethical character, Health, Vocation, Worthy home-membership, and Worthy use of leisure. Of these objectives only "command of fundamental processes" was directly related to intellectual development, and was itself a last-minute addition to the list.[24]

One can only conclude from our present educational state that many schools have failed miserably on every count. Our voting population has not increased with universal education. Our nation is plagued with a vast number of citizens who are illiterate and innumerate.[25] Our schools are showplaces for all of the crimes and depravity of our nation at large. We are increasingly health conscious, but mass media probably influenced this as much or more than education. Many of our graduates must be remedially trained by their employers. Divorce rates and instances of cruelty to children and spouses are staggering. The last principle, taking it to include healthy leisure activities, may be said to have succeeded; but as mentioned earlier, the media has had as much if not more influence in this area as the schools.

The NEA's principles differed markedly from the recommendations of the Committee of Ten.[26] The earlier committee recommended that schools should not distinguish between college-bound students and those who would end their education at the high school level. Instead of providing intellectual stimulation for only a few students, they concluded, all should take the same courses throughout high school.[27] The new principles, however, encouraged separate education for those who would continue their education and those who would end their school careers after high school. The new principles geared education toward socialization, rather than education, of the vast majority of students.

The fact that most of the Cardinal Principles dealt with social rather than purely intellectual issues is traceable to the "progressive" or "new" education, one of the educational developments of the early twentieth century. Basing their approach primarily on the writings of educational philosopher John

Dewey—whose ideas came largely from the French philosopher Rousseau—proponents of this new educational format rejected many of the traditional and authoritarian aspects of the school. Books, structured classes, and grades were set aside in favor of learning by experience, a throwback to the Quakers.[28]

Though he did advocate nontraditional educational methods, Dewey's premise was not that the school should be thought of merely as preparatory for future life. He thought it should instead be immersed in the realities of living, that the school should mirror as closely as possible the vagaries of life outside its walls, instead of being a cloister where the theory of life was taught without reference to the practice of living. Most of the progressivists had missed the subtlety of this premise or neglected it entirely.[29] This idea of school as a looking glass into society is entirely different from the concept of the school as a die through which students are pressed into conformance with society. Dewey saw the school as an invaluable aid in the reform of society, and education as one tool with which to build the most desirable social structure; but the adoption of the NEA's objectives twisted Dewey's purpose for the school into one of adapting or fitting students into society's mold based on someone's idea of what society should be, instead of enabling students to learn enough about society and social structures to build the society they need.[30]

❧

The post-World War II era portended some definite changes for the country's society. Compulsory education laws had been extended and tightened in the 1930s, and most young people were already attending school. As the returning soldiers populated factories and took workplace opportunities from other young people, school was seen as more and more necessary in order to gain competitive advantage. Young people who 20 years earlier would have already joined the workforce were remaining students, and a new class of U.S. citizen came into being: the teenager.

It took some time for teenagers to become recognized as a distinct group; caught between adolescence and adulthood, they struggled for their place in society.[31] By the 1950s it was evident that teenagers were developing a culture all their own. The country's standard of living continued to rise, and teenagers became avid consumers of material goods their parents had never known. Their music was new and different and in years to come would continue to confound and confuse adults. As other media, especially television, increased in importance and influence, they discovered access to wider varieties of information in less depth than any generation before them.[32] Few educators and professionals recognized the unique factors affecting, and special needs of, this new cultural segment. Before they became a separate cultural group, teenagers had been indoctrinated into society and availed themselves of all society had to offer; now they were forced to wait until they graduated from high school or college before they joined the social order.[33] Few foresaw that the unintentional alienation of this age group through sequestration in schools would lead to their rejection of the social elements regarded as important or fundamental by adults.[34]

The most obvious and disturbing manifestation of teenage and young adult alienation was the campus radicalism of the late 1960s. From the beginnings of student activism at the University of California at Berkeley to campus protests at Columbia, the University of Chicago, Harvard, and Cornell, campus activism found students protesting against perceived injustices and fighting for idealistic causes. Of itself, this was not much of a problem. The disturbing trend lay in the dissolution of campus activism into radicalism in which students seized university buildings, disrupted classes, and tried to hide willful destruction of property and other, more serious offenses behind the academic spirit of nonattribution found on the college campuses. The tragic events at Kent State, where four students were killed, and Jackson State College, where two students were killed, only showed that radical behavior is often met with equally radical behavior.[35]

While those events were widely covered by the media, the number of campus radicals who killed themselves making pipe bombs and other explosives almost escaped notice. Indeed, a few weeks *before* the fatal protest at Kent State, three leaders of a leftist student organization "died while making bombs in a luxurious Greenwich Village townhouse."[36] The nagging question behind these particular untimely deaths is: what might those bright young people have accomplished if they had lived? What reforms might they have fostered if they had treated their own lives with less contempt than they treated society in general?

&

Most recently, comparative research has revealed shocking disparities between educational accomplishments in the United States and other industrialized nations. In international comparisons produced in the mid 1970s, U.S. students were never first or second on any of the 19 tests administered; they were last 7 out of 19 times.[37]

Such comparisons are quickly used by enthusiastic reporters, but must be taken with a very large proverbial grain of salt. A serious problem with all such comparisons is the difficulty of specific tests to reliably compare different national groups.[38] Another is the problem of scope, especially of high school comparisons, since many countries weed out high school candidates with comprehensive examinations, accepting only the best students into academic programs.[39]

In response to many of these reports, reform movements have been moving across the United States for the last two decades. Individual states have analyzed their educational problems and implemented efforts to solve the problems. The results have been mixed.

In the 1984 report *The Nation Responds,* the reform efforts of the 50 states and the District of Columbia were presented. At the time, states were either considering or implementing new requirements for high school graduation, improved textbooks and educational materials, different school day and school year lengths, and various professional development programs for teachers.[40]

A private attempt at educational reform, developed by the American Society for Quality Control, started in 1988 with a two-year pilot program. With the koala bear as a mascot, the "Koalaty Kids" program emphasized reading and self-worth, provided a platform for improvement in other areas of school life, and encouraged increased parental and community involvement.[41] While its intentions are good, the program in practice heavily stresses the use of prizes and other rewards for student performance. This reliance on external motivators in such a classic behaviorist fashion can stifle the children's internal motivation (see Chapters 2 and 3). When the pilot program was evaluated in 222   1990, reported results were generally favorable, but several schools dropped out because of the cost of the prizes demanded by the program.[42]

Some schools around the nation have incorporated ideas from the quality philosophy in attempts to improve the education they provide. Partnerships have formed between schools and industries, and some entire communities are working on transforming the way they do business in every sector of community life.[43] Examples of schools adopting quality and participating in the transformation have appeared throughout this book. Perhaps the most remarkable success among schools applying quality improvement is Mount Edgecumbe High School in Sitka, Alaska, which has been using Deming's methods since 1988.[44]

❧

In the final analysis, the U.S. education system may not be in as dire straits as one could infer from recent research and comparisons, especially higher education. The United States continues to attract undergraduate and graduate students from all parts of the world.[45] Graduates of our nation's institutions, while perhaps not as technically competent as graduates of other nations, may find themselves better able to innovate and adapt to new situations because of the inherent flexibility of our higher education curricula. Some research also suggests that the U.S. education system serves the aggregate talent of the nation more effectively than its foreign counterparts.[46]

But in spite of the favorable position of our higher education and the successes of local reforms, the implications of our total educational decline cannot be denied. Already 27 million citizens over 17 years old are functionally illiterate; another 45 million are only marginally literate. Estimates put the fraction of functional illiterates in the workplace at as much as 75 percent of the workforce. (The extent of illiteracy was brought home to me several years ago when I was asked to write down a telephone message for a coworker who had never learned to read and could only write his name. Perhaps saddest of all, he had no desire to learn.) The problem is not getting any better: the Census Bureau estimates that as much as 70 percent of the total U.S. population in the year 2000 will be functionally illiterate if current trends continue.[47]

According to Commerce Department estimates, over 240 billion dollars are lost per year in lost taxes, increased public expenditure for assistance, and other expenses as a result of the number of high school dropouts—whom I prefer to call nongraduates—in this country.[48] Add to this the cost of remedial training programs, the costs of industrial problems caused by workers who cannot learn their jobs, the costs associated with increased accidents because workers cannot read or understand simple health and safety guidelines, and the overall burden on industry and government becomes enormous. I was faced with the onerous task of alleviating one of these burdens by training employees on workplace hazards and safety procedures; some could not decipher a relatively simple Material Safety Data Sheet.

Other industrialized nations, with whom we compete in the world market, do not share this competitive disadvantage. It is not something that has been foisted upon us by our competitors; we saddled ourselves with it voluntarily, in what the National Commission on Excellence in Education called "an act of unthinking, unilateral educational disarmament."[49] My premise throughout this book has been that improved quality in education, by improving graduates' academic skills and ability to learn, will provide industry with workers who can be trained for highly technical jobs without having to go through remedial education, and who can continue to learn and grow as time goes on. In addition, the quality transformation in education will result in more students graduating, and their improved abilities and subsequently improved opportunities will enable them to capitalize on opportunities in the job market and break into the world of industry and trade, greatly enhancing their economic status and improving the entire nation's economy and self-image.

THE DIFFICULTY OF VALUES

Value-added (see Chapter 3) is not the same as values. A complete education must at some point explore societal values in order for the student to adequately address concepts of good and evil, right and wrong, justice and injustice. Apart from the values expressed in the Declaration of Independence and the Constitution—which are often misinterpreted and poorly addressed—values education has been woefully neglected in the United States.[1]

Some might argue that this is proper, that values are more appropriately addressed in other forums such as the family, but the inculcation of the values and norms of society is one of the primary purposes of education. Some have argued the opposite—that instruction in and adoption of values (especially Christian values) is the primary purpose of education, the sole reason for the existence of the school.[2] Most of us presumably stand in the middle, recognizing the need for shared responsibility in values instruction.

Values form the foundation of society and the basis for norms of behavior in all sorts of groups. In developing values in young people, society builds an ideological base upon which the society itself is continually built and modified. If our society is to grow and prosper, it is imperative that values be addressed in education.

Despite their importance, values instruction cannot be the primary emphasis of education. Education should prepare the student for future endeavors through the acquisition of skills, knowledge, and values that are either immediately useful or form the basis for acquiring further knowledge and specialized training. Values education forms an integral part of student preparation; without it, students have no hope of making rational decisions that will positively affect their lives, because values allow such decisions to be made with respect to their perceived outcomes. As stated by philosopher C. I. Lewis, "To be rational, rather than foolish or perverse, means to be capable of constraint by prevision of some future good or ill; to be amenable to the consideration, 'You will be sorry if you don't,' or 'if you do.'"[3]

INESCAPABLE VALUES

The education of young people to take their places in society must include values if society is to prosper and continue. This does not imply that instruction in values is completely absent from our national life. Values education occurs in families, in religious teaching, and in community activities, where either explicitly or implicitly the values of the group are passed on to young people. The values of the nation as a whole, however, are passed on through the schools, which "are the prime instruments for providing our citizens with the common concepts, values, and skills essential for the survival and progress of our democratic society."[4] Professor James Q. Wilson has pointed out that accomplishing effective values education in the United States can be extremely difficult, because "the political constraints on public schools . . . inhibit them from creating the proper ethos [for character development] except where extraordinary principals manage to overcome these constraints."[5]

༄

At the risk of stating a generalization, family and community values generally match the values of the nation as a whole (see *Values for Our Nation*, page 231); they may, however, place greater or lesser emphasis on certain items. A set of national values, however, has been neglected in the same way that a national educational purpose has been neglected. Local control is favored. We must realize that perpetuation of strictly local cultures and values is dangerous for our pluralistic nation's strength, in the same way that fragmentation of our people into separate language groups is dangerous for our nation's unity. This does not belittle local or ethnic culture, but the public education system is not the forum for teaching particular subcultural elements; rather, it must stress subcultural friendliness by teaching tolerance of different peoples through understanding of their history and values. Strictly ethnic elements should remain the responsibility of family and community, not the public school system.

Public education must not, by any means, be used to perpetuate dominance by any cultural group; instead, it must assure that values compatible with the totality of our national ideals are taught. To accomplish this, values education must be a part of the education curriculum; in fact it was demanded in many previous education reform movements by both reformers and employers.[6] And values education does occur in the school system, though educators are quick to deny the presence of any particular value system in their teaching. Theodore R. Sizer points out that "most high schools' formal statements of purpose identify 'ethical conduct' and 'citizenship' as goals for their schools," but "they shy away from specific programs toward these ends or even from carefully defining the words these statements employ."[7] We are told it would be antithetical to their intellectual purity to risk advocating one set of values over another.

But education, despite its claims to the contrary, is never value-neutral.[8] The way the school is organized and operated, how standards of discipline are set and enforced, even which school activities are stressed and which are downplayed are indicative of the values of the teachers and administrators and contribute to the development of student character.[9]

The influence of teachers—and other significant adults—in shaping students' opinions and outlooks is extraordinary, even when values are not discussed outright. All teachers, no matter how well-meaning, display to their students the value system they have chosen. Subtle indicators such as the clothes they wear, the

227

car they drive, the way they talk, and the way they decorate their classroom provide insight into their personal values. More visible indicators such as their relationship to their students and the political and social causes they defend give clear testimony about their beliefs. In discussing current events and issues, whether inside or out of class, and especially in handling emotional or controversial topics, teachers' convictions are shown both in the way they approach the subject and the way they treat students who hold opposing viewpoints.

Beyond the fact that teachers' actions and words betray their own value systems is the innate impressionability of young people. Professional youth workers indicate that the majority of students make their most significant life-determining decisions between the ages of 12 and 18. These decisions, about life, careers, marriage, and faith, can be greatly influenced by significant adults in the students' lives.[10] While this makes teaching exciting, the fact that student decisions affecting their entire lives can be—and are—influenced by the adults with whom they relate carries with it a great responsibility.

Wherever they learn values, whether from home or church or school, as young people grow into adulthood they continually consider the values they have learned and relate them to their own lives. This consideration usually does not involve deep philosophical resolution of issues; it is largely emotional and pragmatic and is influenced by many pressures (for example, social, religious) on the young person. Ultimately it results in either acceptance or rejection of the value system they have learned, usually with personal modifications that suit their temperament and beliefs. At the end of the process of selection and adaptation, students are left with the values that carry them through their entire adult lives. The danger in this process is the possibility that values will be chosen without the benefit of serious study or thought.[11]

The inclusion of values in the school curriculum would provide a much-needed forum for serious considerations of values and beliefs. Analysis of values themselves must come before deeper applications of the values to ethical questions, as pointed out by Lewis:

> Questions of values, for any specific mode of valuation, are empirical questions; and the test of correctness in evaluation is to be found by some reference to experience.

> Valuation is always a matter of empirical knowledge. But what is right and what is just, can never be determined by empirical facts alone.[12]

Once students have learned how their values are formed, they may wrestle with such serious topics as prejudice, corruption, poverty, and other issues and thus gain insight into the problems of society. Such consideration and analysis may also give them the impetus to formulate solutions, fulfilling the vision of the school set forth by John Dewey. Values education would not necessarily give tacit approval to the current society, but would allow students to choose the values necessary to build the society they need to live in.

One main problem with teaching values often stems from the fear that values instruction will be more mechanical than analytical. Values instruction is not meant to *give* students particular values but to allow them to make educated value judgments. Another related fear is that values education, in a zeal to shape unbiased values in students, will destroy the students' accepted values and leave them with a void that may be filled haphazardly. This merely points out the care with which values education must be structured; while giving students tools with which to make judgments, it cannot be allowed to arbitrarily judge the values the students may have already accepted.[13]

GOOD VERSUS EVIL

The concept of good and evil and the conflict between the two have been under attack for many years. Some view the concept as antiquated and belonging to mythology, especially as regards the symbolic evil antagonist. Some believe the concept is unrealistic and does not leave room for such things as various degrees of right and wrong, and the consideration of the motives of the participants. Whatever the difficulty with good and evil, traditional ideas about them seem to have been lost in the modern world.

In his book *The Closing of the American Mind*, Allan Bloom provides a deep and masterful look at the decline of good and evil and their replacement by the tenuous "values" that are the subject of this appendix.[14] Bloom argues that the white-and-black dichotomy between good and evil has been replaced with the full spectrum of available values, values which are capable of chameleonlike shifts to blend in with the background of society.

Many people no longer recognize the importance of the struggle between good and evil, though it is a key part of many modern myths, such as the *Star Wars* and *Indiana Jones* movies. Good and evil are often caricatured in movies and other media. Many audiences automatically recognize and ally themselves with the "good guys," though the recent popularity of purely evil antiheroes has served to confuse the issue. In addition, the struggle between good and evil is often trivialized: the depths of evil and good are generally left unexplored, and the similarities between the two are rarely considered.[15]

Despite the intellectual neglect of good and evil, they are important concepts that play major roles in the development of values. Anyone who has heard a five-year-old ask of a chess board, "Who are the good guys and who are the bad guys?" knows that the struggle between good and evil, between right and wrong, strikes a fundamental chord in children. Sociologist Bruno Bettelheim has argued that good and evil are necessary elements of child behavior and play, and maintains that the outcome of the struggle—good overcoming evil—is important to children's emotional and intellectual development.[16]

Many adults would be hesitant to admit that the struggle between good and evil strikes a similar chord in them, and that the symbolism of good triumphing over evil is important to them. Few would admit that their joy over the U.S. ice hockey team's victory over the Soviet Union in the 1980 Olympics was related to the ideological struggle between the two nations: it was patriotic pride, rather than "good" capitalism winning out over "evil" communism. Few would admit to gloating over the collapse of the Berlin Wall in 1989 or the demise of the Soviet Union in 1991: it was not good being vindicated and evil beaten, it was happiness for the new freedoms of Eastern Europeans and the states of the new Commonwealth. Whether they admit it or not, for many adults the victory of good over evil is both intellectually and emotionally satisfying.

Good and evil—and especially evil—may have become cliché, but they are still powerful influences on people. Whether one believes in their literal existence or their ultimate manifestations, as motivators they deserve to be recognized, and as concepts they need to be explored. Study of historical figures who represent the two, going beyond their popular images to examine them more deeply, would give students better insight into their timeless conflict and greatly enhance students' formation of personal value systems.

VALUES FOR OUR NATION

The importance of values to the continuation and improvement of society has already been discussed. If values are to be included in education, they must either be taught as part of other courses or as separate courses or seminars of their own.[17] Treatment of values in education must include opportunities to study practical cases or apply values in real situations; this conforms to the Aristotelian ideal that moral virtue is developed through practice: "A good character comes about through regular repetition of right actions, not through moral instruction or personal discovery."[18] My experience in values seminars leads me to believe it is better to let values be addressed in all possible forums, for example, as part of history, science, literature, and other classes. What values went into making historical decisions? How does science and art reflect the values of the scientist and the artist?

Regardless of how or when values are included, it is necessary to decide what values will be stressed. Defining a set of values unique to this country is, however, a difficult task, considering the diverse nature of our nation. Currently, whatever national values are taught come from the documents that helped form the United States. The Declaration:

> We hold these truths to be self evident: that all men are created equal; that they are endowed by their creator with certain inalienable rights; that among these are life, liberty, and the pursuit of happiness; that to secure these rights, governments are instituted among men, deriving their just powers from the consent of the governed....And for the support of this declaration, with a firm reliance on the protection of divine providence, we mutually pledge to each other our lives, our fortunes, and our sacred honor.

231

and the Constitution:

> We the people of the United States, in order to form a
> more perfect union, establish justice, insure domestic
> tranquility, provide for the common defense, promote
> the general welfare, and secure the blessings of liberty to
> ourselves and our posterity, do ordain and establish this
> Constitution for the United States of America.

form the basis for not only the existence but also the beliefs of this
nation. In addition to these two, the Bill of Rights provides specific rights to individuals which the government cannot abrogate,
but which can be both misunderstood and misapplied.[19] The support and defense of these ideals requires a forum in which they
can be explored, in which understanding of their historical significance and contemporary applicability can be built.

We have established that ideals and values must be included
in the school curriculum; once included, they can be taught in
many ways. For younger students, stories in which virtues and values are displayed may be read and discussed; for older students,
analytical papers may be written about, for example, historical
treatment of the values or their relation to modern problems.[20]

What are some of these values? The value of courage and
conviction in the face of difficult circumstances or overwhelming
odds. The value of "justice for all" and of truth and honesty. The
value of freedom and the importance of tolerance and respect for
the rights and freedoms of others. The value of kindness and compassion for the less fortunate and the value of service. These values
are almost universally taught in one form or another.[21]

Some individuals and groups may question the placement
of national values over local or minority values. The concern is
legitimate and would carry more weight if the proposed national
values subverted or conflicted with the local values, but the values
just listed should not be contrary to anyone's convictions. We
emphasize national values over local values for the same reason
that earlier we emphasized national needs. Recall that this country
fought a Civil War, still the most devastating war ever waged by
Americans, because the strength of the Union was too important
to be compromised. If it is important for this nation to survive as
a cohesive unit,[22] some set of national values must be propagated.

A final reason for including values in education is that they
can directly contribute to student and school success. Students

"who believe in the value of hard work and responsibility and who attach importance to education are likely to have higher academic achievement and fewer disciplinary problems than those who do not have these ideals." These values have been shown to be far better predictors of academic achievement than the students' family or socioeconomic backgrounds.[23] While these ideals are rooted in the students' experiences with their parents, they can be reinforced and extended by quality education.

THE GIFTED AND TALENTED MYTH

Recently more and more attention has been paid to the educational requirements of "gifted and talented" students. The differences in natural abilities of students has been recognized for as long as schools have functioned, and the question of whether advanced students should receive special opportunities has been addressed many times.[1] The answer has not always been definite.

DISCOVERING GIFTS AND CULTIVATING TALENTS

The recent gifted and talented movement in education is not one in which students with special aptitudes are allowed to simply learn at a faster rate. These programs actually remove certain students from their original classrooms, place them together with other "gifted" students, and focus more attention on their efforts.[2] The students are told explicitly that they are part of the "gifted and talented" program and become increasingly aware of the differences between themselves and other students.

Experience has shown that acceleration of "gifted" students, that is, giving them more advanced subject matter faster, is   235 effective in giving them sufficient scholastic challenges; rather than being overwhelmed, they thrive academically. Typically these students remain as active in extracurriculars as they were prior to entering the special program, and often are more certain of their goals than their peers.[3] Experience with these programs has been overwhelmingly positive; recall, however, that theory of knowledge (Chapter 2) shows that experience teaches nothing without a theory or concept to explain the experience. We are exploring a new theory.

It now seems to be generally accepted that conventional schools are not capable of meeting the needs of gifted and talented students, but at what level does a student simply have a better grasp of a subject as opposed to being "gifted"? The selection of students to participate in such programs is little more than a black art.

Significant lifetime accomplishments are often less a function of pure intelligence or ability than they are of hard work. Selection of highly intelligent young people into gifted and talented programs, by focusing almost exclusively on intellectual strength, cannot guarantee the selectees' later success, and it misses many more young people who could also make contributions to our society.[4] The linking of school status with ability also contributes to the downward spiral of hopelessness in students whose desire to achieve is not matched by their natural ability.[5]

Selection of gifted and talented students rarely recognizes that student performance, like all human performance, is dynamic. It varies over time and is affected by factors, which may be outside our control as educators. Student performance by any measure, if plotted on a run chart, would not follow a straight line; students, like everyone else, have good days and bad days. Many factors (for example, how test questions are worded, too many tests in other subjects, number of papers or other assignments due, fights with parents or boyfriends or girlfriends, extracurricular commitments) can affect a student's performance. Teachers must recognize the natural variation of performance over time and not penalize students for factors beyond their control.

How does this relate to the selection of gifted and talented students? The fact that student performance varies and is influenced by so many unknown factors makes it difficult to predict how a student will perform in the future. Selection or nonselection of students for special programs is a *prediction* that they will either succeed or not, but that prediction is often made without knowledge.[6]

Assuming student populations form a system that approximates the normal distribution, then the vast majority (over 99 percent) of the students will be included within three standard deviations (3 sigma) on either side of the mean. These students form a stable system, and we cannot easily differentiate between them; that is, we cannot easily separate out individual students from the overall system of students, teachers, material, and so on. Figure D.1 illustrates such a system, where only a very few students lying outside the larger system may be identified as being truly superior. Likewise, only a few students lie outside the system on the other end and need special attention.

&. &.

ON THE LOWER END
OF THE DISTRIBUTION OF STUDENTS

The suggestion that 99 percent of the student population forms a stable performance system flies in the face of conventional educational wisdom, which holds more nearly to a figure of 68 percent, or 1 sigma on either side of the mean.[7] This puts 16 percent of the student population in the "above normal" category and relegates the bottom 16 percent to being classed as "below normal" in some manner. But is this more indicative of the students' inability to deal with the subject matter or of the educational system's inability to deal adequately with the needs of these students?

These young people are, after all, young human beings with incredible capacities to learn and grow. They should not be categorized and stigmatized simply because the system has not found a way to nurture them. If equity in education is a cause you believe in, if you recognize that all of us have untapped potential and almost limitless ability to learn,[8] you must realize that most of these students' "failures" are actually failures of the system. Until we include them in our concept of the system, we will remain unable to serve them with the opportunities they crave.

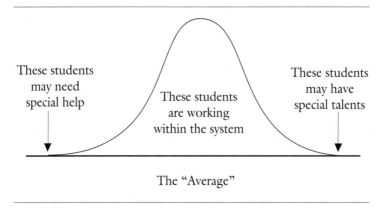

These students
may need
special help

These students
are working
within the system

These students
may have
special talents

The "Average"

Figure D.1   Distribution of Students

Our aim should be to serve all of the students in the system, not to select separate elements of the population and serve them in distinct and special ways.

Arbitrarily taking students out of the central range and labeling them "gifted" belies the fact that the system is stable, but that is precisely what school districts have been doing for a long time. Estimated numbers of gifted and talented students in the 1976–1977 school year placed the percentage of such students at between 3 and 5 percent of the school-age population.[9] [This is less than two standard deviations (2 sigma) from the mean, rather than three.]

Consider two students whose performance is similar; their mastery is almost equal according to many measures. One is selected to participate in the gifted and talented program, the other is not. Are they that much different? One is encouraged and affirmed as special, while the other's specialness is denied. What proof is there that the first is truly more gifted than the second, that the first will succeed and the second could not? What joy in learning is denied to the second student, whose self-esteem may be stricken by losing such an opportunity?

The improved performances of gifted and talented students is often cited as adequate justification for the programs. This hides the fact that the selected students are no longer working within the same system as the rest of the school population. The system within which the "gifted" student learns (consisting of such factors as increased teacher attention, improved quality of textbooks and other learning materials, and more conducive learning environment) is changed to accommodate their perceived superiority, while the system within which nonselected students learn remains the same. As pointed out in previous discussions about stable systems, the performance of a system in control will remain stable *until changes to the system are made*. Of course students placed in gifted and talented programs excel; we have built their learning systems to allow them to do so. How can we justify manufacturing a special learning system for only one segment of the school population? We have given all students the system within which they learn; they did not design or build it. We are arbitrarily denying the benefits of changes in the system to the majority of students based on incomplete knowledge of student performance and a lack of faith in student potential.

୬

The main problem with special programs for gifted and talented students is that they arbitrarily recognize the giftedness of some students and deny the giftedness of others, creating in schools what Deming calls "an artificial shortage of winners." The quality philosophy counters this by recognizing and affirming the value in each student. It recognizes that students are different, that they learn in different ways and at different speeds, but it does not penalize students for those differences.

Schools must play an active role in recognizing the talents in every student. The talents do not have to be monumental. Every art student does not have to be a Michelangelo, every chemistry student does not have to be a Priestley; as Peter Kline states in *The Everyday Genius:* "We don't need more Shakespeares, Mozarts, or Newtons, because their work is already done. We need geniuses uniquely different from them, whose work and contributions we cannot foresee."[10] Every student has some talent, some gift, that can be uncovered and developed. The result? Pride and fulfillment that will go with the student throughout life.

THE NEW ELITE?

The segregation of gifted and talented students, apart from the difficulty of identifying those students who are actually more gifted than others, may have additional interesting and detrimental consequences.

Consider the hypothetical case of a student who is sequestered from other students because she is gifted. Some students faced with such a situation will at first deny their giftedness, because they do not wish to leave their friends. If she accepts admission into the special program, the student may eventually fall away from her previous circle of friends, turning to other gifted students for affirmation. Gradually, however, the student accepts her position in the new class and recognizes the difference between the attention and encouragement she receives there than she previously did. If the increased attention she receives continues to be a motivator, or the new class sparks her internal motivation to learn, the schism between her old and new existences may deepen.

Are we in danger of creating a new elite? Certainly gifted and talented students, whose abilities are cultivated through years of special treatment and attention, can be a powerful force for advancing our knowledge. But if they find too much satisfaction in their separate status and begin to expect more from themselves and less from others, if they learn to think of themselves as superior, their knowledge and abilities may be lost to the society that created them. An intellectual elite, at best they may keep the advances they make to themselves; at worst, they may use them against the masses of people they consider intellectually inferior.

This argument against elitism was one factor that spurred this country's drive toward equal educational opportunities for all. To fulfill our democratic ideal, our institutions could neither recognize nor purposefully develop an elite; free and public education was developed in this country to guarantee that all would have access to similar learning opportunities. The difficulties of educating all members of the population, however, led to compromises that at first allowed certain students to go into academic tracks and sent others into vocational tracks (though the approach to this in the United States has not been as drastic as in other nations). These very real difficulties in providing equity in learning opportunities, rather than being catalysts for innovation in teaching and school administration, have been excuses for taking the easy way out through establishment of even more educational tracks (for example, advanced placement, honors, college preparatory, regular, vocational, and remedial), all in addition to the programs that are the subject of this appendix. The inherent problems of educating a diverse population have not disappeared and will probably never go away completely, but instead of dividing students into categories that destroy their dignity and self-esteem we must improve the education system to allow every student the opportunity to reach her potential.

PROGRAMS AND POSSIBILITIES

"Gifted and talented" programs, as they exist today, should be abolished. Even if the fear of creating an elitist minority is unfounded (and I hope it is), we cannot continue to brand the majority of our students as average and a small portion as gifted.[11] The intent was never to put down students who were not selected; the intent of grading students was never to embarrass those at the bottom. The result is the same—and trying to placate the vast majority of students who are not at the top, by telling them there is really nothing wrong with them, is certainly to damn them with faint praise.

In addition to removing strictly gifted and talented programs, the other segregations of academic level mentioned previously must also be removed. Vocational and academic tracks may still be maintained—although some educational experts have argued that vocational education should also be dropped[12]—but dividing the academic track into so many different categories is ludicrous.[13]

These changes in educational offerings and outlook, as with the other changes demanded by the quality transformation, will certainly be difficult at first; the difficulty is not reason to avoid them—it is evidence of their being worthwhile. The changes will not be impossible. They will require the cooperation and collaboration of all levels of education. For example, being able to offer a uniformly high quality education to all students at the junior high and high school level, without dividing them into arbitrary ability groups, will be incumbent upon adequately preparing them in grade school and before.

৵

It has been pointed out by educational researchers that children's school performance in the early grades is related to many things, and that socioeconomically deprived children often do not perform as well as children from more affluent backgrounds. (Recall our discussion of enumerative and analytic studies in Appendix A; what type of studies produced this information?) The Head Start program was started to help counter the adverse effects of poverty by providing special preschool educational opportunities (such as field trips) and medical and dental care for disadvantaged children. Recently it was suggested that the Head Start program should be expanded with a corps of nurses who perform routine health assessments and provide health and nutritional information for low-income families.[14] It is impossible to quantify how much each dollar spent on Head Start has saved the United States over the lives of the children served; it is also unnecessary if we recall that the most important figures are unknown and unknowable. How can we quantify the benefit, economic or otherwise, to society of a child's development into a responsible adult rather than a hoodlum?[15] Whatever the benefit, it is certainly enough to warrant continued investment in these children.

Preschool attention alone, however, will not prepare all students for junior high and high school. The grade school curriculum itself must be structured to provide not only the *skills* of reading, writing, and basic mathematics, but also the *knowledge* that goes along with the skills. Elementary school learning activities provide a foundation upon which the next six years of education are built. If grade school does not give the student an adequate frame of reference in which to place the more advanced concepts to which he will be introduced, the student will founder.[16] Those students who are well prepared in elementary school should be able to handle the uniform curriculum of junior high and high school.

To suggest that some students simply cannot handle some subjects is far too sweeping a generalization. In his 1968 book *The Learning Society*, Robert M. Hutchins wrote, "The evidence is that every child who has not sustained damage to his brain can learn the basic subjects; that all subjects can be taught at an earlier age than had been suspected; and that it can no longer be said that any member of the human race in ineducable."[17] All students are different, and the education system must recognize the differences and allow students to operate within their capabilities. This does not mean that students cannot be challenged by their subject matter, or that the subjects must be tailored to some minimum standard of performance. It may be difficult for some students to grasp some concepts, but this does not mean we should simply give up on them. In fact, emphasizing academics through advanced subject matter and good textbooks has proven effective in increasing what students learn.[18]

One way to enhance the educational experience for students who can handle the subject matter quickly is to enlist them in helping their peers. Studies have shown that when advanced students tutor other students, both the student and the tutor generally develop a better grasp of the subject. In addition, the student being tutored often has an improved attitude that can lead to further improvement.[19] Making use of students who demonstrate a keen grasp of a subject would not only improve the learning experience for other students, but would develop cooperation and teamwork skills vital to later life.[20]

To make all of this a reality, teachers must also recognize the power their perceptions of student potential have in shaping educational achievements.[21] We have pointed out before that they must recognize the differences between their students. As stated by Sizer, "None of us learns precisely as any other does, and some of us respond better to the styles of teaching familiar in schools than do others. Some learn the same amount, but more slowly; others simply learn less." He continues with a telling indictment of teacher attitudes: "For some, there are low expectations: almost inevitably they learn less."[22] When teachers believe in their students and give their students reason to believe in themselves, the educational experience will be enhanced for all concerned.

We are concerned with transforming education; in the process we have questioned many of the prevalent practices and found them lacking. The conclusion may be simply stated: The aim of *public* education in our semi-democratic society should be to recognize and develop the gifts and/or talents that *each person* possesses. The goal is not to produce uniform automatons, devoid of individuality, but to provide each student with uniformly excellent educational opportunities. The education transformation will bring us closer to reaching that aim.

NOTES

1. Observation made by Dr. Dan Brown in a lecture on educational accountability.

2. I recognize my lack of credibility with the education community; if I were a professional educator, I probably could not have proposed this shift in the educational paradigm. See Joel Arthur Barker, *Discovering the Future* (St. Paul, Minnesota: ILI Press, 1989), pp. 25–29.

3. Clarence Irving Lewis, *An Analysis of Knowledge and Valuation* (LaSalle, Illinois: The Open Court Publishing Company, 1946), p. xi.

4. Barker points out that naivete about the established rules and norms of the field is one of the characteristics of what he calls "paradigm shifters." *Discovering the Future*, p. 26.

INTRODUCTION: AN EDUCATED NATION

1. Mortimer B. Zuckerman, "Brother, Can You Spare a Dime?" *U.S. News & World Report*, 22 August 1988, p. 68.

2. National Center for Education Statistics, *The Condition of Education, Volume 1: Elementary and Secondary Education* (Washington, D.C.: U.S. Department of Education, 1988), p. 32.

3. *The Nation Responds* (Washington, D.C.: U.S. Department of Education, 1984), p. 11.

4. Referring to the six "National Goals for Education" formulated at the "education summit" in Charlottesville, Virginia. These goals will be addressed in detail in Chapter 4. See *National Goals for Education* (Washington, D.C.: Executive Office of the President, 26 February 1990).

5. Students who stop attending school may be one of the most important leads to improving education. See David T. Kearns and Denis P. Doyle, *Winning the Brain Race* (San Francisco: ICS Press, 1989), p. 3.

6. W. Edwards Deming, *Out of the Crisis* (Cambridge, Massachusetts: Massachusetts Institute of Technology Center for Advanced Engineering Study, 1986), p. 5. Dr. Deming credits Dr. Lloyd S. Nelson of the Nashua Corporation with the original observation.

7. Lewis B. Mayhew, Patrick J. Ford, and Dean L. Hubbard, *The Quest for Quality* (San Francisco: Jossey-Bass, 1990), p. 23.
This observation is similar to one Dr. Deming makes about a national referendum on quality. Who would vote against it?

8. *What Works*, 2nd ed. (Washington, D.C.: U.S. Department of Education, 1987), p. 81.

9. William W. Scherkenbach, *The Deming Route to Quality and Productivity* (Washington, D.C.: CEEPress, George Washington University, 1988), pp. 29–31. See also Deming, *Out of the Crisis*.

10. E. D. Hirsch, *Cultural Literacy* (New York: Vintage Books, 1988).

11. Judith E. Lanier and Michael W. Sedlak, "Teacher Efficiency and Quality Schooling," in Thomas J. Sergiovanni and John H. Moore, editors, *Schooling for Tomorrow* (Boston: Allyn and Bacon, 1989), p. 128.

12. "It will not do to blame television for the state of our literacy.... In some respects, such as its use of standard written English, television watching is acculturative. Moreover, ... the schools themselves must be held partly responsible for excessive television watching, because they have not firmly insisted that students complete significant amounts of homework, an obvious way to increase time spent on reading and writing." Hirsch, *Cultural Literacy*, p. 20.

13. Richard N. Bolles, *The Three Boxes of Life* (Berkeley, California: Ten Speed Press, 1981).

14. Jerold W. Apps, *Problems in Continuing Education* (New York: McGraw-Hill Book Company, 1979), p. 60.

15. Wayne Rice at the Youth Specialties' 1990 National Resource Seminar, Pasadena, California.

16. This observation was made by my friend Robert L. Turner.

17. Especially in teaching cardiopulmonary resuscitation, we were often faced with people who had learned enough about AIDS to be afraid of it but not enough to know it was not transmitted via the mannequin. The fear they had developed sometimes bordered on hysteria and was difficult—sometimes impossible—to allay.

18. Joel Arthur Barker, *Discovering the Future* (St. Paul, Minnesota: ILI Press, 1989), p. 14. See also pp. 114–117 for specific references to the educational paradigm.

19. Myron L. Tribus' editorial in *Community Link*, December 1990. (Published by the Community Quality Coalition, Jackson Community College, Jackson, Michigan.)
   See also the October 1991 issue of *Quality Progress*.

20. Robert M. Hutchins, *The Learning Society* (New York: Frederick A. Praeger, 1968), p. 25.

21. Robert L. Church and Michael W. Sedlak, *Education in the United States* (New York: The Free Press, 1976), p. 3.

CHAPTER 1: THE QUALITY SHIFT

1. For a fascinating account of postwar Japan, see William J. Sebald, with Russell Brines *With MacArthur in Japan* (New York: W. W. Norton & Company, 1965).

2. Daniel J. Boorstin, *The Americans: The Democratic Experience* (New York: Vintage Books, 1974), pp. 363–367.

3. Boorstin, *The Americans: The Democratic Experience*, p. 369.

4. Boorstin, *The Americans: The Democratic Experience*, pp. 194–195.

5. Boorstin, *The Americans: The Democratic Experience*, p. 197; and David A. Garvin, *Managing Quality* (New York: The Free Press, 1988).

6. Dr. W. Edwards Deming, personal communication. See also *Out of the Crisis* (Cambridge, Massachusetts: Massachusetts Institute of Technology Center for Advanced Engineering Study, 1986), p. 318.

7. Walter A. Shewhart, *Economic Control of Quality of Manufactured Product* (Princeton, New Jersey: D. Van Nostrand Company, 1931), p. 39.

8. "The present book gave Dr. Shewhart an opportunity to elaborate on a number of principles that he had already stated and applied in his great book *Economic Control of Quality of Manufactured Product*." From Dr. W. Edwards Deming's foreword to the 1986 edition of *Statistical Method from the Viewpoint*

of Quality Control (New York: Dover Publications). The book was originally published in 1939 by the Graduate School of the U.S. Department of Agriculture.

9. Kaoru Ishikawa, *What Is Total Quality Control?* (Englewood Cliffs, New Jersey: Prentice-Hall, 1985), p. 14.

10. Deming, *Out of the Crisis*, p. 29.

11. With regard to piecework and handcrafted goods, increases in quality required more care, more precision, and more time; thus, costs rose accordingly. When manufacturing turned to inter-changeable parts, improved quality actually reduced cost by elimi-nating wasted time and materials on scrap and rework.

12. Sebald, *With MacArthur in Japan*.

13. Deming, *Out of the Crisis*, p. 488.

14. Dr. W. Edwards Deming, personal communication.

15. Peter G. Peterson, "The Morning After." *The Atlantic Monthly*, October 1987, p. 49.

16. Ishikawa, *What Is Total Quality Control?*, p. 19.

17. A. V. Fiegenbaum, *Total Quality Control* (New York: McGraw-Hill Book Company, 1961).

18. Ishikawa, *What Is Total Quality Control?*, p. 22.

19. Lance Ealey, *Quality by Design* (Dearborn, Michigan: ASI Press, 1988).

20. Philip B. Crosby, *Quality Is Free* (New York: McGraw-Hill Book Company, 1979); and *Quality Without Tears* (New York: McGraw-Hill Book Company, 1984).

21. A. C. Rosander, *The Quest for Quality in Services* (Milwaukee, Wisconsin: ASQC Quality Press, 1989).

22. Regarding cultural differences between the United States and Japan, William Ouchi's *Theory Z* (Reading, Massachusetts: Addison-Wesley, 1981) is a fascinating treatment of management and corporate cultures. He includes sections on several U.S. companies whose cultures are more typically Japanese than American.

Dr. Kaoru Ishikawa once believed that quality control circles would only succeed in nations that used the *kanji* writing system, which, because of its inherent difficulty, teaches people to apply extra effort to their endeavors. He examines other differences between Eastern and Western nations in *What Is Total Quality Control?*

More cultural differences are discussed in Leo J. Moser's "Cross-Cultural Dimensions: U.S.–Japan," in *U.S.–Japan Relations* (Washington, D.C.: U.S. Department of State, 1986).

23. Ishikawa, *What Is Total Quality Control?*, p. 6.

24. Ishikawa, *What Is Total Quality Control?*, pp. 18–19.

25. Peterson, "The Morning After," p. 49.

26. When Dr. Ishikawa started them, they were called quality control circles or QC circles.

27. Management indifference was probably the death blow to those quality circle activities.

28. Deming, *Out of the Crisis*, p. 26.

29. Paul Kennedy, "The (Relative) Decline of America." *The Atlantic Monthly*, August 1987, p. 29.

30. See Peterson, "The Morning After," p. 48. The tape and baling wire were strikingly evident on one of the 1940s vintage machines in a factory I worked in. It was amazing the machine ran as well as it did.

See also Robert B. Reich, "The Next American Frontier." *The Atlantic Monthly*, March 1983, p. 50. Reich points out that the inability of American corporations to compete in industrial ventures led to their reliance on "paper entrepreneurialism" to boost profits.

31. Peterson, "The Morning After," p. 44.

32. Mortimer B. Zuckerman, "Weasel Words." *U.S. News & World Report,* 16 May 1988, p. 80.

33. Robert B. Reich, *Tales of a New America* (New York: Vintage Books, 1988), pp. 94–95.

34. Robert B. Reich reported that America had one lawyer for every 400 citizens while Japan had one lawyer for every 10,000. See "The Next American Frontier," p. 68.

Mortimer B. Zuckerman's editorial, "Brother, Can You Spare a Dime?" reported that the United States was training 1,000 lawyers for every 100 engineers while Japan was training 1,000 engineers for every 100 lawyers. *U.S. News & World Report,* 22 August 1988, p. 68. 35.

35. Even after their unmatched investment in infrastructure mainte-nence and improvement, the Japanese still had 80 billion dollars left-over for investment abroad. Peterson, "The Morning After," p. 58.

36. Dr. John Surak, an examiner for the Malcolm Baldrige National Quality Award.

37. Robert R. Ropelewski, "Wave of Quality Initiatives Sweeps Over DOD, Industry." *Armed Forces Journal International,* January 1990, p. 55; Tom Schoop, "Can Quality Be Total?" *Government Executive,* March 1990; *Total Quality Management Master Plan* (Washington, D.C.: U.S. Department of Defense, 1988); and "Improving the Quality of Government Products and Services," in *OMB Circular A-132 (Draft)* (Washington, D.C.: Office of Management and Budget, 1990).

CHAPTER 2: THE QUALITY TRANSFORMATION

1. See David A. Garvin, *Managing Quality* (New York: The Free Press, 1988), pp. 40–41.

2. See Valarie A. Zietheml, A. Parasuraman, and Leonard L. Berry, *Delivering Quality Service* (New York: The Free Press, 1990).

3. Stanley M. Davis suggests the only customer worth considering is "the customer in the marketplace…Employees who think of other employees as their customers lose sight of the business in favor of the organization." *Future Perfect* (Reading, Massachusets: Addison-Wesley, 1987), p. 106.

A. C. Rosander apparently agrees: "The customer is the ultimate buyer, not an intermediate buyer…. 'Customer' is not applied to other organizations or companies. Neither is it ever used…to refer to those persons in any organization who are receiving the output of a preceding sequence of work. It is unfortunate that the word 'customer' is applied to this situation. Some more appropriate term, such as 'sequential workers,' should be used instead." *The Quest for Quality in Services* (Milwaukee, Wisconsin: ASQC Quality Press, 1989), p. 16.

In contrast to this view, I agree with many others that focusing on the external customer to the exclusion of the internal can be disastrous. It reserves the pride of satisfying the customer for those few people who have direct contact with the external customer. In that case, most employees are working for customers they never see and do not get the benefits of customer interaction and feedback. The recognition of internal customers, whether they be called clients or users or any other name, is necessary to the growth and health of the organization.

4. W. Edwards Deming, "A System of Profound Knowledge." 5 May 1990. Originally presented and published as part of the Osaka Paper.

5. My title is not better than Dr. Deming's, but I like it and believe it accurately describes the concepts' relations to the world as we know it.

I characterize this collection of concepts as a metaphysical paradigm, following C. I. Lewis: "[Metaphysics] will seek to determine the nature of the real, as ethics seeks to determine the good, and logic, the valid, purely by critical consideration of what does not transcend ordinary experience. That is, it will seek to *define* 'reality,' not to triangulate the universe." Clarence Irving Lewis, *Mind and the World Order* (New York: Dover Publications, 1956), p. 10.

6. Deming, "A System of Profound Knowledge," p. 1. Other concepts could conceivably be included, but Dr. Deming has settled on these for the time being.

7. Deming, "A System of Profound Knowledge," p. 3.

8. Deming, "A System of Profound Knowledge," p. 4. Dr. Deming explained to me that his work in Japan was to explain this concept of systems and their optimization.

9. The belief that processes could produce the same outcomes again and again with no variation was an outgrowth of early deterministic physics, which stated that events should be specifically predictable by application of scientific laws. The formulation of the Heisenberg uncertainty principle showed that predictions of future events could not be made precisely. Future events can only be thought of as series of possible outcomes, each of which has a different probability of occurring. Thus the outputs of any process cannot be precisely predicted and will vary over time.

For an intriguing discussion of the Heisenberg principle, see Steven W. Hawking's *A Brief History of Time* (New York: Bantam Books, 1988), pp. 53–61.

10. Dr. Shewhart continues: "We accept our human limitations and say that likely there are many other factors. If we could but name all the reasons why we cannot make the a's alike, we would most assuredly have a better understanding of a certain part of nature than we now have. Of course, this conception of what it means to be able to do what we want to do is not new; it does not belong exclusively to any one field of human thought; it is commonly accepted." *Economic Control of Quality of Manufactured*

Product (Princeton, New Jersey: D. Van Nostrand Company, 1931), pp. 5–6.

11. Deming, "A System of Profound Knowledge," p. 8.

12. See Lewis, *Mind and the World Order*.

13. Lewis, *Mind and the World Order*, p. 230.

14. Lewis, *Mind and the World Order*, p. 44. (Author's emphasis.)

15. Deming, "A System of Profound Knowledge," p. 1.

16. "No one, child or other, can enjoy learning if he must constantly be concerned about grading and gold stars for his performance." Deming, "A System of Profound Knowledge," p. 12.
    See also Frederick Herzberg, "One More Time: How Do You Motivate Employees?" *Harvard Business Review*, September–October 1987, pp. 109–120. (Reprinted from January–February 1968.)

17. Deming, "A System of Profound Knowledge," p. 12.

18. Rosander, *The Quest for Quality in Services*, p. 21.

19. W. Edwards Deming, *Out of the Crisis* (Cambridge, Massachusetts: Massachusetts Institute of Technology Center for Advanced Engineering Study, 1986). *Out of the Crisis* is an updated version of Deming's 1982 book *Quality, Productivity, and Competitive Position*.
    You are also referred to Howard S. Gitlow and Shelly J. Gitlow, *The Deming Guide to Quality and Competitive Position* (Englewood Cliffs, New Jersey: Prentice-Hall, 1987); Nancy R. Mann, The *Keys to Excellence* (Los Angeles: Prestwick Books, 1989); and William W. Scherkenbach, *The Deming Route to Quality and Productivity* (Washington, D.C.: CEEPress, George Washington University, 1988).

20. Mann, *The Keys to Excellence*, p. 62.
    "As has often enough been emphasized, common-sense is

itself a naive metaphysics and one which frequently breaks down on examination." Lewis, *Mind and the World Order*, p. 18.

21. Mann, *The Keys to Excellence*, p. 51.

The latest version of the 14 Points is distributed at Dr. Deming's seminars and is available from Quality Enhancement Seminars, Inc., 1081 Westwood Boulevard, Suite 218, Los Angeles, CA 90024, (213) 681-6396.

I have taken considerable license with the presentation of the 14 Points. Some are verbatim from *Out of the Crisis*, some verbatim from Dr. Deming's seminar, and some are combinations of the two or personally edited versions. I believe I have preserved their original meanings in a format more amenable to this work.

22. Technical discussion on minimizing the cost of inspection is beyond the scope of this book. Suffice it to say that Dr. Deming developed the kp rule for inspection, where k is cost (k_1 being cost to inspect and k_2 being cost to repair the damage done by acceptance of a defective part) and p is the fraction of defective items in an incoming lot. See Deming, *Out of the Crisis*, pp. 407–411.

The kp rule is also addressed in detail in Gitlow and Gitlow, *The Deming Guide to Quality and Competitive Position*.

23. Scherkenbach, *The Deming Route to Quality and Productivity*.

24. People have seen so many programs come and go that they are naturally suspicious of new ones. Leaders must demonstrate that the quality initiative is not a program but a cultural change; they must also be the first to change.

25. Dr. Deming has recently changed his terminology and calls this point *institute management of people*. He prefers to reserve the title "leader" for those who drive the transformation effort. I prefer the original wording, believing that leadership skills should be developed in as many members of our organizations as possible. (See the Conclusion for more discussion on leadership.)

26. "Why do we create an artificial shortage of winners?" is one of Dr. Deming's frequently asked questions at his seminars.

27. Most appraisals do not address teamwork and cooperation but measure the employee's performance in relation to a fixed job description. The job descriptions themselves typically relate only to the employee's tasks, not to the success or failure of the entire organization. (My friend Rob Gray has often suggested that the quickest way for employees to cripple an organization is for everyone to do only what is in their job description.)

The performance appraisal itself is an external motivator, usually linked to other external rewards like promotions and bonuses. These reward systems often stifle innovation by concentrating on the past instead of the future, as pointed out by Rosabeth Moss Kanter in her book *The Change Masters* (New York: Touchstone, 1983), p. 33.

28. Deming, *Out of the Crisis*, p. 64.

29. Gitlow and Gitlow, *The Deming Guide to Quality and Competitive Position*.

30. Kaoru Ishikawa, *What Is Total Quality Control?* (Englewood Cliffs, New Jersey: Prentice-Hall, 1985).

31. It is up to management to give all employees a picture of how their efforts at meeting the needs of their internal customers contribute to the satisfaction of the end user, that is, to give them "the big picture."

32. Deming, "A System of Profound Knowledge," p. 4.

33. Kanter, *The Change Masters*, p. 153.

34. Dr. Deming credits Dr. Lloyd S. Nelson with this challenging question. *Out of the Crisis*, p. 20.

35. Dr. Deming recognizes that Murphy's Law will always apply.

36. Daniel J. Boorstin, *The Americans: The Democratic Experience* (New York: Vintage Books, 1974), p. 198.

37. One 1989 estimate put annual expenditures by industries and businesses for training and retraining employees at 30 billion dollars. John T. Correll, "Unskilled and Unprepared." *Air Force Magazine*, October 1989, p. 6.

38. Mann, *The Keys to Excellence*, p. 43.

39. J. M. Juran, editor, *Juran's Quality Control Handbook*, 4th ed. (New York: McGraw-Hill Book Company, 1988), p. 10.

Dr. Shewhart's production cycle was composed of specification, production, and inspection. "In this sense, specification, production, and inspection correspond respectively to making a hypothesis, carrying out an experiment, and testing the hypothesis. The three steps constitute a dynamic scientific process of acquiring knowledge. From this viewpoint, it might be better to show them as forming a sort of spiral gradually approaching a circular path which would represent the idealized case where no evidence is found...to indicate a need for changing the specification (or scientific hypothesis) no matter how many times we repeat the three steps." Walter A. Shewhart, *Statistical Method from the Viewpoint of Quality Control* (New York: Dover Books, 1986), pp. 44–45.

For a more detailed discussion of the plan-do-study-act cycle, see William W. Scherkenbach, *Deming's Road to Continual Improvement* (Knoxville, Tennessee: SPC Press, 1991), especially pp. 62–81.

40. While problems requiring the collection of data should start with *plan*, situations where large amounts of data are on hand or may be quickly assembled may allow beginning the cycle with *do* or *study*. (Pointed out by Dr. Brian Joiner.)

41. Adapted from Joseph M. Juran, *Juran on Planning for Quality* (New York: The Free Press, 1988), p. 14.

42. I thank my friend Robert L. Turner for this observation.

43. Presented at the Instituting Dr. Deming's Methods for Management of Productivity and Quality seminar, Atlanta, Georgia, 5 September 1991.

44. Sud Ingle, *Quality Circle Master Guide* (Englewood Cliffs, New Jersey: Prentice-Hall, 1982).

45. Ingle, *Quality Circle Master Guide*, pp. 28–32.

46. This has been one of the perils of American management: without benefit of the theory of knowledge, it succumbs to the urge to copy what is successful elsewhere without studying it to see why it was successful. Dr. Deming writes, "An example is no help in management unless studied with the aid of theory. To copy an example of success, without understanding it with the aid of theory, may lead to disaster." "A System of Profound Knowledge," p. 10.

47. Ingle, *Quality Circle Master Guide*, pp. 32–34.

CHAPTER 3: DEFINING QUALITY IN EDUCATION

1. Lewis B. Mayhew, Patrick J. Ford, and Dean L. Hubbard, *The Quest for Quality* (San Francisco: Jossey-Bass, 1990), p. 25.

2. Alexander W. Astin, "When Does a College Deserve to Be Called 'High Quality?'" *Current Issues in Higher Education*, 3 September 1980, pp. 1, 4.

3. Astin, "When Does a College Deserve to Be Called 'High Quality?'" p. 4.

4. The reader is encouraged to investigate the educational philosophies further. Be wary of comparative analyses, as it is difficult for an author who espouses a particular philosophy to be completely objective when considering the others. (This caveat applies equally to the book you are now reading.)

5. Please do not confuse this emphasis on reality with the philosophy of realism.

6. Benefit may be measured in several ways. For example, the ultimate benefit of *successful* education may be the successfulness in later life of graduates and nongraduates. See Roger Kaufman, *Planning Educational Systems* (Lancaster, Pennsylvania: Technomic Publishing Co., 1988), pp. 25, 72.

7. Ronald D. Moen, "The Deming Philosophy for Improving the Educational Process." Presented at the Third Annual International Deming Users Group Conference, Cincinnati, Ohio, 22 August 1989; revised 25 May 1991; p. 3.

8. Knowledge, comprehension, and application are three levels in the taxonomy of the cognitive (thinking) domain. See Benjamin S. Bloom, editor, *Taxonomy of Educational Objectives* (New York: Longman, 1956).

9. Sidney Hook, *Convictions* (Buffalo, New York: Prometheus Books, 1990), p. 83.

10. Lewis A. Rhodes, "Why Quality Is Within Our Grasp ... If We Reach." *School Administrator*, November 1990, p. 34.

11. As Jefferson wrote in his *Notes on the State of Virginia*, "The general objects...are to provide an education adapted to the years, to the capacity, and the condition of every one, and directed to their freedom and happiness."

12. Daniel J. Boorstin, *The Discoverers* (New York: Vintage Books, 1985), p. 489.

13. The realization that the customers of education cannot be ignored was recently pointed out: "The legitimate stakeholders in public education must be identified, an analysis made of their participation in the policymaking process, and the impact of the reform in question assessed." Douglas E. Mitchell, "Measuring Up: Standards for Evaluating School Reform," in Thomas J. Sergiovanni and John H. Moore, editors, *Schooling for Tomorrow* (Boston: Allyn and Bacon, 1989), p. 56.

14. For example, see Milton Friedman and Rose Friedman, *Free to Choose* (New York: Avon Books, 1981), p. 147.

15. Included in the community are the children and families of those who choose to work in the home.

16. The system flowchart was first used by Dr. Deming to depict an industrial model; he used it to teach the Japanese in 1950. See W. Edwards Deming, *Out of the Crisis* (Cambridge, Massachusetts: Massachusetts Institute of Technology Center for Advanced Engineering Study, 1986), p. 4.

17. A similar educational system flowchart appears on page 15 of Ronald D. Moen's "The Deming Philosophy for Improving the Educational Process."

18. *Statistical Abstract of the United States*, 1985, 105th ed. (Washington, D.C.: U.S. Bureau of the Census, 1984), p. 405.
   Dr. Deming points out that a large number of people who work in manufacturing industries are actually performing service functions; however, "in spite of the relatively few people that are engaged in manufacturing and in agriculture, it is they that are almost wholly responsible for our balance of trade.
   "It is obvious...that because there are so many people engaged in service in the United States, improvement in our standard of living is highly dependent on better quality and productivity in the service sector. The cost of living, if it is high, is high because we pay more than necessary for what we get. This is pure inflation." *Out of the Crisis*, p. 185.

19. *What Works*, 2nd ed. (Washington, D.C.: U.S. Department of Education, 1987), p. 81.

20. Students "criticized the university as a soulless 'knowledge factory,' using Clark Kerr's *The Uses of the University* as a text to prove that the university was an adjunct of industry and government and that students were no more than raw material for the mass production process." Diane Ravitch, *The Troubled Crusade* (New York: Basic Books, 1983), p. 194.

21. See Kaufman, *Planning Educational Systems*; Bela H. Banathy, *Instructional Systems* (Belmont, California: Fearon Publishers, 1968); Martin R. Wong and John D. Raulerson, *A Guide to Systematic Instructional Design* (Englewood Cliffs, New Jersey: Educational Technology Publications, 1974); and Rita Richey, *The Theoretical and Conceptual Bases of Instructional Design* (London: Kogan Page, Ltd., 1986).

22. National Commission on Excellence in Education, *A Nation at Risk* (Washington, D.C.: U.S. Department of Education, 1983), p. 7.

23. "What has Japan? Nothing except people and good management." William W. Scherkenbach, *The Deming Route to Quality and Productivity* (Washington D.C.: CEEPress, George Washington University, 1988), p. 127.

24. Joseph M. Juran, *Juran on Planning for Quality* (New York: The Free Press, 1988), p. 61.

25. "Skills Employers Want." *Safety & Health*, December 1989, p. 56. For more information, write the American Society for Training and Development, 1630 Duke Street, Box 1443, Alexandria, VA 22313.

26. Mike Yaconelli and Jim Burns, *High School Ministry* (Grand Rapids, Michigan: Youth Specialties Books, 1986), p. 99.

Another viewpoint on the importance of listening: "It's been said that communication is what's heard, not what's said. As active listeners, we hold the responsibility to insure that what's being said and what's being heard are the same." Rich Van Pelt, *Intensive Care* (Grand Rapids, Michigan: Youth Specialties Books, 1988), p. 50.

For practical exercises aimed at improving listening and thinking skills, see Peter Kline, *The Everyday Genius* (Arlington, Virginia: Great Ocean Publishers, 1990).

27. Scherkenbach, *The Deming Route to Quality and Productivity*, p. 128. See also Alfie Kohn, *No Contest* (Boston: Houghton Mifflin, 1986).

28. Scherkenbach, *The Deming Route to Quality and Productivity*, p. 128.

29. Theodore R. Sizer, *Horace's Compromise* (Boston: Houghton Mifflin Company, 1984), p. 151.

30. Through motivation with grades and other rewards, the student is "ruled by external forces." W. Edwards Deming, "A System of Profound Knowledge," 5 May 1990. Originally presented and published as part of the Osaka Paper.

31. *What Works*, p. 37.

32. The other favorite is: "Is this going to be on the test?" Discussed by Wayne Rice at Youth Specialties' 1990 National Resource seminar in Pasadena, California.

33. Having learned it in geometry class, I had never thought of the Pythagorean Theorem as being useful until I worked as a carpenter. The contractor I worked for showed us how to use it to be sure the corners we had laid out for the house we were building were square.

34. See E. D. Hirsch, Jr., *Cultural Literacy* (New York: Vintage Books, 1988).

35. The results of a positive self-fulfilling prophecy can be significant. See Robert Rosenthal and Lenore Jacobsen, *Pygmalion in the Classroom* (New York: Holt, Rinehart and Winston, 1968).

36. Anne D. Forester, "An Examination of Parallels Between Deming's Model for Transforming Industry and Current Trends in Education." Submitted to the Total Quality Education/Total Quality Management Taskforce, 1 July 1991, p. 21.

37. William Glasser, *The Quality School* (New York: Harper & Row, 1990); and *Control Theory in the Classroom* (New York: Harper & Row, 1986); Kline, *The Everyday Genius*.

38. This would require the formation of a body of teachers who would self-regulate the teaching profession and set standards for preparation and certification. More discussion on professional development for educators is found in Chapter 5.

39. This misuse of statistics is further discussed in an amusing book by Darrell Huff, *How to Lie with Statistics* (New York: W. W. Norton & Company, 1954).

40. For the purposes of this work, administrators include principals as well as guidance counselors, superintendents, and others who manage the education system.

41. Cliff Schimmels, *Parents' Most-Asked Questions About Kids and Schools* (Wheaton, Illinois: Victor Books, 1989), p. 1.

42. Many teenage crises (for example, substance abuse, suicide) have warning signs that, in retrospect, were quite clear and could have signaled trouble if recognized. See Jim Burns, *The Youth Builder* (Eugene, Oregon: Harvest House Publishers, 1988); Yaconelli and Burns, *High School Ministry,* and Van Pelt, *Intensive Care.*

43. *What Works,* p. 5.

44. Harry G. Good, *A History of American Education,* 2nd ed. (New York: The Macmillan Company, 1962), p. 74.

45. Hirsch, *Cultural Literacy,* pp. 147–151.

46. Many of the educational references used for this book have included curriculum suggestions. Most have been vague, some more specific, but taken together they are all reminders of the problems of reaching a consensus on the issue.

47. A *Nation at Risk,* pp. 70–72.

48. One of the strongest opposing views to including physical education in the curriculum is found in Sizer, *Horace's Compromise.*

49. Physical education classes have often been sources of anxiety for young people who are not particularly strong, graceful, or athletic. Games that do not require great athletic prowess, give no advantages to "jocks," and are played just for fun can relieve the stresses on young people and make these classes more enjoyable. This provides an extra advantage in that more students may continue playing games and participating in healthy exercise after they leave school. Wayne Rice made this point at the Youth Specialties' 1990 National Resource Center in Pasadena, California.

See also Kohn, *No Contest*, pp. 93–95.

50. I apologize to those readers familiar with curriculum development who may be offended by my approach. My intent is to fuel debate and discussion, in hopes that an informed consensus may be reached and decisive action taken.

51. Michael W. Kirst, "Who Should Control the Schools? Reassessing Current Policies," in Thomas J. Sergiovanni and John H. Moore, editors, *Schooling for Tomorrow* (Boston: Allyn and Bacon, 1989), p. 75.

For an eye-opening discussion of school boards, their limitations, and educational equity, see Jonathan Kozol, *Savage Inequalities* (New York: Crown Publishers, 1991), pp. 210–213.

52. National Center for Education Statistics, *The Condition of Education, Volume 1: Elementary and Secondary Education* (Washington, D.C.: U.S. Department of Education, 1988), pp. 34–35.

53. I owe thanks for this observation to my friend James H. Galt-Brown.

Kozol explains the economics of disparities in funding between rich and poor areas in *Savage Inequalities*, especially pp. 54–56, 66, 121–123.

54. See Hirsch, *Cultural Literacy.*

According to C. I. Lewis, "We use language to convey thought. If language really conveys anything, then there must be

something which is identical in your mind and mine when we

understand each other." *Mind and the World Order* (New York: Dover Publications, 1956), p. 73.

55. It is important that boards not succumb to the political temptation to apply weaker curriculum requirements, for by doing so they risk their children's futures in order to gain temporary favor with voters. Colleges and universities can significantly impact this, as discussed in Chapter 6.

I thank my friend David O'Nan for help with this point.

56. *A Nation at Risk*, pp. 25, 50–51.

57. Leonard L. Baird, "Value Added," in *Performance and Judgment* (Washington, D.C.: U.S. Department of Education, 1988), p. 205.

58. Usually, the second measurement is used to determine if the student is ready to progress. This is too much like a final inspection (see Chapters 2 and 4).

59. Baird, "Value Added," in *Performance and Judgment*, pp. 206–208.

60. One data point cannot be used to predict future performance. Only a series of measurements that show statistical control provides enough information on which to base a reasonable prediction.

CHAPTER 4: THE EDUCATION TRANSFORMATION

1. Diane Ravitch wrote that the 1970's Experimental Schools Program "intended to demonstrate that comprehensive, holistic change of an entire district or subdistrict was possible and that extensive community involvement would strengthen the process of comprehensive change. *These goals were not attained because they were inherently unattainable.*" (Emphasis added.) *The Troubled Crusade* (New York: Basic Books, 1983), pp. 259–260.

Is the quality transformation fated to follow this pattern? Are its goals "inherently unattainable?" More than any other reform movement, this education transformation proposes change that is nothing if not "comprehensive." It will require a change in the way we think about education and the way we think about leading and managing education; this is a cultural change, not the implementation of a program or project. It requires trust and cooperation among all participants. If we cannot move beyond our individual empires, unlearn our prejudices, and work together to accomplish the necessary changes, then perhaps not only our education system but our nation itself is doomed to failure.

2. As stated many times, acting without the benefit of knowledge can be disastrous. Perhaps this is why the Bible tells us to seek understanding at all cost.

3. Dr. Deming writes, "The 14 points are the basis for the transformation of American industry....The 14 points apply anywhere, to small organizations as well as to large ones, to the service industry as well as to manufacturing." *Out of the Crisis* (Cambridge, Massachusetts: Massachusetts Institute of Technology Center for Advanced Engineering Study, 1986), p. 23.

Several people and groups have also worked on adapting Dr. Deming's points to education. Notable among these are the work of Dr. David Bayless and his associates at Westat, Inc.; Dr. Anne Forester in Victoria, British Columbia; Richard Hail in Blountville, Tennessee; Bruce Hunter of the American Association of School Administrators; David Langford and his entrepreneurship classes at Mount Edgecumbe High School in Sitka, Alaska; Ron Moen of Associates in Process Improvement; Dr. Jacob O. Stampen of the University of Wisconsin–Madison; the Johnston County Schools in North Carolina; the Petersburg Public Schools in Virginia; the Oregon, Beloit-Turner, Brodhead, and Parkview School Districts in Wisconsin.

For a discussion of the 14 Points in relation to higher education, see Richard I. Miller, editor, *Applying the Deming Method to Higher Education* (Washington, D.C.: College and University Personnel Association, 1991).

4. The National Educational Quality Initiative has operated for several years under the auspices of ASQC though it is now a separate entity. Its members operate several committees, dedicated to

spreading the quality philosophy throughout the educational system. For more information, contact NEQI at 1819 S. Green Bay Road, Grafton, WI 53204, (414) 229-6259.

The first symposium on "The Role of Academia in National Competitiveness and Total Quality Management" was held in July 1990 at West Virginia University and was an interesting example of good intentions. The tone of the announcements and invitations indicated that it was designed to introduce academia to the quality philosophy for the benefit of industry and government, rather than for the improvement of education itself. The second symposium, held July 1991 at the University of Southern California, focused on visions and carried a similar message. While this approach is not inherently bad, it may not engender the kind of trust that is required to accomplish the transformation. The third symposium, at Lehigh University in July 1992, was the first to include workshops for K–12 educators.

The Total Quality Alliance was formed in October 1991, and brought together industry representatives familiar with quality improvement efforts with educators working on quality in schools. Coordinated by the National Learning Foundation, its aim was to foster improved understanding between the groups and build a foundation for cooperation and action. Representatives from the National Educational Quality Initiative and the previously mentioned symposia were in attendance and are working together to build a national vision and a coherent approach to quality in education.

5. Leaders must take care not to get wrapped around the axle in this effort. Too much time spent developing and refining a vision may be as bad as too little, diluting support and fragmenting efforts that could be channeled into quality improvements.

6. William W. Scherkenbach, *The Deming Route to Quality and Productivity* (Washington, D.C.: CEEPress, George Washington University, 1988), p. 11.

Thomas J. Sergiovanni writes, "Leaders who are remiss in expressing and articulating a vision in terms of values and dreams miss the very point of leadership. The vision of a school must also reflect the hopes and dreams, the needs and interests, the values and beliefs of the group. When a school vision embodies the   267 sharing of ideals, a covenant is created that bonds together leader and followers in a common cause." "The Leadership Needed for Quality Schooling," in Thomas J. Sergiovanni and John H. Moore, editors, *Schooling for Tomorrow* (Boston: Allyn and Bacon, 1989), p. 220.

7. Myron Tribus, "The Application of Quality Management Principles in Education." November 1990, p. 3. Available from Dr. Tribus at 350 Britto Terrace, Fremont, CA 94539.

8. Anne D. Forester, "An Examination of Parallels Between Deming's Model for Transforming Industry and Current Trends in Education." Submitted to the Total Quality Education/Total Quality Management Taskforce, 1 July 1991, p. 9.

9. W. James Popham and T. R. Husek, "Implications of Criterion-Referenced Measurement," in W. James Popham, editor, *Criterion-Referenced Measurement* (Englewood Cliffs, New Jersey: Educational Technology Publications, 1971), pp. 19–21.

10. Carl Sommer, *Schools in Crisis* (Houston, Texas: Cahill Publishing Company, 1984), p. 38.
    Alfie Kohn refutes this idea in *No Contest* (Boston: Houghton Mifflin Company, 1986), pp. 26–27, 50.

11. Bruce Hunter, "Some Random Thoughts on Education Reform." Draft 4, 16 December 1990 (unpublished).

12. Anthony Campolo, *Growing Up in America* (Grand Rapids, Michigan: Youth Specialties Books, 1989), p. 19.
    "Most of American education is highly individualistic, fueled by a competitive structure of evaluation." Kohn, *No Contest*, p. 50. Earlier on the same page, Kohn writes, "So far from making us more productive,...a structure that pits us one against the other tends to inhibit our performance. Children simply do not learn better when education is transformed into competitive struggle."

13. Theodore R. Sizer, *Horace's Compromise* (Boston: Houghton Mifflin Company, 1984), p. 169.

14. National Commission on Excellence in Education, *A Nation at Risk* (Washington, D.C.: U.S. Department of Education, 1983), p. 73.

15. W. Edwards Deming, "A System of Profound Knowledge." 5 May 1990, p. 12. Originally presented and published as part of the Osaka Paper.

16. William W. Scherkenbach, *Deming's Road to Continual Improvement* (Knoxville, Tennessee: SPC Press, 1991), pp. 241–245.

17. William Glasser, *The Quality School* (New York: Harper & Row, 1990).

18. Tribus, "The Application of Quality Management Principles in Education," p. 5.
    In Mount Edgecumbe High School's adaptation of Dr. Deming's philosophy, point 3 was considered so important they split it into two parts and dedicated the first part specifically to the elimination of competitive grading. Thus, their entire version has 15 Points. David Paul Langford, "Changing Education Systems Through Management and Cooperation." Presented at the 1990 Third Northern Regions Conference: Cooperation in a Changing World, Anchorage, Alaska, 18 September 1990.

19. "Legally, we may be headed for a serious crisis: Tests that are declared inadequate for assessing individual student problems are being relied on as instruments for controlling school performance and staff rewards." Douglas E. Mitchell, "Measuring Up: Standards for Evaluating School Reform," in Thomas J. Sergiovanni and John H. Moore, editors, *Schooling for Tomorrow* (Boston: Allyn and Bacon, 1989), p. 53.

20. Langford, "Changing Education Systems Through Management and Cooperation."

21. For an extensive list of purchasing considerations, see A. C. Rosander, *The Quest for Quality in Services* (Milwaukee, Wisconsin: ASQC Quality Press, 1989), p. 8.

22. I am indebted to my friend James H. Galt-Brown for this insight.

23. What better way for schools to practice what they preach about environmental responsibility?

24. The quality of the teachers' professional service would include moral uprightness and adherence to a code of ethics as well as classroom activities.

25. These divisions of the teaching profession are explained in detail in Chapter 5.

26. See Peter Kline, *The Everyday Genius* (Arlington, Virginia: Great Ocean Publishers, 1990).
   I am grateful to Doug Webb for information on interactive video and center-indexed references.

27. *The Nation Responds* (Washington, D.C.: U.S. Department of Education, 1984).

28. Sergiovanni, "The Leadership Needed for Quality Schooling," in *Schooling for Tomorrow*, p. 214.

29. As mentioned, some students are "brains" in remedial classes.

30. Roland S. Barth, "A Personal Vision of a Good School." *Phi Delta Kappan*, March 1990, p. 516.

31. David L. Bayless, Gabriel Massaro, and Nancy W. Bayless, "Quality Improvement in Education Today and the Future." Progress Report of a project of the Center for Research on Educational Accountability and Teacher Evaluation of Western Michigan University, 1991, pp. 29–30.

32. *What Works*, 2nd ed. (Washington, D.C.: U.S. Department of Education, 1987), p. 67.

33. Tribus, "The Application of Quality Management Principles in Education," p. 5.

34. Forester, "An Examination of Parallels Between Deming's Model for Transforming Industry and Current Trends in Education," p. 17.

35. Perhaps the most blatant example of exhortative slogans aimed at young people is the overused and ineffective "Just Say No" campaign against drugs. Tell the girl whose father's sole purpose in life seems to be to get drunk, beat her mother and her brothers, and molest her and her sisters that temporarily escaping through drugs is no way out. Tell the boy who goes to bed every night hungry, or in pain from neglected tooth decay, with five brothers and sisters in a one room apartment, to "Just Say No" when the local drug lord drives a fancy car and has money to spend and nubile companions to spend it on. The slogan does nothing to improve any child's present situation or future potential.

36. Without an understanding of variation in the performance of a system, how can the teacher hope to gauge the student's ability correctly, except as a snapshot in time, with no value for predicting future success?

37. Charles A. Melvin III, "School Restructuring the Deming Way." Presented at the Fourth Annual Hunter Conference on Quality, Madison, Wisconsin, 10-12 April 1991, p. 6.

38. Sidney Hook, "A Philosophical Perspective," in Annelise Anderson and Dennis L. Bark, editors, *Thinking About America* (Stanford, California: Hoover Institution Press, 1988), p. 447.

39. Hook, "A Philosophical Perspective," in *Thinking About America*, p. 447.

40. It looks good to the innumerate populace to set such goals—they are momentarily appealing and easily forgotten. Who remembers when the targets are not met? One's political opponents may remember, but often may be silenced with doubletalk.

41. "National Goals for Education" (Washington, D.C.: Executive Office of the President, 26 February 1990). All of the goals are quoted from this paper.

42. Glasser, *The Quality School* and *Control Theory in the Classroom*. See also Kohn, *No Contest*.

43. Willis D. Hawley, "Traveling Old Roads Deeper Into the Woods Leaves Promises to Keep." *Theory Into Practice*, Winter 1990, p. 15.

CHAPTER 5: STRATEGY

1. *The Nation Responds* (Washington, D.C.: U.S. Department of Education, 1984); and Dennis P. Doyle and Terry W. White, *Excellence in Education* (Washington, D.C.: American Enterprise Institute for Public Policy Research, 1985), p. 19.

2. This will be the major obstacle to implementing any nation-wide reform.

3. Diane Ravitch, *The Troubled Crusade* (New York: Basic Books, 1983), pp. 259–260.

4. Theodore R. Sizer, *Horace's Compromise* (Boston: Houghton Mifflin Company, 1984), p. 98.

5. For example, the 1990 National Symposium on the Role of Academia in National Competitiveness and Total Quality Management at West Virginia University.

6. "There is no substitute for knowledge. Enlargement of a committee is not a way to acquire profound knowledge....As a good rule, profound knowledge must come from the outside and by invitation. Profound knowledge can not be forced on to anybody." W. Edwards Deming, "A System of Profound Knowledge," 5 May 1990, p. 9. Originally presented and published as part of the "Osaka Paper."

7. An example of what Dr. Deming calls tampering. See *Out of the Crisis* (Cambridge, Massachusetts: Massachusetts Institute of Technology Center for Advanced Engineering Study, 1986).

8. James A. Kimple, et al, "Applying Quality Principles in Public Education," in *1991 ASQC Quality Congress Transactions* (Milwaukee, Wisconsin: American Society for Quality Control, 1991), p. 698.

9. Thomas Toch, "Drafting the Best and Brightest." *U.S. News & World Report*, 29 January 1990, p. 52. See also "Eager Ingenues." *The Economist*, 6 July 1991, p. 26; Marcus Mabry, "The New Teacher Corps." *Newsweek*, 16 July 1990, pp. 62–63.

10. William Glasser, *The Quality School* (New York: Harper & Row, 1990). See also Dr. Glasser's *Control Theory in the Classroom* (New York: Harper & Row, 1986).

11. Sidney Hook, "A Philosophical Perspective," in Annelise Anderson and Dennis L. Bark, editors, *Thinking About America* (Stanford, California: Hoover Institution Press, 1988), p. 449.

12. Anne D. Forester, "An Examination of Parallels Between Deming's Model for Transforming Industry and Current Trends in Education." Submitted to the Total Quality Education/Total Quality Management Taskforce, 1 July 1991, p. 19.

13. Updates will be necessary simply because of the changes in our world and how we relate to the world. For example, an interesting discussion of the changes in language over time is found in E. D. Hirsch, *Cultural Literacy* (New York: Vintage Books, 1988).

14. This is not a given.

15. See Hirsch, *Cultural Literacy*; Diane Ravitch, *The Schools We Deserve* (New York: Basic Books, 1985); and *What Works*, 2nd ed. (Washington, D.C.: U.S. Department of Education, 1987).

16. R. Earl Hadady, *How Sick Is Uncle Sam?* (Pasadena, California: Key Books Press, 1986).
    The reader who is interested in learning more about the plight of poor children in the United States is urged to read Jonathan Kozol's *Savage Inequalities* (New York: Crown Publishers, 1991).

17. Ravitch, *The Schools We Deserve*, p. 79.

18. Bruno Bettelheim and Karen Zelan, "Why Children Don't Like to Read." *The Atlantic Monthly*, November 1981, p. 27.

19. Sidney Hook, *Convictions* (Buffalo, New York: Prometheus Books, 1990), p. 76.

20. I thank my friend James H. Galt-Brown for his assistance with this section.

21. National Commission on Excellence in Education, *A Nation at Risk* (Washington, D.C.: U.S. Department of Education, 1983).

22. Not to the exclusion of other language(s), but as the national language.

23. Clarence Irving Lewis, *Mind and the World Order* (New York: Dover Publications, 1956), pp. 202–204.

24. I remember enjoying my high school chemistry and physics classes mostly because we regularly considered practical applications of what we were learning.
    Many schools, however, do not have the equipment or other resources to give students the experience with scientific methodology that they require. Kozol, *Savage Inequalities*, pp. 27–28, 139–140.

25. R. Earl Hadady, *How Sick Is Uncle Sam?* Hadady would require participation in such family life classes for all students.

26. I thank Brad Lego for his help with this point, and for reemphasizing to me the importance of family life schooling.

27. David T. Kearns and Denis P. Doyle, *Winning the Brain Race* (San Francisco: ICS Press, 1989), p. 95.

28. Sizer, *Horace's Compromise*, p. 115.

29. "Mastery" is the term most used by Theodore R. Sizer in suggesting what the focus of the students' educational achievements should be, though it is notoriously difficult to define in operational terms. See *Horace's Compromise.*

30. Kearns and Doyle, *Winning the Brain Race*, p. 41.

31. National Center for Education Statistics, *The Condition of Education, Volume 1: Elementary and Secondary Education* (Washington, D.C.: U.S. Department of Education, 1988), pp. 66–67.

32. *Japanese Education Today* (Washington, D.C.: U.S. Department of Education, 1987).

33. William W. Scherkenbach, *The Deming Route to Quality and Productivity* (Washington, D.C.: CEEPress, George Washington University, 1988), p. 128.

34. I thank Theresa May Hicks for this observation.

35. Robert E. Slavin, "Learning Together." *The American School Board Journal*, August 1990, p. 23.

36. Pointed out by LtCol George S. Beall, USAF (Ret), in an educational accountability lecture.

37. I thank my colleague Dr. John Surak for his help with this section.

38. Myron Tribus, "The Application of Quality Management Principles in Education." November 1990, p. 7. Available from Dr. Tribus at 350 Britto Terrace, Fremont, CA 94539.

39. L. Edwin Coate, "Implementing Total Quality Management in a University Setting." Oregon State University, July 1990. Of the 25 institutions examined in this paper, fewer than half were using the quality philosophy in academic areas, though most were teaching the philosophy.

See also Suzanne Axland, "Looking for a Quality Education?" *Quality Progress*, October 1991, p. 61.

40. Gerald A. Dorfman and Paul R. Hanna, "Can Education Be Reformed?" in Annelise Anderson and Dennis L. Bark, editors, *Thinking About America* (Stanford, California: Hoover Institution Press, 1988), p. 386.

41. *The Condition of Education*, pp. 70–71.

42. Their report stated that "taking and even passing college and university courses are no guarantees that the material has been learned. Thus, all instructors [the Holmes Group's first level of certification—GR] should also pass a written test in each subject they will teach, prior to certification" as well as a test in pedagogy and a test in communication skills. *Tomorrow's Teachers* (East Lansing, Michigan: The Holmes Group, 1986), p. 11.

This passage seems to contain a hopeless dichotomy. If taking and passing a *course* does not guarantee that a teacher candidate has learned the material, does taking and passing a *test* guarantee it? No—no such guarantee exists in any form.

43. Dennis Lawton, "Teacher Education," in Max Morris and Clive Griggs, editors, *Education—The Wasted Years?* (London: The Falmer Press, 1988), p. 170.

44. Dorfman and Hanna, "Can Education Be Reformed?," p. 386.

45. Marcus Mabry, et al, "The New Teacher Corps."

46. See W. Edwards Deming, "On Teaching," in Cecelia S. Killian, *The World of W. Edwards Deming* (Washington, D.C.: CEEPress, George Washington University, 1988). See also *Out of the Crisis*, pp. 173–174.

I thank my friend Sharon O'Nan for her help with this section.

47. *Tomorrow's Teachers*, p. 64.

48. Sidney Hook describes an experiment in which the power of a fake teacher's personality fooled a classroom full of professionals

into thinking he was a competent professional, thus pointing out the dire need for substance in teaching. See Hook, *Convictions*, p. 78.

49. Kearns and Doyle, *Winning the Brain Race*, p. 57.

50. Robert L. Church and Michael W. Sedlak, *Education in the United States* (New York: The Free Press, 1976).

51. See *The Nation Responds, Tomorrow's Teachers*, the National Institute for Education's Reaching for Excellence (Washington: U.S. Department of Education, 1985); Doyle and Hartle, *Excellence in Education*, p. 21; and Phillip C. Schlechty, "Career Ladders: A Good Idea Going Awry," in Thomas J. Sergiovanni and John H. Moore, editors, *Schooling for Tomorrow* (Boston: Allyn and Bacon, 1989).

52. *The Condition of Education*, pp. 40–41, 100.
The difference in teacher salaries between affluent areas and poor areas can be staggering. See Kozol, *Savage Inequalities*, p. 69.

53. John D. Shingleton, "Economics of the Job Market for the 1992 Grad," in *CPC Annual*, 35th ed. (Bethlehem, Pennsylvania: College Placement Council, 1991), p. 17.

54. *What Works*, p. 39.

55. Some suggest even more days. See R. Earl Hadady, *How Sick Is Uncle Sam?*.

56. Dorfman and Hanna, "Can Education Be Reformed?" in *Thinking About America*, p. 387.

57. Bettelheim and Zelan, "Why Children Don't Like to Read."

58. For example, the American National Standards Institute: "An American National Standard implies a consensus of those substantially concerned with its scope and provisions. An American National Standard is intended as a guide to aid the manufacturer,

the consumer and the general public. The existence of an American National Standard does not in any respect preclude anyone, whether he has approved the standard or not, from manufacturing, marketing, purchasing, or using products, processes or procedures not conforming to the standard. American National Standards are subject to periodic review and users are cautioned to obtain the latest editions." This message is printed in the front of every such standard.

59. Donald Marquardt, et al, "Vision 2000: The Strategy for the ISO 9000 Series Standards in the 90's." *Quality Progress*, May 1991, p. 30; and "Quality Management and Quality System Elements—Guidelines." *ANSI/ASQC Q94-1987*, p. 2.

60. George Q. Lofgren, "Quality System Registration." *Quality Progress*, May 1991, p. 35.

61. Harrison M. Wadsworth, "Relationship of U.S. Registration Activities to European Requirements," in *1991 ASQC Quality Congress Transactions* (Milwaukee, Wisconsin: American Society for Quality Control, 1991), p. 718.

62. Robert W. Peach, "State of Quality System Certification in the United States," in *1991 ASQC Quality Congress Transactions* (Milwaukee, Wisconsin: American Society for Quality Control, 1991), p. 709.

63. Robert K. Branson and F. Craig Johnson, "Total Quality Management: The New Look at Accountability, School Improvement Programs, and Site-Based Management." Center for Educational Technology, Florida State University, July 1991, p. 5.

64. Branson and Johnson, "Total Quality Management: The New Look at Accountability, School Improvement Programs, and Site-Based Management," p. 6.

65. Dr. Brian Joiner, conversation at the Instituting Dr. Deming's Methods for Management of Productivity and Quality seminar, Atlanta, Georgia, 5-6 September 1991.

66. "Quality Improvement in Engineering." *Quality Progress*, September 1991, p. 16.

67. Peter Scholtes of Joiner Associates, Inc., at the Instituting Dr. Deming's Methods for Management of Productivity and Quality seminar, Atlanta, Georgia, 5-6 September 1991.

68. "Planning a Total Quality School District in Johnston County, North Carolina." Johnston County Schools, 1991.

69. *The Condition of Education*, pp. 46–47.

70. Robert M. Hutchins, *The Learning Society* (New York: Frederick A. Praeger, 1968), p. 7.

CHAPTER 6: ROLES AND RESPONSIBILITIES

1. "Total quality must begin with top management, and Board [sic] of Education, Superintendent, and each school principal.... creating a climate of growth through education/training and understanding change through sources of power." From "Planning a Total Quality School District in Johnston County, North Carolina." Johnston County Schools, 1991.

2. *What Works*, 2nd ed. (Washington, D.C.: U.S. Department of Education, 1987), p. 64.

3. Roland S. Barth, "The Principal and the Profession of Teaching," in Thomas J. Sergiovanni and John H. Moore, editors, *Schooling for Tomorrow* (Boston: Allyn and Bacon, 1989), p. 242.

4. See Seymour B. Sarason, *The Predictable Failure of Educational Reform* (San Francisco: Jossey-Bass, 1990).

5. Valarie A. Zietheml, A. Parasuraman, and Leonard L. Berry, *Delivering Quality Service* (New York: The Free Press, 1990), p. 35.

6. Lewis A. Rhodes, "The Deming Superintendent." *School Administrator*, December 1990, pp. 24–25.

7. Theodore R. Sizer, *Horace's Compromise* (Boston: Houghton Mifflin Company, 1984), p. 174.

8. Two days suspension or two licks with the paddle. This brings back fond memories of the vice principal at Winyah High School.

9. Jim Burns, *The Youth Builder* (Eugene, Oregon: Harvest House Publishers, 1988).

10. Cliff Schimmels, *Parents' Most Asked Questions About Kids and Schools* (Wheaton, Illinois: Victor Books, 1989), p. 10.

11. Torsten Husen, *The Learning Society* (London: Methuen & Co., Ltd., 1974), p. 25.
See also David T. Kearns and Denis P. Doyle, *Winning the Brain Race* (San Francisco: ICS Press, 1989), p. 95.

12. For more information, contact Gary Goldman at Quality Improvement Associates, Inc., 645 North Michigan Avenue, Suite 800, Chicago, IL 60611, (312) 929-9094.

13. One of my high school teachers once threatened to call a "gathering of eagles" to force me out of some of my extracurricular commitments. It didn't work, and I resented the intrusion. Later, I realized I was prone to overextend myself (a trait I have unfortunately carried with me since).

14. James H. Brown, "Baden-Powell's Boy Scouts: The Premiere Youth Organization of Edwardian England." Master's Thesis, Murray State University, Murray, Kentucky, 1989.

15. *What Works*, p. 5.

16. This has been pointed out by many people. For an interesting discussion on the medieval roots of the "traditional" family structure, see Anthony Campolo, *Growing Up in America* (Grand Rapids, Michigan: Youth Specialties Books, 1989).

17. How many children have gone into a particular line of work at the urging of parents, only to be supremely unhappy in the pursuit?

18. Ron Lee Davis, "The Servant Leader and His Family." Morning Bible Study, 1987 National Youth Workers' Convention, Los Angeles, California.

19. See Burns, *The Youth Builder*, and Mike Yaconelli and Jim Burns, *High School Ministry* (Grand Rapids, Michigan: Youth Specialties Books, 1986).

20. *Improving Schools and Empowering Parents* (Washington, D.C.: U.S. Department of Education, 1989), p. 12.

21. *Improving Schools and Empowering Parents*, p. 14.

22. *Japanese Education Today* (Washington D.C.: U.S. Department of Education, 1987); and Jonathan Kozol, *Savage Inequalities* (New York: Crown Publishers, 1991.

23. *Improving Schools and Empowering Parents*, p. 14. See also Kozol, *Savage Inequalities*, pp. 59–63.

24. William Bennett on C-SPAN, 10 April 1991.

25. *Improving Schools and Empowering Parents*, p. 15.

26. Milton Friedman and Rose Friedman, *Free to Choose* (New York: Avon Books, 1981), pp. 150–152.

27. W. Edwards Deming, *Out of the Crisis* (Cambridge, Massachusetts: Massachusetts Institute of Technology Center for Advanced Engineering Study, 1986), p. 20.

28. Susan Beatty, "Why I Believe in Home Schooling." *Focus on the Family*, April 1991, p. 5.

29. Comments from Bob Brown, principal at Sue Cleveland Elementary School in Piedmont, South Carolina, who enjoys an excellent relationship with the parents of his students.

See Cheri Fuller, "How to Improve the Parent-Teacher Connection." *Focus on the Family*, September 1989, p. 4.

30. For example, preparation may include better initial orientation to the college environment. See Lewis B. Mayhew, Patrick J. Ford, and Dean L. Hubbard, *The Quest for Quality* (San Francisco: Jossey-Bass, 1990), pp. 110–111.

31. John W. Harris, Jr., "Assessing Institutional Effectiveness," in Susan Cooper Cowart, *Project Cooperation* (Washington, D.C.: American College Testing Program, 1990).

32. "Managing Total Quality for Education: Meeting the Challenge." Independent School District 832, Mahtomedi, Minnesota.
   "Task Force Action Plan: Business and Education Working Together for the Future." The Lehigh Valley Business-Education Partnership, Allentown, Pennsylvania, June 1991.
   "Total Quality Education at George Stone Center." George Stone Center, Pensacola, Florida.

33. Dennis P. Doyle and Terry W. Hartle, *Excellence in Education* (Washington, D.C.: American Enterprise Institute for Public Policy Research, 1985), p. 2.
   Some of the problems of local school boards are discussed in Michael W. Kirst, "Who Should Control the Schools? Reassessing Current Policies," in Thomas J. Sergiovanni and John H. Moore, editors, *Schooling for Tomorrow* (Boston: Allyn and Bacon, 1989).

34. National Commission on Excellence in Education, *A Nation at Risk* (Washington, D.C.: U.S. Department of Education, 1983), pp. 78–79.

35. Once again I express my gratitude to my friend James H. Galt-Brown for his insight.
   See also Kozol, *Savage Inequalities*.

36. R. Earl Hadady, *How Sick Is Uncle Sam?* (Pasadena, California: Key Books Press, 1986.

37. My thanks go to Brad Lego for these examples.

38. This will require guidance and a national effort to equalize opportunities and resources.

CHAPTER 7: PROBLEMS AND PROSPECTS

1. For a more in-depth discussion of the changes involved in the transformation, see William W. Scherkenbach, *Deming's Road to Continual Improvement* (Knoxville, Tennessee: SPC Press, 1991). Mr. Scherkenbach's treatment of the physical, logical, and emotional aspects of change and human needs is especially thorough.

2. See Jim Burns, *The Youth Builder* (Eugene, Oregon: Harvest House Publishers, 1988); and Rich Van Pelt, *Intensive Care* (Grand Rapids, Michigan: Youth Specialties Books, 1989).

3. See Van Pelt, *Intensive Care*; and Burns, *The Youth Builder*.

4. Joel Arthur Barker, *Discovering the Future* (St. Paul, Minnesota: ILI Press, 1989), pp. 30–32.
    I fully expected to incur the wrath of educators everywhere by taking on this project, but have been pleasantly surprised by the responses and help I have received in preparing the book.
    See also Seymour B. Sarason, *The Predictable Failure of Educational Reform* (San Francisco: Jossey-Bass, 1990), p. 108.

5. Paul Hersey and Kenneth L. Blanchard, *Management of Organizational Behavior* (Englewood Cliffs, New Jersey: Prentice-Hall, 1982).

6. Hersey and Blanchard, *Management of Organizational Behavior*.

7. W. Edwards Deming, *Out of the Crisis* (Cambridge, Massachusetts: Massachusetts Institute of Technology Center for Advanced Engineering Study, 1986), pp. 86–87.

8. Most of the inhibitors to the transformation mentioned in the text were adapted from Howard S. Gitlow and Shelly J. Gitlow, *The Deming Guide to Quality and Competitive Position* (Englewood Cliffs, New Jersey: Prentice-Hall, 1987).

9. "Deming's ideas took root in Japan because the Japanese industrialists committed themselves to actions coherent with Deming's beliefs, even when they did not agree with those beliefs. Later on, actual results made believers out of them." Lewis A. Rhodes, "Beyond Your Beliefs: Quantum Leaps Toward Quality Schools." *School Administrator*, December 1990, p. 26.

10. Gitlow and Gitlow, *The Deming Guide to Quality and Competitive Position*.

11. Gitlow and Gitlow, *The Deming Guide to Quality and Competitive Position*; Deming, *Out of the Crisis*; and William W. Scherkenbach, *The Deming Route to Quality and Productivity* (Washington, D.C.: CEEPress, George Washington University, 1988).

12. Gitlow and Gitlow, *The Deming Guide to Quality and Competitive Position*; and Deming, *Out of the Crisis*.

13. Gitlow and Gitlow, *The Deming Guide to Quality and Competitive Position*; and Deming, *Out of the Crisis*.

14. For example, the sociology teacher who, for whatever reason, skirts the important subject of analytical methods.

15. Gitlow and Gitlow, *The Deming Guide to Quality and Competitive Position*.

16. Jim Burns, *The Youth Builder* (Eugene, Oregon: Harvest House Publishers, 1988), p. 31.

17. Mike Yaconelli and Jim Burns, *High School Ministry* (Grand Rapids, Michigan: Youth Specialties Books, 1986), p. 9.

18. Daniel J. Boorstin, *The Americans: The Democratic Experience* (New York: Vintage Books, 1974), p. 233.

19. Burns, *The Youth Builder*, p. 31.

20. Gitlow and Gitlow, *The Deming Guide to Quality and Competitive Position*.

21. This is also pointed out by Morris Massey in "What You Are is Where You Were When." *The Massey Triad, Part One: The Past* (Video Publishing House, 1986).

22. Wayne Rice, at the Youth Specialties' 1990 National Resource Seminar, Pasadena, California.

23. Burns, *The Youth Builder*.

24. Burns, *The Youth Builder*; and Anthony Campolo, *Growing Up in America* (Grand Rapids, Michigan: Youth Specialties Books, 1989).

25. I am indebted to David O'Nan for his assistance in this area.

26. Gerald A. Dorfman and Paul R. Hanna, "Can Education Be Reformed?" in Annelise Anderson and Dennis L. Bark, editors, *Thinking About America* (Stanford, California: Hoover Institution Press, 1988), p. 389.

27. Dr. Deming attributes the phrase to Mr. James K. Bakken of the Ford Motor Company. See *Out of the Crisis*, p. 126.

28. Joseph M. Juran, *Juran on Leadership for Quality* (New York: The Free Press, 1989).

29. Juran, *Juran on Leadership for Quality*.

30. Burns, *The Youth Builder*; and Van Pelt, *Intensive Care*.

31. Rosabeth Moss Kanter, *The Change Masters* (New York: Touchstone, 1984).

32. Myron Tribus, "The Application of Quality Management Principles in Education," November 1990, p. 7.

CONCLUSION: OF LEADERS AND THE FUTURE

1. My friend Rob Gray made this point to me several times.

2. John H. Zenger, *Leadership* (San Jose, California: Zenger-Miller, 1985).

3. *I Ching*, Hexagram 7.

4. Donelson R. Forsyth, *An Introduction to Group Dynamics* (Monterey, California: Brooks/Cole Publishing Company, 1983); D. R. Hampton, C. E. Summer, and R. A. Webber, *Organizational Behavior and the Practice of Management*, 5th ed. (Glenview, Illinois: Scott, Foresman and Company, 1987); Sun Tzu, *The Art of War* (London: Oxford University Press, 1963).

5. Miyamoto Musashi, *Go Rin No Sho (A Book of Five Rings)* (Woodstock, New York: Overlook Press, 1974), p. 42.

6. See Zenger, *Leadership*.

7. John Keegan, *The Mask of Command* (New York: Viking Penguin, 1987), p. 318.

8. Sun Tzu, *The Art of War*, p. 123.

9. Lao Tzu, 3rd century B.C.

10. Musashi, *Go Rin No Sho*, p. 42.

11. John W. Gardner, *On Leadership* (New York: The Free Press, 1990), p. 157.

12. Forsyth, *An Introduction to Group Dynamics*.

13. Thomas Jefferson, *Notes on the State of Virginia.*

14. Musashi, *Go Rin No Sho*, p. 66.

15. I remember being told this at Palmetto Boys State and the Governor's School of South Carolina (summer programs for rising high school seniors). While it stirred some feelings of pride at the time, I had trouble believing it was true. With the benefit of hindsight and improved understanding, I believe it not at all now.

16. Ecclesiastes 3:1.

APPENDIX A: TOOLS AND TECHNIQUES

1. Two of the problems encountered by school boards are (1) public ignorance and indifference about their functions, and (2) their own lack of education and training. See Michael W. Kirst, "Who Should Control the Schools? Reassessing Current Policies," in Thomas J. Sergiovanni and John H. Moore, editors, *Schooling for Tomorrow* (Boston: Allyn and Bacon, 1989).

2. This developmental step is most pronounced in early adolescents, and makes adolescent (i.e., junior high school) education one of the most critical steps in student development. See Wayne Rice, *Junior High Ministry* (Grand Rapids, Michigan: Youth Specialties Books, 1987).

3. Myron Tribus, "The Application of Quality Management Principles in Education." November 1990, p. 5. Available from Dr. Tribus at 350 Britto Terrace, Fremont, CA 94539.

4. Kaoru Ishikawa, *Guide to Quality Control* (Tokyo: Asian Productivity Organization, 1982), pp. 18–29.

5. Dr. Deming points out that Dr. Shewhart originally used "assignable" cause instead of "special," and adds "I prefer the adjective special for a cause that is specific to some group of workers, or to a particular production worker, or to a specific machine,

or to a specific local condition. The word to use is not important; the concept is." *Out of the Crisis* (Cambridge, Massachusetts: Massachusetts Institute of Technology Center for Advanced Engineering Study, 1986), p. 310.

6. "In general there must be the possibility of arguing from past to future; not with certainty, but with probability.... No better basis for statistical generalization could be devised than the known fact that certain constituents of the situation are distributed in a genuinely 'random' fashion. Since any departure from 'pure chance' is itself subject to generalization of some sort, a statistical basis for probable judgment cannot conceivably fail to be afforded." Clarence Irving Lewis, *Mind and the World Order* (New York: Dover Publications, 1956), pp. 346, 384.

7. Dr. Shewhart originally used 3 sigma as an achievable, *economical* measure of success. See Walter A. Shewhart, *Statistical Method from the Viewpoint of Quality Control* (New York: Dover Publications, 1986.)

8. William Scherkenbach, *The Deming Route to Quality and Productivity:* (Washington: CEEPress, George Washington University, 1988), pp. 68–69.
See also Shewhart, *Statistical Method from the Viewpoint of Quality Control,* p. 54.

9. My friend Rob Gray has joked that this country needs a new support group called "Single Data-Point Managers Anonymous."

10. *Statistical Quality Control Handbook,* 2nd ed. (Indianapolis, Indiana: Western Electric Company, 1958). The handbook may be ordered by contacting AT&T Technologies, Commercial Sales Clerk, P. O. Box 19901, Indianapolis, IN 46219, 1-800-432-6600. Specify Select Code 700-444.

11. Deming, *Out of the Crisis,* p. 318.

12. Bruce Hunter, "Some Random Thoughts on Education Reform." Draft 4, 16 December 1990 (unpublished).

13. W. Edwards Deming, "Boundaries of Statistical Inference," in Norman L. Johnson and Harry Smith, Jr., editors, *New Developments in Survey Sampling* (New York: Wiley Interscience, 1969).

14. Deming, "Boundaries of Statistical Inference," in *New Developments in Survey Sampling.*

15. Tribus, "The Application of Quality Management Principles in Education," p. 2.

16. See A. C. Rosander, *The Quest for Quality in Services* (Milwaukee, Wisconsin: ASQC Quality Press, 1989).

17. Strong emphasis on *enough data*. A competent statistician is invaluable in planning data acquisition and teaching statistical methods.

18. "The definition of any characteristic, whether it be age, employment status, income from interest, change in liquid assets, yield per acre, quality of being defective, or anything else, must be given in terms of an *operation* or *procedure* for the *measurement* of this characteristic." W. Edwards Deming, *Some Theory of Sampling* (New York: John Wiley & Sons, 1950), p. 15.
See also *Out of the Crisis*, p. 279.

19. Remarks by LtCol George S. Beall, USAF (Ret), in a lecture on educational accountability.

20. W. Edwards Deming, "A System of Profound Knowledge," 5 May 1990, p. 12. Originally presented and published as part of the Osaka Paper.

21. The importance of careful selection of the variables cannot be overstressed. The variables must have some logical connection in order for a scatter diagram to be effective in visualizing the relationship.

22. Scherkenbach, *The Deming Route to Quality and Productivity*, p. 111.

23. The $\bar{x}$-R chart is a type of control chart used to study variables data. Instead of plotting every individual value, the values are grouped together in sets and the average ($\bar{x}$) of each set is plotted. Below the $\bar{x}$ plot, the range (R) is plotted; the range is the difference between the highest value in the set and the lowest. The control limits are then calculated using the range average ($\bar{R}$) and numerical constants based on the number of data points in each set. See Ishikawa, *Guide to Quality Control*, Chapter 7; and Henry L. Lefevre, *Quality Service Pays* (Milwaukee, Wisconsin: ASQC Quality Press, 1989).

24. Deming, *Out of the Crisis*, p. 313.

25. Dr. Juran named the principle after Vilfredo Pareto, an Italian economist. *Juran on Leadership for Quality*, p. 136.

APPENDIX B: AN EDUCATION PRIMER—A QUALITY SHIFT?

1. Harry G. Good, *A History of American Education*, 2nd ed. (New York: The Macmillan Company, 1962), p. 29; and Daniel J. Boorstin, *The Americans: The Colonial Experience* (New York: Vintage Books, 1974), p. 300.

2. "... no part of the country sent more students of law and classics to England than Charleston, South Carolina." Good, *A History of American Education*, p. 53.

3. Boorstin, *The Americans: The Colonial Experience*, p. 307.

4. Good, *A History of American Education*, pp. 13–14.

5. Good, *A History of American Education*, pp. 66–67; and Patrick J. Ryan, *Historical Foundations of Public Education in America* (Dubuque, Iowa: William C. Brown Company, 1965), p. 207.

6. Robert L. Church and Michael W. Sedlak, *Education in the United States* (New York: The Free Press, 1976), p. 10.

7. Church and Sedlak, *Education in the United States*, p. 3.

8. Edmund S. Morgan, *The Birth of the Republic, 1763–1789*, revised ed. (Chicago: University of Chicago Press, 1977), p. 120.

9. Good, *A History of American Education*, pp. 93–94; and Boorstin, *The Americans: The Colonial Experience*, p. 183.

10. Daniel J. Boorstin, *The Americans: The National Experience* (New York: Vintage Books, 1974), p. 34.

11. E. D. Hirsch, Jr., *Cultural Literacy* (New York: Vintage Books, 1987), p. 95.

12. Good, *A History of American Education*, pp. 72–76, 110–116.

13. "In 1848 [the Connecticut Commissioners of Common Schools] reported that of the 1663 schoolhouses in the state only 873 had outhouses and 745 had no sanitary facility at all." Boorstin, *The Americans: The National Experience*, p. 44.

14. Church and Sedlak, *Education in the United States*, pp. 55–56, 60.

15. Milton Friedman and Rose Friedman, *Free to Choose* (New York: Avon Books, 1981), pp. 143–144.

16. Boorstin, *The Americans: The National Experience*; pp. 314–318, and Good, *A History of American Education*, p. 187.

17. Hirsch, Cultural Literacy, pp. 116–118; and Good, *A History of American Education*, pp. 256–257.

18. Church and Sedlak, *Education in the United States*, p. 26.

19. Disparities in school facilities and socioeconomic status have been blamed for many of the educational problems of black children. The Coleman Report of 1966 was used to defend the hypothesis that the academic achievements of black children were related to their being segregated from white children in school. It "shifted the issue under investigation from equal opportunity to equal results." Diane Ravitch, *The Troubled Crusade* (New York: Basic Books, 1983), p. 168.

According to Professor E. D. Hirsch, the report's major finding (that achievement was more related to family background than to school quality) "is not surprising. Common sense predicts that children from literate households can more readily gain the literate culture necessary for reading than those from illiterate households." (*Cultural Literacy*, p. 114.) He continues, "We might infer from [the results] that the schools have not done much to compensate for cultural deprivations; that the significant part of our children's education has been going on outside rather than inside the schools; and finally, that this state of affairs is not inevitable." The last phrase is significant: the disparities between schools are not inevitable; they can be overcome. The quality initiative gives educators, parents, and students the tools they need to provide first-class education to all students.

20. "Southern emphasis on an educated leadership was of a piece with Southern unconcern for popular instruction." Boorstin, *The Americans: The National Experience*, p. 217.

21. Church and Sedlak, *Education in the United States*, p. 289.

22. "The establishment of the school system in the United States as an island of socialism in a free market sea reflected...the early emergence among intellectuals of a distrust of the market and of voluntary exchange.... Needless to say, the public school system was not viewed as 'socialist' but simply as 'American.'" Friedman and Friedman, *Free to Choose*, p. 144.

23. Church and Sedlak, *Education in the United States*, p. 301.

24. Ravitch, *The Troubled Crusade*, p. 48.

The original order of the principles was: (1) Health, (2) Command of fundamental processes, (3) Worthy home-membership, (4) Vocation, (5) Citizenship, (6) Worthy use of leisure, and (7) Ethical character.

25. Mathematically illiterate. See John Allen Paulos, *Innumeracy* (New York: Vintage Books, 1988).

26. Hirsch, *Cultural Literacy*, p. 118.

27. Church and Sedlak, *Education in the United States*, p. 294.

28. Ravitch, *The Troubled Crusade*, p. 44.

29. "Because Dewey's ideas were complex, they were more easily misunderstood than understood, and his disciples proved better at discrediting traditional methods and curricula than at constructing a pedagogically superior replacement." Ravitch, *The Troubled Crusade*, p. 47.
   Again: "The misunderstandings of Dewey's educational philosophy are legion and it may be that if Dewey had written with greater precision, some of them could have been obviated.... Many of the criticisms of Dewey's views are really more properly addressed to the pronouncements of self-styled disciples." Sidney Hook, *Convictions* (Buffalo, New York: Prometheus Books, 1990), p. 90.

30. Dewey "believed that the school might become a fundamental lever of social progress by virtue of its capacity to improve the quality of life for individuals and for the community." Ravitch, *The Troubled Crusade*, p. 47.
   "The school, Dewey argued, must now provide what the industrial revolution has placed beyond the ordinary experience of children. The school must become a community .... Children do not become moral, that is, social, without a society. The school must be a society." Good, *A History of American Education*, p. 359.

31. "Too young to fight, too old to stay at home, youth became its own subculture." Morris Massey, "What You Are Is Where

You Were When," *The Massey Triad, Part One: The Past* (Schaumberg, Illinois: Video Publishing House, 1986).

32. Massey, "What You Are Is Where You Were When." Massey points out the startling (1986) statistic that 99.9 percent of American households have television sets, while only 97 percent have indoor plumbing.

33. Torsten Husen, *The Learning Society* (London: Methuen & Co., Ltd., 1974), p. 9; and Theodore R. Sizer, *Horace's Compromise* (Boston: Houghton Mifflin Company, 1984), p. 50.

34. "In the late 1960s and early 1970s some adolescents ... organized against the very notion of a school. They treated any institutionalized education, in fact any institution, as oppressive." Daniel J. Boorstin, *The Americans: The Democratic Experience* (New York: Vintage Books, 1974), pp. 233–234.

35. Many of the movements that turned violent and radical started as protests lobbying peaceably for change in the spirit of "Civil Disobedience" (for example, "sit-ins"). When the changes did not materialize according to the desired timetable, the protesters grew impatient and demanded attention to their causes, often through violence. Massey ("What You Are Is Where You Were When") ascribes this demand for immediate gratification of demands to people who were "value-programmed" in the television era.

Ravitch chronicles the protest movements in Chapter 6 of *The Troubled Crusade*, "From Berkeley to Kent State."

36. Ravitch, *The Troubled Crusade*, p. 220.

37. National Commission on Excellence in Education, *A Nation at Risk* (Washington, D.C.: U.S. Department of Education, 1983), p. 8.

38. Alex Inkeles, "National Differences in Scholastic Performance," in Philip G. Altbach, et al, editors, *Comparative Education* (New York: Macmillan Publishing Company, 1982), p. 211.

39. Comparisons of the United States with foreign countries often "relate the performance of a vast majority in one place with that of a carefully screened elite in another." Husen, *The Learning Society*, pp. 43–44.

40. *The Nation Responds*, p. 16.

41. *Koalaty Kid Pilot Program* (American Society for Quality Control, 1988).

I am grateful to Bob Brown, Principal of Sue Cleveland Elementary School in Piedmont, South Carolina, for comments on his experience with the program. Mr. Brown credits the program with substantial improvements in his school's image and atmosphere.

42. I thank Dr. Paul Messier of the National Learning Foundation for this observation.

43. For more information on community quality efforts, write the Community Quality Coalition, c/o Jackson Community College, 2111 Emmons Road, Jackson, MI 49201.

44. David Paul Langford, "Changing Education Systems Through Management and Cooperation." Presented at the 1990 Third Northern Regions Conference: Cooperation in a Changing World, Anchorage, Alaska, 18 September 1990.

See also Myron Tribus, "The Application of Quality Management Principles in Education." November 1990. Available from Dr. Tribus at 350 Britto Terrace, Fremont, CA 94539.

45. This was abundantly clear when I was an undergraduate student. Foreign students made up most of the graduate students in my department.

46. *A Nation at Risk*, p. 38.

47. John T. Correll, "Unskilled and Unprepared." *Air Force Magazine*, October 1989, p. 6; and Jim Castelli, "How to Close Tomorrow's Literacy Gap." *Safety & Health*, December 1989, p. 55.

48. Correll, "Unskilled and Unprepared," p. 6.

49. *A Nation at Risk*, p. 5.

APPENDIX C: THE DIFFICULTY OF VALUES

1. For example: William J. Bennett, "Educators Must Teach Morality." *Citizen*, September 1988, p. 16; John W. Gardner, *The Recovery of Confidence* (New York: Pocket Books, 1971); R. Earl Hadady, *How Sick Is Uncle Sam?* (Pasadena, California: Key Books Press, 1986); David T. Kearns and Denis P. Doyle, *Winning the Brain Race* (San Francisco: ICS Press, 1989); Carl Sommer, *Schools in Crisis* (Houston, Texas: Cahill Publishing Company, 1984).

2. See Gordon H. Clark, *A Christian Philosophy of Education*, 2nd ed. (Jefferson, Maryland: The Trinity Foundation, 1988). Originally published in 1946.

3. Clarence Irving Lewis, *An Analysis of Knowledge and Valuation* (LaSalle, Illinois: The Open Court Publishing Company, 1946), p. 480.

4. Gerald A. Dorfman and Paul R. Hanna, "Can Education Be Reformed?" in Annelise Anderson and Dennis L. Bark, editors, *Thinking About America* (Stanford, California: Hoover Institution Press, 1988), p. 389. They hold that only the government can ensure that common values and beliefs continue throughout society.

5. James Q. Wilson, "Public Policy and Personal Character," in Annelise Anderson and Dennis L. Bark, editors, *Thinking About America* (Stanford, California: Hoover Institution Press, 1988), pp. 494–495.

6. Robert L. Church and Michael W. Sedlak, *Education in the United States* (New York: The Free Press, 1976), pp. 69–70.

7. Theodore R. Sizer, *Horace's Compromise* (Boston: Houghton Mifflin Company, 1984), p. 122.

8. "Education is by its very definition an enterprise in preparing people for a future. To do this, someone has to guess about what that future is to be and how is the best way to prepare for it. Those guesses constitute values. We just can't escape it." Cliff Schimmels, *Parents' Most-Asked Questions About Kids and Schools* (Wheaton, Illinois: Victor Books, 1989), p. 35.

Morris Massey suggests that whether or not to teach values is a stupid question: the only question is how to teach them. "What You Are Is Where You Were When," *The Massey Triad, Part One: The Past* (Schaumberg, Illinois: Video Publishing House, 1986).

9. *What Works*, 2nd ed. (Washington, D.C.: U.S. Department of Education, 1987), p. 59.

10. Wayne Rice explained that the challenge of positively influencing young people and introducing them to the Gospel keeps him in youth work. (Youth Specialties' 1990 National Resource Seminar, Pasadena, California.)

There is some difference of opinion on the actual age bracket. Massey ("What You Are Is Where You Were When") suggests 7 to 20, with 10 being the key age at which we are "value-programmed." What matters, however, is the fact that young people are impressionable: the actual age is irrelevant.

11. Hadady, *How Sick Is Uncle Sam?*.

12. Lewis, *An Analysis of Knowledge and Valuation*, p. 554.

13. "It has become increasingly clear that large numbers of people never find anything to replace [their] shattered early beliefs." Gardner, *The Recovery of Confidence*, p. 89.

14. "…there is now an entirely new language of good and evil, originating in an attempt to get 'beyond good and evil' and preventing us from talking with any conviction about good and evil anymore…. The new language is that of value relativism…." Allan

Bloom, *The Closing of the American Mind* (New York: Touchstone, 1988), p. 141.

15. For instance, one rarely sees good struggling with the possibility of being or becoming evil through the necessity of using evil's methods, even to attain what are considered good ends.

16. Bruno Bettelheim, "The Importance of Play." *The Atlantic Monthly*, March 1987.

17. Hadady suggests that values education should be separate, and a higher priority than the Three R's. He also suggests that separate courses on parenting be included in the school curriculum. See *How Sick Is Uncle Sam?*

18. Wilson, "Public Policy and Personal Character," in *Thinking About America*, p. 492.

19. The First Amendment is the one most often abused. The first clause is used repeatedly to strangle church participation in society, when it actually provides that "Congress shall make no law respecting an establishment of religion, or prohibiting the free exercise thereof." Is not activity in the community free exercise?

The second clause, in which Congress is forbidden to enact legislation "abridging the freedom of speech or of the press," is used to defend all manner of obscenities when it appears to have been aimed at freedom to express political viewpoints.

It is imperative that these constitutional guarantees be studied in detail if they are to be interpreted correctly.

20. My good friend Rob Gray has suggested that every high school student should write at least one analytical paper, instead of concentrating all of their efforts on term (such as research) papers. Research is important and worthy, but analysis and in-depth consideration of alternatives are skills that education should develop. The curriculum presented in Chapter 5 makes this more possible.

21. Bennett, "Educators Must Teach Morality"; Gardner, *The Recovery of Confidence*; and Hadady, *How Sick Is Uncle Sam?*

22. It may not be necessary for us to survive. As Dr. Deming has said many times in his seminars, "I know of no government regulation that says we must survive."

23. *What Works*, p. 15.

APPENDIX D: THE GIFTED AND TALENTED MYTH

1. For example, in his *Notes on the State of Virginia*, Jefferson proposed sending all students to school for three years, but reserved higher public education for those with special aptitude.

2. Harry G. Good, *A History of American Education*, 2nd ed. (New York: The Macmillan Company, 1962); and Diane Ravitch, *The Troubled Crusade* (New York: Basic Books, 1983).

3. *What Works*, 2nd ed. (Washington, D.C.: U.S. Department of Education, 1987), p. 78.

4. *What Works*, p. 14.

5. *What Works*, p. 37.

6. Or on the superficial knowledge of the single data point.

7. Michael John Horvath, *Statistics for Educators* (Seattle, Washington: Special Child Publications, 1985), p. 53.

8. See Peter Kline, *The Everyday Genius* (Arlington, Virginia: Great Ocean Publishers, 1990).

9. Sandra Stencel, "Educating Gifted Children," in Hoyt Gimlin, editor, *Editorial Research Reports on Education in America, Quality vs. Cost* (Washington, D.C.: Congressional Quarterly, Inc., 1981).

10. Kline, *The Everyday Genius*, p. 14.

11. This indicates only that we misunderstand what the average is. It is amazing how many people seem astonished to find that about half the population is above average, while the other half is below.

12. For example, Theodore R. Sizer suggests that technical and junior colleges take over vocational training completely. See *Horace's Compromise* (Boston: Houghton Mifflin Company, 1984).

13. Is the student who is top of the class in the general curriculum really any less gifted than the student who is in the middle of the advanced class? How do you know?

14. R. Earl Hadady, *How Sick Is Uncle Sam?* (Pasadena, California: Key Books Press, 1986), pp. 274–275.

15. Of course, we also cannot determine how much participation in a program such as Head Start actually encourages positive development in children.

16. See E. D. Hirsch, Jr., *Cultural Literacy* (New York: Vintage Books, 1988).

17. Robert M. Hutchins, *The Learning Society* (New York: Frederick A. Praeger, 1968), p. 12.

18. *What Works*, p. 75.

19. *What Works*, p. 46.

20. The benefits of using cooperative learning teams in which students of mixed abilities are put together in teams are discussed in William Glasser, *The Quality School* (New York: Harper & Row, 1990), and *Control Theory in the Classroom* (New York: Harper & Row, 1986).

21. See Robert Rosenthal and Lenore Jacobsen, *Pygmalion in the Classroom* (New York: Holt, Rinehart and Winston, 1968).

22. Sizer, *Horace's Compromise*, p. 39.

BIBLIOGRAPHY

Altbach, Philip G., Robert F. Arnove, and Gail P. Kelly, editors, *Comparative Education*. New York: Macmillan Publishing Company, 1982.

Anderson, Annelise, and Dennis L. Bark, *Thinking About America: The United States in the 1990s*. Stanford, California: Hoover Institution Press, 1988.

Apps, Jerold W., *Problems in Continuing Education*. New York: McGraw-Hill Book Company, 1979.

Astin, Alexander W., "When Does a College Deserve to Be Called 'High Quality?'" *Current Issues in Higher Education* (3 September 1980): 1–9.

Axland, Susan, "Looking for a Quality Education." *Quality Progress* (October 1991): 61–72.

Baird, Leonard L., "Value Added: Using Student Gains as Yardsticks of Learning." In *Performance and Judgment: Essays on Principles and Practice in the Assessment of College Student Learning*. Washington, D.C.: U.S. Department of Education, 1988.

Banathy, Bela H., *Instructional Systems*. Belmont, California: Fearon Publishers, 1968.

Barker, Joel Arthur, *Discovering the Future: The Business of Paradigms.* St. Paul, Minnesota: ILI Press, 1989.

Barth, Roland S., "A Personal Vision of a Good School." *Phi Delta Kappan* (March 1990): 512–516.

———, "The Principal and the Profession of Teaching." In Thomas J. Sergiovanni and John H. Moore, editors, *Schooling for Tomorrow.* Boston: Allyn and Bacon, 1989.

Bayless, David L., Gabriel Massaro, and Nancy W. Bayless, "Quality Improvement in Education Today and the Future." Progress report of a project of the Center for Research on Educational Accountability and Teacher Evaluation of Western Michigan University, 1991.

Beatty, Susan, "Why I Believe in Home Schooling." *Focus on the Family* (April 1991): 4–5.

Bennett, William J., "Educators Must Teach Morality." *Citizen* (September 1988): 16.

Bettelheim, Bruno, "The Importance of Play." *The Atlantic Monthly* (March 1987): 35–46.

———, and Karen Zelan, "Why Children Don't Like to Read." *The Atlantic Monthly* (November 1981): 25–31.

Bloom, Allan, *The Closing of the American Mind.* New York: Simon & Schuster, 1987.

Bloom, Benjamin S., editor, *Taxonomy of Educational Objectives: The Classification of Educational Goals. Handbook 1: Cognitive Domain.* New York: Longman, 1956.

Bolles, Richard N., *The Three Boxes of Life, and How to Get Out of Them.* Berkeley, California: Ten Speed Press, 1981.

Boorstin, Daniel, *The Americans: The Colonial Experience.* New York: Vintage Books, 1974.

————, *The Americans: The Democratic Experience*. New York: Vintage Books, 1974.

————, *The Americans: The National Experience*. New York: Vintage Books, 1974.

————, *The Discoverers*. New York: Vintage Books, 1985.

Branson, Robert K., and F. Craig Johnson, "Total Quality Management: The New Look at Accountability, School Improvement Programs, and Site-Based Management." Center for Educational Technology, Florida State University, July 1991.

Brown, James H., "Baden-Powell's Boy Scouts: The Premiere Youth Organization of Edwardian England." Masters Thesis; Murray State University, Murray, Kentucky, 1989.

Burns, Jim, *The Youth Builder: Today's Resource for Relational Youth Ministry*. Eugene, Oregon: Harvest House Publishers, 1988.

Campolo, Anthony, *Growing Up in America: A Sociology of Youth Ministry*. Grand Rapids, Michigan: Youth Specialties Books, 1989.

Castelli, Jim, "How to Close Tomorrow's Literacy Gap." *Safety & Health* (December 1989): 54–57.

Church, Robert L., and Michael W. Sedlak, *Education in the United States*. New York: The Free Press, 1976.

Clark, Gordon H., *A Christian Philosophy of Education*, 2nd ed. Jefferson, Maryland: The Trinity Foundation, 1988.

Coate, L. Edwin, "Implementing Total Quality Management in a University Setting." Oregon State University, July 1990.

Correll, John T., "Unskilled and Unprepared." *Air Force Magazine* (October 1989): 6.

Cowart, Susan Cooper, *Project Cooperation: Designing and Implementing Models of Outcome Assessments for Two-Year Institutions*. Washington, D.C.: American College Testing Program, 1990.

Crosby, Philip B., *Quality Is Free: The Art of Making Quality Certain*. New York: McGraw-Hill Book Company, 1979.

———, *Quality Without Tears: The Art of Hassle-Free Management*. New York: McGraw-Hill Book Company, 1984.

Davis, Stanley M., *Future Perfect*. Reading, Massachusetts: Addison-Wesley, 1987.

Deming, W. Edwards, "A System of Profound Knowledge." 5 May 1990. Originally presented and published as part of the Osaka Paper.

———, "Boundaries of Statistical Inference." In Normal L. Johnson and Harry Smith, Jr., editors, *New Developments in Survey Sampling*. New York: Wiley Interscience, 1969.

———, *Out of the Crisis*. Cambridge, Massachusetts: Massachusetts Institute of Technology Center for Advanced Engineering Study, 1986.

———, *Some Theory of Sampling*. New York: John Wiley & Sons, 1950.

Dorfman, Gerald A., and Paul R. Hanna, "Can Education Be Reformed?" In Annelise Anderson and Dennis L. Bark, editors, *Thinking About America*. Stanford, California: Hoover Institution Press, 1988.

Doyle, Dennis P., and Terry W. Hartle, *Excellence in Education: The States Take Charge*. Washington, D.C.: American Enterprise Institute for Public Policy Research, 1985.

"Eager Ingenues." *The Economist* (6 July 1991): 26.

Ealey, Lance A., *Quality By Design: Taguchi Methods and U.S. Industry.* Dearborn, Michigan: ASI Press, 1988.

Feigenbaum, A. V., *Total Quality Control: Engineering and Management.* New York: McGraw-Hill Book Company, 1961.

Forester, Anne D., "An Examination of Parallels Between Deming's Model for Transforming Industry and Current Trends in Education." Submitted to the Total Quality Education/Total Quality Management Taskforce, 1 July 1991.

Forsyth, Donelson R., *An Introduction to Group Dynamics.* Monterey, California: Brooks/Cole Publishing Company, 1983.

Friedman, Milton, and Rose Friedman, *Free to Choose.* New York: Avon Books, 1981.

Fuller, Cheri, "How to Improve the Parent-Teacher Connection." *Focus on the Family* (September 1989): 2–5.

Gardner, John W., *On Leadership.* New York: The Free Press, 1990.

———, *The Recovery of Confidence.* New York: W. W. Norton & Company, 1970.

Garvin, David A., *Managing Quality: The Strategic and Competitive Edge.* New York: The Free Press, 1988.

Gimlin, Hoyt, editor, *Editorial Research on Education in America, Quality vs. Cost.* Washington, D.C.: Congressional Quarterly, Inc., 1981.

Gitlow, Howard S., and Shelly J. Gitlow, *The Deming Guide to Quality and Competitive Position.* Englewood Cliffs, New Jersey: Prentice-Hall, 1987.

Glasser, William, *Control Theory in the Classroom.* New York: Harper & Row, 1986.

————, *The Quality School*. New York: Harper & Row, 1990.

Good, Harry G., *A History of American Education*. 2nd ed. New York: The Macmillan Company, 1962.

Hadady, R. Earl, *How Sick Is Uncle Sam? A New Perspective*. Pasadena, California: Key Books Press, 1986.

Hampton, D. R., C. E. Summer, and R. A. Webber, *Organizational Behavior and the Practice of Management*, 5th ed. (Glenview, Illinois: Scott, Foresman and Company, 1987).

Harris, John W. Jr., "Assessing Institutional Effectiveness," in Susan Cooper Cowart, *Project Cooperation: Designing and Implementing Models of Outcome Assessments for Two-Year Institutions*. Washington, D.C.: American College Testing Program, 1990.

Hawking, Steven W., *A Brief History of Time*. New York: Bantam Books, 1988.

Hawley, Willis D., "Traveling Old Roads Deeper Into the Woods Leaves Promises to Keep." *Theory Into Practice* (Winter 1990): 13–20.

Hersey, Paul, and Kenneth H. Blanchard, *Management of Organizational Behavior: Utilizing Human Resources*. Englewood Cliffs, New Jersey: Prentice-Hall, 1982.

Herzberg, Frederick, "One More Time: How Do You Motivate Employees?" *Harvard Business Review* (September–October 1987): 109–120. (Reprinted from January–February 1968.)

Hirsch, E. D., Jr., *Cultural Literacy: What Every American Needs to Know*. New York: Vintage Books, 1988.

Hook, Sidney, *Convictions*. Buffalo, New York: Prometheus Books, 1990.

————, "A Philosophical Perspective." In Annelise Anderson and Dennis L. Bark, editors, *Thinking About America*. Stanford, California: Hoover Institution Press, 1988.

Horvath, Michael John, *Statistics for Educators*. Seattle, Washington: Special Child Publications, 1985.

Huff, Darrell, *How to Lie With Statistics*. New York: W. W. Norton & Company, 1954.

Hunter, Bruce, "Some Random Thoughts on Education Reform, the Management Philosophy of W. Edwards Deming and the Application of Total Quality Management in Education." Draft 4, 16 December 1990 (unpublished).

Husen, Torsten, *The Learning Society*. London: Methuen & Co., Ltd., 1974.

Hutchins, Robert M., *The Learning Society*. New York: Frederick A. Praeger, 1968.

Improving Schools and Empowering Parents: Choice in American Education. Washington, D.C.: U.S. Department of Education, 1989.

"Improving the Quality of Government Products and Services," in *OMB Circular A-132 (Draft)*. Washington, D.C.: Office of Management and Budget, 1990.

Ingle, Sud, *Quality Circle Master Guide: Increasing Productivity with People Power*. Englewood Cliffs, New Jersey: Prentice-Hall, 1982.

Inkeles, Alex, "National Differences in Scholastic Performance." In Philip G. Altbach, et al, editors, *Comparative Education*. New York: Macmillan Publishing Company, 1982.

Ishikawa, Kaoru, *Guide to Quality Control*. Tokyo: Asian Productivity Organization, 1982.

————, *What Is Total Quality Control? The Japanese Way.* Translated by David J. Lu. Englewood Cliffs, New Jersey: Prentice-Hall, 1985.

Japanese Education Today. Washington, D.C.: U.S. Department of Education, 1987.

Juran, Joseph M., editor, *Juran's Quality Control Handbook,* 4th ed. New York: McGraw-Hill Book Company, 1988.

————, *Juran on Leadership for Quality: An Executive Handbook.* New York: The Free Press, 1989.

————, *Juran on Planning for Quality.* New York: The Free Press, 1988.

Kanter, Rosabeth Moss, *The Change Masters: Innovation and Entrepreneurship in the American Corporation.* New York: Touchstone, 1983.

Kaufman, Roger, *Planning Educational Systems: A Results Based Approach.* Lancaster, Pennsylvania: Technomic Publishing Co., 1988.

Kearns, David T., and Denis P. Doyle, *Winning the Brain Race: A Bold Plan to Make Our Schools Competitive.* San Francisco: ICS Press, 1989.

Keegan, John, *The Mask of Command.* New York: Viking Penguin, Inc., 1987.

Kennedy, Paul, "The (Relative) Decline of America." *The Atlantic Monthly* (August 1987): 29–38.

Killian, Cecelia S., *The World of W. Edwards Deming.* Washington, D.C.: CEEPress, George Washington University, 1988.

Kimple, James A., Saul A. Rubinstein, Dennis Murray, and Edward Blair, "Applying Quality Principles in Public Education." In *1991 ASQC Quality Congress Transactions*. Milwaukee, Wisconsin: American Society for Quality Control, 1991.

Kirst, Michael W., "Who Should Control the Schools? Reassessing Current Policies." In Thomas J. Sergiovanni and John H. Moore, editors, *Schooling for Tomorrow*. Boston: Allyn and Bacon, 1989.

Kline, Peter, *The Everyday Genius: Restoring Children's Natural Joy of Learning—And Yours, Too.* Arlington, Virginia: Great Ocean Publishers, 1990.

Koalaty Kid Pilot Program. American Society for Quality Control, 1988.

Kohn, Alfie, *No Contest: The Case Against Competition.* Boston: Houghton Mifflin Company, 1986.

Kozol, Jonathan, *Savage Inequalities: Children in America's Schools.* New York: Crown Publishers, 1991.

Langford, David Paul, "Changing Education Systems Through Management and Cooperation." Presented at the 1990 Third Northern Regions Conference: Cooperation in a Changing World, Anchorage, Alaska, 18 September 1990.

Lanier, Judith E., and Michael W. Sedlak, "Teacher Efficiency and Quality Schooling." In Thomas J. Sergiovanni and John H. Moore, editors, *Schooling for Tomorrow*. Boston: Allyn and Bacon, 1989.

Lawton, Dennis, "Teacher Education." In Max Morris and Clive Griggs, editors, *Education—The Wasted Years?* London: The Falmer Press, 1988.

Lefevre, Henry L., *Quality Service Pays: Six Keys to Success.* Milwaukee, Wisconsin: ASQC Quality Press, 1989.

Lewis, Clarence Irving, *An Analysis of Knowledge and Valuation*. La Salle, Illinois: The Open Court Publishing Company, 1946.

––––––, *Mind and the World Order: Outline of a Theory of Knowledge*. New York: Dover Publications, 1956.

Lofgren, George Q., "Quality System Registration." *Quality Progress* (May 1991): 35–37.

Mabry, Marcus, "The New Teacher Corps." *Newsweek* (16 July 1990): 62–63.

"Managing Total Quality for Education: Meeting the Challenge." Independent School District 832, Mahtomedi, Minnesota.

Mann, Nancy R., *The Keys to Excellence: The Story of the Deming Philosophy*. Los Angeles: Prestwick Books, 1989.

Marquardt, Donald, Jacque Choré, K. E. Jensen, Klaus Petrick, James Pyle, and Donald Strable, "Vision 2000: The Strategy for the ISO 9000 Series Standards in the 90's." *Quality Progress* (May 1991): 25–31.

Massey, Morris, "What You Are Is Where You Were When." *The Massey Triad, Part One: The Past*. Schaumburg, Illinois: Video Publishing House, 1986.

Mayhew, Lewis B., Patrick J. Ford, and Dean L. Hubbard, *The Quest for Quality: The Challenge for Undergraduate Education in the 1990s*. San Francisco: Jossey-Bass, 1990.

Melvin, Charles A. III, "School Restructuring the Deming Way." Presented at the Fourth Annual Hunter Conference on Quality, Madison, Wisconsin, 10-12 April 1991.

Miller, Richard I., editor, *Applying the Deming Method to Higher Education (for More Effective Human Resource Management)*. Washington: College and University Personnel Association, 1991.

Mitchell, Douglas E., "Measuring Up: Standards for Evaluating School Reform." In Thomas J. Sergiovanni and John H. Moore, editors, *Schooling for Tomorrow*. Boston: Allyn and Bacon, 1989.

Moen, Ronald D., "The Deming Philosophy for Improving the Educational Process." Presented at the Third Annual International Deming Users Group Conference, Cincinatti, Ohio, 22 August 1989. Revised 25 May 1991.

Morgan, Edmund S., *The Birth of the Republic, 1763–1789*, revised ed. Chicago: University of Chicago Press, 1977.

Morris, Max, and Clive Griggs, editors, *Education—The Wasted Years? 1973–1986*. London: The Falmer Press, 1988.

Moser, Leo J., "Cross-Cultural Dimensions: U.S.–Japan." In *Toward a Better Understanding: U.S.–Japan Relations*. Washington, D.C.: U.S. Department of State, 1986.

Musashi, Miyamoto, *Go Rin No Sho (A Book of Five Rings)*. Translated by Victor Harris. Woodstock, New York: Overlook Press, 1974.

National Center for Educational Statistics, *The Condition of Education, Volume 1: Elementary and Secondary Education*. Washington, D.C.: U.S. Department of Education, 1988.

National Commission on Excellence in Education, *A Nation at Risk: The Imperative for Educational Reform*. Washington, D.C.: U.S. Department of Education, 1983.

"National Goals for Education." Washington, D.C.: Executive Office of the President, 26 February 1990.

National Institute for Education, *Reaching for Excellence: An Effective Schools Sourcebook*. Washington, D.C.: U.S. Department of Education, 1985.

The Nation Responds: Recent Efforts to Improve Education. Washington, D.C.: U.S. Department of Education, 1984.

Ouchi, William, *Theory Z: How American Business Can Meet the Japanese Challenge*. Reading, Massachusetts: Addison-Wesley, 1981.

Paulos, John Allen, *Innumeracy: Mathematical Illiteracy and its Consequences*. New York: Vintage Books, 1988.

Peach, Robert W., "State of Quality System Certification in the United States." In *1991 ASQC Quality Congress Transactions*. Milwaukee, Wisconsin: American Society for Quality Control, 1991.

Peterson, Peter G., "The Morning After." *The Atlantic Monthly* (October 1987): 43–69.

"Planning a Total Quality School District in Johnston County, North Carolina." Johnston County Schools, 1991.

Popham, W. James, Editor, *Criterion-Referenced Measurement: An Introduction*. Englewood Cliffs, New Jersey: Educational Technology Publications, 1971.

——, and T. R. Husek, "Implications of Criterion-Referenced Measurement." In W. James Popham, editor, *Criterion-Referenced Measurement*. Englewood Cliffs, New Jersey: Educational Technology Publications, 1971.

"Quality Improvement in Engineering." *Quality Progress* (September 1991): 16.

"Quality Management and Quality System Elements—Guidelines." *ANSI/ASQC Q94-1987*. Milwaukee, Wisconsin: ASQC Quality Press, 1987.

Ravitch, Diane, *The Schools We Deserve*. New York: Basic Books, 1985.

——, *The Troubled Crusade: American Education, 1945–1980*. New York: Basic Books, 1983.

Reich, Robert B., "The Next American Frontier." *The Atlantic Monthly* (March 1983): 43–58ff.

———, *Tales of A New America: The Anxious Liberal's Guide to the Future.* New York: Vintage Books, 1988.

Rhodes, Lewis A., "Beyond Your Beliefs: Quantum Leaps Toward Quality Schools." *School Administrator* (December 1990): 23–26.

———, "The Deming Superintendent." *School Administrator* (December 1990): 24–25.

———, "Why Quality is Within Our Grasp...If We Reach." *School Administrator* (November 1990): 31-34.

Rice, Wayne, *Junior High Ministry*, 2nd ed. Grand Rapids, Michigan: Youth Specialties Books, 1987.

Richey, Rita, *The Theoretical and Conceptual Bases of Instructional Design.* London: Kogan Page, Ltd., 1986.

Ropelewski, Robert R., "Wave of Quality Initiatives Sweeps Over DOD, Industry." *Armed Forces Journal International* (January 1990): 54–56.

Rosander, A. C., *The Quest for Quality in Services.* Milwaukee, Wisconsin: ASQC Quality Press, 1989.

Rosenthal, Robert, and Lenore Jacobsen, *Pygmalion in the Classroom: Teacher Expectation and Pupils' Intellectual Development.* New York: Holt, Rinehart and Winston, 1968.

Ryan, Patrick J., *Historical Foundations of Public Education in America.* Dubuque, Iowa: William C. Brown Company, 1965.

Sarason, Seymour B., *The Predictable Failure of Educational Reform: Can We Change Course Before It's Too Late?* San Francisco: Jossey-Bass, 1990.

Scherkenbach, William W., *Deming's Road to Continual Improvement*. Knoxville, Tennessee: SPC Press, 1991.

———, *The Deming Route to Quality and Productivity: Road Maps and Roadblocks*. Washington: CEEPress, George Washington University, 1988.

Schimmels, Cliff, *Parents' Most-Asked Questions About Kids and Schools*. Wheaton, Illinois: Victor Books, 1989.

Schlechty, Phillip C., "Career Ladders: A Good Idea Going Awry." In Thomas J. Sergiovanni and John H. Moore, editors, *Schooling for Tomorrow*. Boston: Allyn and Bacon, 1989.

Schoop, Tom, "Can Quality Be Total?" *Government Executive* (March 1990): 20–25.

Sebald, William J., with Russell Brines, *With MacArthur in Japan: A Personal History of the Occupation*. New York: W. W. Norton & Company, 1965.

Sergiovanni, Thomas J., "The Leadership Needed for Quality Schooling." In Thomas J. Sergiovanni and John H. Moore, editors, *Schooling for Tomorrow*. Boston: Allyn and Bacon, 1989.

———, and John H. Moore, Editors, *Schooling For Tomorrow: Directing Reforms to Issues That Count*. Boston: Allyn and Bacon, 1989.

Shewhart, Walter A., *Economic Control of Quality of Manufactured Product*. Princeton, New Jersey: D. Van Nostrand Company, 1931.

———, *Statistical Method from the Viewpoint of Quality Control*. New York: Dover Publications, 1986.

Shingleton, John D., "Economics of the Job Market for the 1992 Grad." In *CPC Annual*, 35th ed. Bethlehem, Pennsylvania: College Placement Council, 1991.

Sizer, Theodore R., *Horace's Compromise: The Dilemma of the American High School*. Boston: Houghton Mifflin Company, 1984.

"Skills Employers Want," *Safety & Health* (December 1989): 56.

Slavin, Robert E., "Learning Together." *The American School Board Journal* (August 1990): 22–23.

Sommer, Carl, *Schools in Crisis: Training for Success or Failure?* Houston, Texas: Cahill Publishing Company, 1984.

Stampen, Jacob O., "Improving the Quality of Education: W. Edwards Deming and Effective Schools." *Contemporary Education Review* (Winter 1987): 423–433.

Statistical Abstract of the United States, 1985. 105th ed. Washington, D.C.: U.S. Bureau of the Census, 1984.

Statistical Quality Control Handbook, 2nd ed. Indianapolis, Indiana: Western Electric Company, 1958.

Stencel, Sandra, "Educating Gifted Children." In Hoyt Gimlin, editor, *Editorial Research Reports on Education in America, Quality vs. Cost*. Washington, D.C.: Congressional Quarterly, Inc., 1981.

"Task Force Master Plan: Business and Education Working Together for the Future." Lehigh Valley Business-Education Partnership, Allentown, Pennsylvania, June 1991.

Toch, Thomas, "Drafting the Best and Brightest." *U.S. News & World Report* (29 January 1990): 52.

Tomorrow's Teachers: A Report of the Holmes Group. East Lansing, Michigan: The Holmes Group, 1986.

"Total Quality Education at George Stone Center." George Stone Center, Pensacola, Florida.

Total Quality Management Master Plan. Washington, D.C.: U.S. Department of Defense, 1988.

Toward a Better Understanding: U.S.–Japan Relations. Washington, D.C.: U.S. Department of State, 1986.

"Toward a System of Total Quality Management (The Deming Way)." Petersburg Public Schools, Petersburg, Virginia.

Tribus, Myron, "The Application of Quality Management Principles in Education, at Mt. Edgecumbe High School, Sitka, Alaska." November 1990. (Available from Dr. Tribus at 350 Britto Terrace, Fremont, CA 94539.)

————, editorial in *Community Link* (December 1990): 1.

Tzu, Sun, *The Art of War.* Translated by Samuel B. Griffith. London: Oxford University Press, 1963.

Van Pelt, Rich, *Intensive Care: Helping Teenagers in Crisis.* Grand Rapids, Michigan: Youth Specialties Books, 1988.

Wadsworth, Harrison M., "Relationship of U.S. Registration Activities to European Requirements." In *1991 ASQC Quality Congress Transactions.* Milwaukee, Wisconsin: American Society for Quality Control, 1991.

What Works: Research About Teaching and Learning, 2nd ed. Washington, D.C.: U.S. Department of Education, 1987.

Wilson, James Q., "Public Policy and Personal Character." In Annelise Anderson and Dennis L. Bark, editors, *Thinking About America.* Stanford, California: Hoover Institution Press, 1988.

Wong, Martin R., and John D. Raulerson, *A Guide to Systematic Instructional Design.* Englewood Cliffs, New Jersey: Educational Technology Publications, 1974.

Yaconelli, Mike, and Jim Burns, *High School Ministry.* Grand Rapids, Michigan: Youth Specialties Books, 1986.

Zeitheml, Valarie A., A. Parasuraman, and Leonard L. Berry, *Delivering Quality Service: Balancing Customer Perceptions and Expectations.* New York: The Free Press, 1990.

Zenger, John H., *Leadership: Management's Better Half.* San Jose, California: Zenger-Miller, 1985.

Zuckerman, Mortimer B., "Brother, Can You Spare a Dime?" *U.S. News & World Report* (22 August 1988): 68.

———, "Weasel Words." *U.S. News & World Report* (16 May 1988): 80.

INDEX